VOTING, INTEREST GROUPS, AND PARTIES

VOTING, INTEREST GROUPS, AND PARTIES

VOTING, INTEREST GROUPS, AND PARTIES

SCOTT, FORESMAN'S AMERICAN GOVERNMENT READINGS SERIES   Joseph C. Palamountain, Jr., Academic Editor

BRADBURY SEASHOLES

TUFTS UNIVERSITY

SCOTT, FORESMAN AND COMPANY

Library of Congress Catalog Card No. 66-14833
Copyright © 1966 by Scott, Foresman and Company, Glenview, Illinois 60025
All rights reserved. Printed in the United States of America
Regional offices of Scott, Foresman and Company are located in Atlanta,
Dallas, Glenview, Palo Alto, and Oakland, N.J.

FOREWORD

The American Government Readings Series has been designed to meet the need of American government courses and other courses in political science for broader, more imaginative selections of supplementary readings than those found in the traditional single-volume collection. All too often, the conventional reader is sadly uneven, thoroughly unimaginative, and so inadequate that the instructor is forced to create his own syllabus to achieve satisfactory, up-to-date coverage.

The American Government Readings Series avoids these weaknesses by substituting for the chapters in the single-volume effort individual volumes edited by specialists. By providing separate readers on specific subjects, such as the presidency, Congress, and civil rights, the series offers the instructor new variety and flexibility in constructing his course. By drawing on the resources of a group of specialists rather than a single generalist, the series promises both authority and originality.

The readings in each volume are derived from a variety of sources: books and monographs, professional and popular journals, and historical documents. They introduce stimulating dialogs between advocates of conflicting points of view, thereby involving the student in significant controversy over important issues. Each collection represents a range of difficulty and includes a balance of articles chosen for general interest, research significance, and theoretical import. Chapter introductions provide essential background information, and full headnotes lead the student into the individual selections.

A unique feature of the series is the original essay with which each editor closes his volume. Analyzing current issues and research, the essays point out their relevance for the student and, in the process, heighten his awareness of what a political scientist does and how he does it.

The Publishers

CONTENTS

PREFACE

"Civics texts would have us believe that the problem facing the citizen in a democracy is, to quote the title of a recent book in the field, *How to Be an Active Citizen*. According to this . . . view, a successful democracy requires that citizens be involved and active in politics, informed about politics, and influential. . . .

". . . [C]itizens in democracies rarely live up to this model. They are not well informed, not deeply involved, not particularly active; and the process by which they come to their voting decision is anything but a process of rational calculation."

In these few sentences, Gabriel A. Almond and Sidney Verba in *The Civic Culture* (Princeton University Press, 1963, pp. 473-474) catch the essence of what this volume of readings intends to investigate. The ideology of American democracy calls for the involvement of all citizens in politics and government on the basis of a genuine and informed interest. The consensus on the desirability and duty of participating is complete in the United States; even those who believe themselves powerless to affect the course of public policy feel compelled to vote.

Americans are taught at an early age that competition in politics, as well as in economics, is a "good thing." Even though children and adults alike shy away from the possible tension that open competition for public honor can create — witness all the club elections that involve only a single slate of candidates — most of us nevertheless subscribe to the importance of "the two-party system." Partisanship, then, accompanies participation as a fundamental component of our ideology.

Voting, Interest Groups, and Parties assesses the reality of American politics against the standards of our "activist" intentions. It does this not only by exploring the major avenues through which people can and do pursue their commitment to participate but also by indicating the dimensions of nonparticipation.

While there are numerous ways in which an individual can take part in democratic government — running for office, for example — many are by their nature not suitable for widespread participation. Others, though widespread, are too unimportant or, like "discussing politics," too diffuse for focused examination here. Accordingly, primary attention in this volume is given to three major avenues for mass participation in a democracy — voting, working as members of interest groups, and joining in party-related activity.

Bradbury Seasholes
Medford, Massachusetts

CHAPTER 1

TAKING PART

Voting forms the foundation of democratic politics. It is the basic art of democracy: first, because it is that mode of formal governmental action taken by the greatest number of people; and second, because it is the operational link between democratic theory and the real world.

This chapter deals mainly with voting and nonvoting. It is important to establish at the outset the extent of public participation through voting, compared with some of the other modes of participation. Fifteen years ago Julian Woodward and Elmo Roper reported the results of a national survey dealing with just this matter. Some of their findings are shown on page 2.[1] Even allowing for a certain amount of exaggeration in the answers, a picture of relatively high participation in voting emerges — at least in quadrennial presidential elections. But membership in an interest group or similar organization was claimed by less than a third of the sample, and party activity, even of the most rudimentary variety, attracted less than a ninth of the adult population.

Figures such as these do not exist independent of the context in which they occur. Part of that context is the political culture Almond and Verba describe in the quotation used in the Preface. Another part is historical: current data reflect the convergence of at least three voting trends in America — liberalization of requirements for voting eligibility, population growth, and changes in the distributions of relevant demographic characteristics. In the first selection in this chapter, Robert Lane traces the history of suffrage in the United States, examines current subgroup differences in voting and nonvoting, and speculates about trends for the future.

Because nonvoting conflicts with democratic ideology, its occurrence generates considerable alarm. For some people, the alarm takes the form of expressed disgust with "lazy voters." Others seek to explain nonvoting, or nonparticipation generally, as symptomatic of deep-seated pathology — alienation, resentment, disillusion, and so forth. Against this background of alarm,

[1]Julian L. Woodward and Elmo Roper, "Political Activity of American Citizens," *American Political Science Review*, XLIV (December 1950), 874.

	Per cent of total sample qualifying
Voting	
Once or more in last four years	75
Three times or more	47
Five times or more	21
Discussing public issues with others	
Discusses frequently and takes an equal share in the conversation	21
Discusses frequently and usually tries to convince others he is right	6
Belonging to organizations that take stands on public issues	
Belongs to one or more such organizations	31
Belongs to two or more	7
Written or talked to congressman or other public official to give own opinion on a public issue	
One or more times in the past year	13
Two or more times in the past year	7
Worked for election of a political candidate in last four years	11
Contributed money to a party or candidate in last five years	7

Morris Rosenberg explores the subject of nonparticipation with reference to the responses he obtained during a series of interviews and catalogues what he feels are the more significant causes. These causes should be carefully scrutinized and judged as valid or invalid bases for alarm.

Alienation as one source of nonparticipation has received a great deal of attention in recent years. Political alienation is viewed as an outcome of a severe disparity between ideals and reality. All of us respond to some extent to any disparity. Up to a point, a gap between ideals and reality provides desirable motivation and purpose for living. A society in which ideals and reality coincided would be a static and unchallenging kind of utopia. Problems arise when the gap becomes too great.

When too great a gap between ideals and reality opens, most Americans are likely to blame reality rather than ideals. This is the immediate response of the reformer, an admirable breed in our country's history. Despite his sense of outrage and anger, the reformer is fundamentally an optimist who believes that the solution to disparity between ideals and reality is to improve reality.

An alternative solution, however, is to lower ideals. Unattractive as this sounds at first, it must be given serious consideration. Although there is always the danger in a self-satisfied society that it will be chosen as the first course of action, it should be recognized as a reasonable second course, after reality seems to have been improved as much as possible. The third alternative, to conclude that ideals and reality are hopelessly unrelated, is by far the most damaging possibility, since it carries the seeds of personal and societal disintegration—unrelieved frustration for the individual and destructive behavior by individuals against society.

This understanding of the character of alienation leaves unanswered the crucial questions: To what extent are Americans alienated from politics? To what extent are their nonvoting and other forms of nonparticipation traceable to a fundamental resentment that causes them to reject the whole political system as an object of confidence and trust? The Rosenberg selection implicitly answers part of these questions by indicating a wide variety of causes of nonparticipation, most of which do not have components of alienation. Allen Schick pursues the matter further, carefully scrutinizing the nature of American negativism toward government and politics.

The chapter ends on two startling notes. First, William Andrews proposes that data on voting and nonvoting have been misinterpreted by those who see nonvoting as a substantial feature of our political life; re-examining voting figures, Andrews concludes that—at least in regard to this particular form of participation—the American record is quite good. Finally, Anthony Downs asks whether it is rational for a citizen to vote.

POLITICAL INVOLVEMENT THROUGH VOTING
Robert E. Lane

The historical facts about who could and who could not vote in the United States have always seemed surprising when juxtaposed with a fairly constant ideology concerning "popular" government. In general, elitist positions have been received coolly by Americans. But at the several junctures of our history when extension of the right to vote occurred, numerous voices have been heard defending the exclusion of a particular group from full participation in the political arena. The extension of suffrage by abandoning property or wealth as a prerequisite was effected rather quietly, but opposition to the inclusion of Negroes in the electorate has induced some startling rhetoric from a nation that defines itself as a democracy:

"Gentlemen concede that idiots and lunatics have not either a natural right or an artificial right to vote or to hold office. I ask them how they can give this right to a race of men who throughout their whole history, in every condition in which they have ever been placed, have demonstrated their utter inability for self-government."*

Women, too, were subjected to abuse of this unhappy character, but both groups nevertheless entered the electorate through constitutional amendment.

Securing the right to vote and exercising that right are entirely different matters, however. Lane's data show that groups newly admitted into the potential electorate have been slow to use their votes. Uncertainty about and unfamiliarity with political events are not dispelled quickly. And, of course, Southern Negroes repeatedly have been deterred from voting by psychological, economic, and physical intimidation, as well as by legal and administrative devices.

The Civil Rights Act of 1965 has at long last begun an assault on the remaining forces of repression that have kept Negro voting participation abnormally low. Lane shows that in the population at large, phenomena such as increasing education, assimilation of immigrant groups, and greater affluence all seem to indicate an end to the downward trend in American voting activity that persisted through the 1920's, but that, at the same time, contemporary subgroup differences in voting participation continue.

POLITICAL INVOLVEMENT: THE LESSONS OF HISTORY

Several generalizations, relating to sectional versus class conflict, the effect of candidate appeal, and the relationship of issues to turnout, are suggested by [Figures 1 and 2]. The most striking feature of the over-all picture is the persistent decline in the proportion of eligible voters making use of the franchise from 1896 to 1924. This trend appears to be independent of the periodic fluctuations in turnout from one election to the next, or at least seems to result from different causes. The plateau of participation from 1876 to 1896 was, in the first place, sustained by the sectional tensions associated with the Civil War, when the bloody shirt was flourished frequently as the symbol of the great conflict between North and South. Then, as the Civil War faded as a sectional issue, it was succeeded by the East-West split dramatized by the free silver fight. In the 'eighties and 'nineties party coalitions aligned the rural, debtor, and Democratic West and South against the urban, creditor, Republican East. The parties represented broadly opposed interests and causes, and were supported as such in each area. After 1896, however, growing industrialization, urbanization, concentration of wealth, and increased immigration, began to break up the Republican solidarity of the East. At the same time, some alleviation of economic discontent and a growth of commercial centers reduced the tendency of the West to make the sectional struggle the center of politics. With the parties presenting less sharp choices of policies, say Schlesinger and Eriksson,[1] voter interest dropped off.

While this explanation minimizes the appeal of the Progressive movement and the "New Freedom" (which were in large part middle-class movements), it obviously needs to be revised in light of the politics of the New Deal era. From 1932 onward, there has been a tendency to emphasize class interests in politics and to make the differences between them more meaningful. However, even with this modified class conflict, voting has not regained the high level of the late nineteenth century. The advent of female suffrage [in 1920] is one reason for this slump, but another may be the more equivocal incentive to

Reprinted with permission of The Free Press from *Political Life* by Robert E. Lane, pp. 23-52. Copyright © 1959 by the Free Press, a Corporation.
*Senator Garret Davis of Kentucky, quoted in the *Congressional Globe*, 40th Congress, 3rd Session, p. 1630.
[1]Arthur M. Schlesinger and Erik M. Eriksson, "The Vanishing Voter," *New Republic*, 40 (1924), 162-167.

FIGURE 2 PER CENT OF ELIGIBLE VOTERS VOTING IN PRESIDENTIAL ELECTIONS, 1856-1952

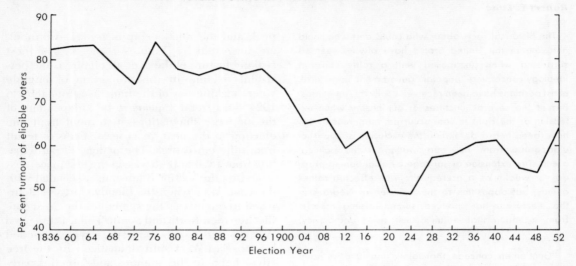

political participation in class as opposed to sectional conflict. In the United States sectional conflict tends to produce greater turnout for several reasons. For lower-class individuals, there is an implicit humiliation in acceptance of their relatively lower status, and hence a reluctance to participate in politics on a basis which emphasizes this lower status. An objective appraisal of one's interests is often distasteful and frequently not necessary. Both the reality of mobility and the illusions of classlessness fostered by American society contribute to the ease with which a person can avoid seeing politics in terms of socio-economic status. Failing to perceive these socio-economic ties to political life, a person may well regard a non-sectional

political alignment as relatively meaningless. Moreover, class conflict, because it involves geographical neighbors, is more unpleasant in many respects than is sectional conflict, which, within the local community, has uniting, rather than divisive tendencies. . . .

A second generalization—which we shall partially reject—attributes the major reason for variation in turnout to the intrinsic features of the candidates' personalities. This is an element of the more general theory of "resonance" between leaders and followers, that is, a belief that the characterological needs (moralistic, aggressive, etc.) of a group of followers are "satisfied" by the personality of the leader. There is no doubt but that this force is operative and that

FIGURE 1 PER CENT OF TOTAL POPULATION VOTING IN PRESIDENTIAL ELECTIONS, 1824-1952

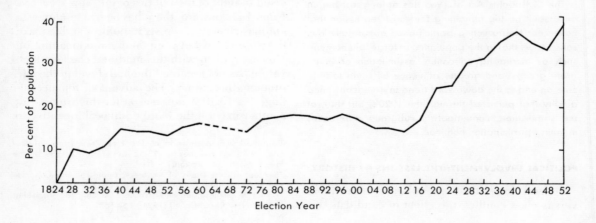

candidate appeal includes some such element. Moreover, it is probably a force somewhat independent of issues — but not nearly so independent of issues as has been supposed. Let us consider some historical problems associated with an excessive reliance upon this view as the basis for variations in turnout. One of these relates to the difference in apparent appeal of the same leader: Grant in 1868 and 1872, Roosevelt in 1932 and 1936, and, for a losing candidate, Bryan in his three elections. (On the other hand, note the identical turnout in Cleveland's two winning elections and also in the two FDR elections in 1936 and 1940, after he was better known and before we were in the war.) These considerations are, of course, only suggestive inasmuch as *two* major candidates are involved in each election.

Another such difficulty has to do with special features of public personality which are said to be especially appealing. If here one refers to a special resonance with the common man in the sense of mirroring the common man's own qualities, we cannot fail to note not only the appeal of the patrician Roosevelt, but also the marked increase in turnout in 1916 when the contest was between a reserved professor and an upper-class lawyer. Furthermore, on these grounds, how can we account for the poor drawing power evident in Bryan's last two campaigns? The Great Commoner had lost none of his capacity for identification with the man in the street, but he never again could rouse the country as he had in 1896.

One key to Bryan's differential appeal lies in the area of the campaign issues. In 1896 Bryan found in the silver issue a symbol of the desires and resentments of the agricultural West. To the dissatisfied, free coinage of silver was the solution to all their problems. Bryan's background, personality, and abilities were perfectly suited to exploit such an issue and thus bring him into close contact with the common man. But after 1896 free silver lost its political appeal, and, as Hofstadter says, "Bryan's political career after 1896 was a long, persistent search for an issue comparable in effect to free silver."[2] One can only conclude from such evidence that candidate appeal is closely related to the issues of the time; the two interact to produce varying degrees of interest, depending upon their interrelationship with each other and with the public mood. Candidates are appealing and issues are electrifying only with respect to the nature of the public involved and the time of the election

under analysis. Hence it may be said of Eisenhower, not that intrinsic features of his personality have a capacity to stir the electorate at any time, but rather that in 1952 and 1956 "For a great many voters, it was a happy combination of the man and the hour."[3]

As for the nature of the issues which seem most closely associated with a higher turnout, it is normally true that domestic and economic issues attract the greatest attention. Slavery, reconstruction, free land, monetary policies including the monetization of silver, tariff, control of trusts, labor, social security, relief, all seem to have been historically more salient than foreign policy. And current survey material in the last twenty years reinforces this impression of the greater weight given by the public to domestic issues. But the impact of wars upon electoral turnout seems nevertheless to be significant:

In general these data support the hypothesis that turnout tends to be high on the eve of wars and lower in post-war periods. This pattern has a certain logic. Periods just prior to major wars (not the Spanish-American war) are likely to be times of crisis, with problems of foreign policy and defense becoming salient and pressing. The issues attendant upon such crises tend to draw voters to the polls. The slumps in turnout generally associated with post-war elections can perhaps be partially accounted for by the natural letdown and diminution of interest which follow such periods of sustained participation. In fact, the evidence suggests that it is generally difficult to maintain political enthusiasm and emotion and that a relaxation of tension, sometimes accompanied by a reaction against the party which conducted the war (1918 and 1920, 1946), is inevitable in politics. People get tired of politics, and, being quick to lose interest, are more difficult to arouse no matter how appealing the candidates or how exciting the issues.

The above discussion suggests a [major] conclusion. . . . : few political events have single causes; different and often interrelated factors account for any single phenomenon. Thus candidates, issues, the public mood, party dispositions, and numerous other points must be considered in order to post a theory which adequately ac-

[2]Richard Hofstadter, *The American Political Tradition* (New York: Alfred A. Knopf, Inc., 1948), p. 193.
[3]Angus Campbell, Gerald Gurin, and Warren E. Miller, *The Voter Decides* (Evanston, Ill.: Row, Peterson & Co., 1954), p. 176.

TABLE I   THE IMPACT OF WAR ON ELECTORAL TURNOUT

Turnout in Presidential Elections

Four American Wars*	Election prior to outbreak of war	Election after conclusion of war
Civil War	slightly higher in 1860 than in 1856	markedly lower in 1868 than in 1864 or 1856
Spanish-American War	markedly higher in 1896 than in 1892	markedly lower in 1900 than in 1896 or 1892
World War I	markedly higher (reversal of trend) in 1916 than in 1912	markedly lower in 1920 than at any previous time (but woman suffrage accounts for most of this decline)
World War II	sustained high in 1940 compared to 1936 and before	markedly lower in 1944 and 1948 than in 1940 or 1936

* Because the 1952 election occurred during a period of truce in the Korean War, and hence is partially a war-year election, the Korean War is omitted from this table.

counts for historical fluctuations in level of electoral participation.

In summary, therefore, we may say:

■ The proportion of the population voting has increased almost continuously from the period of the Revolution to the present.

■ The proportion of the eligible voters making use of their franchise declined from the post-Civil War election of 1876 to 1928, when the trend (interrupted by the war) was reversed, and this proportion shows a tendency to increase.

■ Historically, periods of sectional conflict in the United States (North against South, East against West) have experienced greater electoral turnout than periods of class conflict.

■ Although the personal qualities of a candidate exert great influence on popular interest in politics, these qualities are dependent for their effect upon the issues associated with the candidate and the political mood of the public at the time.

■ The politics of pre-war periods attract popular interest and participation in public affairs; the politics of post-war periods fail to attract such interest and participation. . . .

VOTING IN ELECTIONS

The formal nature of the election will create situations with quite different meanings for the electors. First, consider the difference between voting on issues and voting for people, that is, referenda and constitutional amendments on the one hand and the election of candidates on the other. The whole complex of personal attraction (and repulsion) is a feature of the election of candidates but not of the referendum. Secondly, the difference between primaries and elections in two-party areas offers a distinction between a contest where a well-worn and familiar (party) loyalty is usually called into play and one where this is not present. Or, finally, consider the difference between local elections and national elections. The tangible material rewards at stake in the local election, combined with a more clear-cut ethnic appeal, evoke responses very different from the broader and more policy-oriented appeals involved in national elections. The voting in elections for aldermen or constable may represent popularity contests when these elections are separated from other elections; they may merely represent exercises in party loyalty when these offices are part of a long list of offices to be filled at a general mayoralty election. In this sense, although the marking of the ballot may be the same in every case, the type of election will, in large measure, structure the types of attitude, knowledge, and skills associated with electoral participation.

Yet the act of voting, however it may differ in the above respects, will almost universally require certain qualities of the voter. We refer to these here because such requisite qualities represent a kind of threshold which an individual must be able to pass before he can exercise the franchise; they sift the population for "culls" although not all non-voters are "culls" in this sense, by any means. In the first place, voting should be understood as an *act* involving an expenditure of energy and time, the coordination of muscles and mind, scheduling the event among other events, and partaking of the nature of a positive act in other ways. Second, voting requires a *decision;* perhaps a decision on a very low level of decisiveness, but nevertheless a positive commitment to one side or the other (with ticket splitters committing themselves

Demographic characteristics	Per Cent of Group Non-Voting Election year 1940	1948	1952
Sex			
Male	25%	31%	21%
Female	39	41	31
Age			
21-34		44	32
35-44		34	24
45-54		25	21
55 and over		37	23
Religion			
Protestant		42	32
Catholic		21	15
Jewish		—	—
No religion		—	—
Race			
White	32	34	21
Negro	64	64	67
Type of community			
Metropolitan areas	25	17	21
Towns and cities	32-35	37	27
Rural areas	39	59	32
Education			
Grade School		45	38
High School		33	20
College		21	10
Occupation of head of family			
Professional and managerial	22	25	12
Other white collar		19	19
Skilled and semi-skilled		29	26
Unskilled	40	50	40
Farm operators	39	58	33

Demographic characteristics	Per Cent of Group Non-Voting Election year 1940	1948	1952
Trade union affiliation of head of family			
Member		27%	23%
Non-member		38	27
Income			
Under $2,000		54	47
$2,000 — 2,999		39	32
$3,000 — 3,999		26	24
$4,000 — 4,999		25	17
$5,000 and over		18	12
Region			
Northeast		—	16
Midwest		—	15
South		—	51
Far West		—	23
Ethnic background (non-native born)			
Scandinavian		—	17
German		—	20
English-Scotch		—	19
Irish Catholic		—	5
Italian		—	11
Polish		—	13
Generation time in America (Omits Negroes)			
First (Foreign born American citizens)			
Second		—	19
Third		—	14
Fourth or more		—	16
Fourth or more		—	29

SOURCES: For 1948 and 1952: Angus Campbell, Gerald Gurin, Warren E. Miller, *The Voter Decides* (New York: Row, Peterson, 1954), pp. 70-4, 76, 77, 78; for 1940, Gordon M. Connelly and Harry H. Field, "The Non-Voter—Who He Is, What He Thinks," *Public Opinion Quarterly*, VIII (1944), 175-87.

more to individuals than parties). Third, the voting decision implies a certain *relatedness to society,* an awareness of surroundings, a listening to radio and reading of the newspaper, an awareness that *this* Tuesday is election day. Fourth, a voting decision usually implies the *implementation of an emotion.* The emotion may be fear of non-conformity, a partisan loyalty to a symbol or group, a dedication to a program, but whatever it is, the act of voting goes beyond the stage of merely experienced feeling. The person who cannot do this, remains to "stew in his own juice." Finally, the voting act is an *affirmation,* an interpretation that democracy is not a sham; the votes are counted, they do make a difference.

Some of these "threshold factors" along with many other social and psychic forces are reflected in the analysis of non-voting in 1948 and 1952 by various demographic groups, as revealed in Table II. This table tells a familiar story: non-voting is generally higher among women, the youngest eligible age group, Negroes, rural communities, non-union members, lower status (income, education, occupation) groups, and Southerners. Of all the states, Mississippi and South Carolina had the lowest rate of participation; of several occupations, service workers had the lowest rates of electoral participation.[4]

These relations do not hold true everywhere, of course, and indeed they are spurious in the sense that some third intervening variable, such as education, may cause the apparent differences in the rate of voting. A few of the areas where such third factors are operating will be perceived at once; others may be revealed by studies in which such third factors were controlled.

Since education, income, and urbanization are among the most significant social forces affecting non-voting, one would naturally examine these factors to see if they might account for other relationships, or exaggerate or conceal "true" relationships.

Age. Probably part of the reason why the younger group votes less than the middle group is their relatively lower income, although their relatively higher education would tend to increase turnout. Other reasons connected with age differences are certainly also at work, however. Among these are the fluidity of occupational interests, greater geographic mobility, less clearly defined reference and membership groups, greater emphasis on entertainment, and lower frequencies of home ownership.

Religion. The Catholic population tends to be both more urban (therefore in a higher voting milieu) and poorer (therefore in a lower voting group). Consequently there is no clear evidence in these data on the effect of religious affiliation or even ethnic grouping on the turnout. . . .

Race. Negro participation is depressed by external pressures and customs in the South, and by the lower income strata to which most Negroes everywhere belong. It is increased by the urbanization of the Northern Negro, but, since two-thirds of the Negroes live in the South, the urbanization factor will be much the smaller of the influences.

Type of Community. Metropolitan areas are more heavily immigrant, ethnic, Catholic, and Jewish; most of these groups have a higher than average voting rate. Hence the higher rate in Metropolitan areas will be a product of the presence of these groups—just as the voting

TABLE III PERCENTAGE VOTING IN 1944 PRESIDENTIAL ELECTION BY EDUCATION AND INCOME

| | Income | | |
Education	Upper Quarter	Middle Half	Lower Quarter
College	87%	76%	70%
High School	83	68	54
Grade School	83	67	54

SOURCE: Connelly and Field, "The Non-Voter—Who He Is, What He Thinks," *Public Opinion Quarterly*, VIII (1944), 179-80.

rates of these groups will be influenced by their urbanization.

Income and Education. Both of these elements are forces associated with higher voting rates, and each has an influence on voting independent of the other, as illustrated in Table III.

First, note that with reference to education it is college education that makes the difference in every income group; the high school and grade school groups being almost identical in their participation rates. More importantly, income and status roles are much more important than education: those with maximum income but minimum education scoring 83 per cent while those with maximum education but minimum income scoring only 70 per cent.

Although it is easy enough to get figures on the changing proportion of the total population voting over the years, data on the changing proportions within each group are not so readily accessible. Three sources of information, however, give us clues as to what is happening to this phase of participation: the above comparative figures for 1940, 1948, and 1952, a study covering three elections in New York City, and a comparison between 1924 and 1948 voting rates in identical groups in Delaware, Ohio.[5]

On the whole the following changes seem to be taking place:

Increases:
Negroes both in the North and South have greatly increased their rate of voting.
The foreign born population has greatly increased its rate of voting.

[4]Gordon M. Connelly and Harry M. Field, "The Non-Voter—Who He Is, What He Thinks," *Public Opinion Quarterly*, 8 (1944), pp. 175-87.
[5]Campbell and associates, *The Voter Decides*, pp. 70-74; Gerhart Saenger, "Social Status and Political Behavior," *American Journal of Sociology*, 51 (1945-1946), 103-113; Ben A. Arneson and William H. Eells, "Voting Behavior in 1948 as Compared with 1924 in a Typical Ohio Community," *American Political Science Review*, 44 (1950), 432-34.

Women have so increased their rate of voting that when education level is controlled they come rather close to voting in the same proportions as men.

In Northern cities their [the Negroes] voting rate approximates or exceeds the white rate.

The most poorly educated group (no schooling) have greatly increased their voting rate.

Jews have increased their rate of voting since the 1920's.[6]

Decreases:

Farmers and others in agricultural occupations have decreased their voting rate.

Young voters (21-29) have decreased their rate of voting.

People in certain trades closely associated with government, such as railroad and traction and. public service employees, have decreased their rate of voting.

One other question arises, not with respect to the incidence of non-voting in different groups, but with regard to the proportion of people who never vote: those who do not merely skip a particular election, but skip all elections. Unfortunately, we do not have data on the nature of this group—only its size. Warren Miller, in a discussion of the political profile of the electorate, finds that 10 per cent of the electorate old enough (age twenty-nine and over) to have voted in the presidential elections of 1944, and 1952 failed to vote in *any* of these elections.[7] Another interpretation by Samuel Eldersveld of a study which includes all ages, estimates that 17 per cent of the electorate have never voted.[8]

In reviewing this material, we find certain general relationships as well as information on the history and the incidence of voting behavior in society. Some of our conclusions may be set forth as follows:

■ The act of voting in different situations, although identical in form has different meanings and evokes different motives for the electors according to whether it involves (a) a choice of issues (referendum) or of men (elections), (b) a primary or inter-party election, (c) a local or national election, (d) a contest between men known "personally" to an elector or men known, if at all, largely through some identifying labels, etc.

■ The act of voting partially defines the electorate in imposing certain minimum requirements on the voter: energy and time for going to the polls, capacity to decide among conflicting claims, sufficient relatedness to society for awareness of the election, capacity to implement emotional predispositions, an affirmative view of the electoral process.

■ On the basis of relatively short-term and localized evidence, it seems probable that, as contrasted to twenty-five years ago, the following groups vote more frequently: foreign-born, women, Negroes, Jews, and least well educated. The following probably vote less frequently: farmers, youth, persons in government-related occupations.

■ At mid-century, on a national basis, non-voting was higher in the following classes of people: women, youth, Protestants, rural, Negro, lower income, less skilled occupations, less well educated, Southern. These incidences of non-voting are misleading, however, since overlapping third factors often account for the higher incidence of non-voting in a given group.

[6]Saenger, Loc. cit.
[7]Warren E. Miller, *The Political Profile of the American Electorate* (Ann Arbor, Mich.: Survey Research Center, undated), p. 10.
[8]Samuel J. Eldersveld, "The Independent Vote: Measurement, Characteristics, and Implications for Party Strategy," *American Political Science Review*, 46 (1952), 739.

SOME DETERMINANTS OF POLITICAL APATHY

Morris Rosenberg

For most people it is not enough to know that a certain proportion of the American citizenry choose not to participate in politics, even to the simple extent of voting. Most of us, whether out of mere curiosity or from a sense that revelation can aid reformation, feel compelled to determine who the nonparticipants are and why they do not participate.

The nonparticipants can be identified fairly simply by correlating nonparticipation with standard demographic characteristics such as age, sex, education, and religion. Both kinds of data — demographic and voting — are relatively easily obtained from respondents to political questionnaires or surveys. In addition, a great deal can be learned about, for example, the relationship of a person's age to his likelihood of not voting — without relying on surveys, because of the availability of both election and Census statistics for comparable geographic areas. We know with some certainty that the young person and the old person are both less likely to vote than someone who is middle-aged. Similarly, the positive relationship between the amount of a person's education and his likelihood of voting is a standard finding in political research. This kind of information was verified in the studies Lane summarized.

But demographic characteristics say nothing about *why* a person abstains from voting. To answer this question, we can either speculate about the psychological implications of these characteristics, or we can embark upon a specifically psychological investigation of nonparticipation. The following selection reports on the large number of interviews that Rosenberg conducted in an attempt to clarify the range of motivations leading to nonparticipation.

The classification of people into demographic groups is uncomplicated in that the categories are generally few in number and widely recognized; an interviewer and a respondent have little difficulty agreeing on the respondent's sex, age, income, and so forth. But categorization into politically relevant psychological groups is a different matter. Deciding what the categories should be is one substantial problem. Psychological categories can be developed at various "depths"; in one context it may be useful to classify people as "liberals" or "conservatives" and in another context to group them according to childhood fixations. The other problem is to decide what category best fits a particular respondent. Elaborate sets of indirect questions are usually required to determine this factor, and, unlike demographic classification, the respondent is usually unaware both of the possible categories and of the category in which he "belongs."

Because Rosenberg uses categories from various psychological levels, his list of "determinants of political apathy" lacks complete cohesion or undimensionality. Nevertheless, he presents a thoroughly plausible checklist and thereby lays the groundwork for further investigation into the frequency with which each type of determinant is found in the population as a whole.

It has been observed that political apathy is a very widespread phenomenon in American culture. Whether one measures apathy by the criterion of political involvement, knowledge or activity, the number of people who satisfy the culturally defined desiderata of participation is small.

There are those who consider this a serious malfunctioning of democracy. If men are to maintain control over their political destinies, they must be aware of what is going on, and must take a hand in determining public policy. On the other hand, there are some political theorists who find such apathy a favorable, rather than an unfavorable, sign. They interpret it to mean that the society is fundamentally contented, is characterized by consensus rather than by broad cleavages, and is basically stable.

If we accept the view that the democratic ideal encourages political interest and participation, then the question naturally arises: what are the factors which bring about this absence of political interest and activity? . . .

Limitations of space prohibit a discussion of the total range of factors . . . but three general factors merit discussion: (1) the threatening consequences of political activity, (2) the futility of political activity, and (3) the absence of spurs to interest and participation. Let us note how these factors are expressed concretely in [depth interviews conducted by the author].

THE THREATENING CONSEQUENCES OF POLITICAL ACTIVITY

It is generally felt that any restriction on the individual's right to express his political views freely represents a violation of the value of free-

"Some Determinants of Political Apathy," *Public Opinion Quarterly,* XVIII (Winter 1954), 349-366.

dom of speech. It is assumed that the uninhibited airing of ideas, viewpoints, and facts is conducive to the attainment of rational democratic decisions. It may thus be argued that loyalty investigations which frighten innocent people into silence represent a limitation on freedom of speech.

The issue of freedom of speech is usually posed in terms of whether the *government* applies pressure on the individual to restrain him from expressing his political views. Yet there are social factors which may be far more significant than governmental restraint in limiting the expression of social and political ideas. The sociological issue of freedom of speech boils down to the question of whether one is willing to take the *consequences* of expressing one's political ideas and working in their behalf; governmental restraint, expressed in physical coercion, is only *one* such possible consequence.

Our predominantly middle class respondents expressed many fears of presenting their own political views freely, but very rarely were these fears of political authority. In view of the present congressional investigations, it was surprising how few respondents seemed reluctant to reveal their political attitudes openly out of fear of governmental action. One respondent, it is true, carefully checked on the identity of the interviewer; he was reluctant to express his political views frankly to an unknown person who, for all he knew, might actually be an official investigator trying to draw him out. This is a telling commentary on how the current [McCarthy era] governmental investigations may immobilize certain people from the very minimum of political action. But such people proved to be rarities. The reason probably is that in any society, authoritarian or democratic, the individual is always free to stand up and express his views frankly in favor of the government; it is only when people desire to express views which challenge constituted authority that freedom of speech becomes an issue. Most of our respondents were Republicans or Democrats, and it did not appear to occur to them that *their* rights might be threatened by such investigations. Whether different results would appear among a more representative sample of respondents is a question requiring further research.

Our particular respondents, however, did express many fears of uninhibitedly expressing their political views, but the threats they mentioned tended to be of a social or psychological sort rather than of a political nature. The point to be stressed here is that political participation does not simply involve the relationship of the citizen to his government. Political participation may to a considerable extent involve *interpersonal interaction*. Consequently the dynamics of interpersonal relationships may have important implications for the operation of the democratic process. . . .

Threats to interpersonal harmony

One of the characteristics of politics in a democracy is that they are *controversial*. This establishes potentialities for interpersonal disagreement which may threaten the individual in many ways — particularly when the individual has an image of himself as a likeable, agreeable personality. Similarly, there are those who are so insecure that they are terrified of aggression or hostility of any sort directed against them.

Political discussion may threaten to alienate one's friends and neighbors.

" . . . When politics comes up in conversation, I always say — 'Let's talk about something else,' . . . especially when ——— is around. She's such a Democrat and gets so riled up."

Political discussion posed threats to a recent marriage:

". . . Right now I want to avoid friction — *we were just married last June* — so we try not to get into political discussions."

Political discussion may endanger one's position in a group and threaten one's sense of belongingness. For example, a woman who was very much wrapped up in the ——— organization feared that political discussion might jeopardize her position there. When asked why she did not discuss politics more, she replied: "Well, you see, a lot of local political wives are in ——— and I have to be careful.". . .

Thus people may impose a powerful self-censorship on political expression in order to avoid threats to friendship, marriage relationships, and group solidarity. While they are legally free to say what they please, many are unwilling to face the interpersonal consequences of such expression. Whether the situation is actually threatening or whether it is simply interpreted as such by the individual, the effect is the same.

Threats to occupational success

The economic processes of production and exchange in a complex industrial-commercial society involve interpersonal relations at almost every point. If political discussion has a potentially divisive and disharmonious interpersonal effect, then it may be avoided because of its threats to the important area of occupational success. This is particularly likely to occur among those engaged in the sale of products where the salesman must maintain harmonious relations with his customer; it is not, however, restricted to this area. In brief, politics fosters argument and dispute, whereas business success thrives on harmony and goodwill. Consequently, people may fear to talk politics because of the threat it poses to their occupational success.

Political discussion may threaten the harmonious relations essential to economic production. . . .

One respondent, a manager of a plant, was asked whether he had helped any candidates in the most recent campaign. He replied:

"No, because I never like to express my political views in public. . . . Since I have to deal with so many men, both in the plant and in the buying of (raw materials), there is no sense in making people angry at you over a local election.". . .

. . . The man engaged in commerce cannot afford to alienate *either* Democrats or Republicans; in this sense business is not merely apolitical but anti-political. Similarly an employer may be reluctant to alienate his workers, and a worker may be unwilling to jeopardize his job, in defense of his political principles. These factors may be extremely significant to the free expression of political ideas.

Threat of ego-deflation

While political discussion may ostensibly represent a form of intellectual intercourse designed to evaluate alternative principles, it cannot escape implicating the self. An attack on a man's principles may often be seen as a blow to his self-esteem. While some people may enhance their egos through victory in political argument, there are others who, facing the prospect of revealing factual ignorance or committing gross logical errors, seek to avoid the feeling of defeat, abashment, humiliation, or other discomfiture by staying far away from such dis-

cussions. An individual with a highly vulnerable ego may impose a censorship upon himself which is as rigid as any imposed in an authoritarian state.

One woman, observing that her husband and in-laws discussed politics, was asked whether she joined in these discussions. . . .

. . . "My husband and I talk it over, of course, but I don't talk about it in public because I don't know enough. I wish I knew more. Sometimes I'd like to say something."

Although these statements reflected a faith in expertism, combined with a rational insistence that a person should have some basis for his expressed opinions, they suggest that an individual may prefer to avert the danger of exposing himself to public ridicule rather than to freely and openly express his political ideas. . . .

THE FUTILITY OF POLITICAL ACTIVITY

In most cases a precondition for political activity is the conviction that what one does will make a difference, will have an effect of some sort. It is true, of course, that people may engage in some noninstrumental, goal activity such as political discussion simply because they are interested in the subject and enjoy talking about it. In most cases, however, political participation beyond the level of discussion probably has the aim of *getting one's will translated into political action*. But, people tend to be motivated to action only if they feel that this action leads to the desired goal.

One general factor contributing to political apathy is the feeling that activity is futile. The individual feels that even if he were active, the political results he desires would probably not come to pass. There is consequently no point in doing anything.

In expressing this sense of futility, the individual can focus on either the subject or the object of action. On the one hand, he can focus on certain characteristics of himself; e.g., he is insignificant, powerless, or incompetent. On the other hand, he can focus on the characteristics of the objects to be influenced; e.g., political representatives pay no attention to him, political machines run things just as they please, and so on. But if his representative pays no attention to him, this may be either because *he* is too unimportant or because *the representative* is unresponsive to the public will. In other words, each "reason" for feeling that political activity is futile implies both a characteristic of the individual effort and a characteristic of the agents to be influenced. For analytical purposes it is important to distinguish between reasons phrased in terms of the self and those phrased in terms of the nature of the political structure, although these should not be interpreted as representing alternative reasons.

Futility based on the sense of personal inadequacy

It is rather easy to see why, in a mass society characterized by broad disparities in power, an individual may tend to develop a sense of personal insignificance and weakness.

The feeling of the futility of action, deriving from a sense of personal insignificance, is likely to be particularly strong when the individual feels himself to be either (a) only one in relation to a great many, or (b) a weak person in relation to strong and powerful forces.

Simmel has noted that as the size of the group increases, each individual alone makes less of a difference to the totality.[1] Although the proportion of potential voters who actually go to the polls in the United States is relatively small, the absolute number is extremely large; the 1952 national elections attracted over sixty million voters. Many of our respondents appeared overwhelmed by this huge number of participants and felt that their vote would have little effect on the outcome of the election one way or the other.

. . . "My vote will always count, yet one vote one way or the other doesn't make much difference." . . .

People may also tend to consider any serious political efforts on their parts as futile because they feel that they have very little individual power. They feel that their own voices are too weak, their own strength too puny, to make much political difference. . . .

"What does the working man care about politics, anyway? What can he do, even if he did care? That's probably it. . . . What can he do? Nothing should bother him anyway. The country will still go on just the same for the average working man.". . .

In some cases, the *individual's self-image* does not correspond to his picture of the re-

quirements of political activity. His sense of inadequacy is based on special personality characteristics.

One respondent was asked whether he would care about campaigning. "No, I don't think so. Unless I felt strongly enough about something, I would. I'm not much of a salesman. I never cared about buttonholing."

"I don't really go in for it that much. I don't know. I guess I'm more of a listener in that line."

The unmanageability of political forces

Many of the respondents who expressed a sense of futility that their own political action would culminate in a desired political result placed less stress on their own impotence and more on the unresponsiveness of political powers to their pressure. The feeling was that (1) the political representative, (2) the political machine, (3) the "government," or (4) some anonymous agencies of power simply ignored the will of the people; they made their own decisions almost completely uninfluenced by the people.

Under these circumstances, political activity was viewed as futile. Respondents expressing these views tended to feel that they had lost control over the political decision-making process; their political destinies lay in the hands of others.

Many people felt that their *elected representatives* were unconcerned with, and unresponsive to, the will of the people.

. . . "You say to a guy, 'I don't like you; I'm not going to vote for you.' He say, 'If you vote for me I'm your friend, and if you don't vote for me, I'm still your friend.' But if he get elected, he don't do nothing for you. . . . This politics is really a funny thing."

Many respondents appear to feel that once the *political machines* gain power, the citizens' control over the political process tends to be lost.

"The machine is too strong to do what you want."

"The machines run things all around. . . .

[1] *The Sociology of Georg Simmel,* tr. and ed. by Kurt H. Wolff (Glencoe, Ill.: The Free Press, 1950), Part II.

Working to stop the machine could go on and on and still get no place. They'll always be there."

The centralization and concentration of government may produce a sense of remoteness from the decision-making process. The individual feels that he cannot maintain control over political decisions made by powerful figures hundreds and even thousands of miles away. . . .

Finally, there are some people who feel that action is futile because the basic political decisions are in the hands of certain *powerful anonymous forces*. The citizen cannot influence them, not simply because they are remote or unresponsive, but because he does not even know who they are. . . .

It is relevant to note the influence of the time factor in politics. At election time the citizen's sense of power and incentive for action is likely to be maximal. If the individual wishes to get his will translated into political action, he can do something about it, secure in the conviction that he is making some contribution toward that end. Not only may he vote for the candidate who propounds his views and position, but he may also seek to persuade others to do the same. He may thus feel some sense of control over the political process.

However, the *periodicity* of American elections requires the citizen to exercise his power at arbitrarily predetermined times, not when it suits his mood. Thus the individual who is angry at an incumbent or enthusiastic about a candidate may often have to wait a year or more before he can vote again. It is difficult for the human organism to maintain a high level of emotional ardor and involvement over a long period of time. The more characteristic reaction, therefore, is to withdraw one's emotional involvement from politics. Once emotion is withdrawn, of course, vigorous political activity becomes difficult. In other words, *electoral periodicity is not resonant with human reactions*. The individual has power at election time but tends to consider action futile at other times.

. . . "Once a man is elected and he turns out no good, it is too late to do anything about it."

"They might not do what they say. Either they can't do it, or they say, 'I'm in now, so I don't have to do it.'"

The citizen thus feels a *discontinuous* sense of control over the political process. He has some power at the periodic intervals of election time, but most of the time he sees no relationship between his desires and action and actual political results. In addition, he cannot work to translate his will into action immediately but must "save up" his irritations, desires, or enthusiasms until the next election. This characteristic of the political structure may often cause him to feel that there is no point in getting excited or doing anything about political matters, i.e., it encourages apathy. It is true, of course, that citizens can write to their congressmen or participate in pressure groups, but these alternatives seldom appeared to have occurred to our respondents.

The foregone conclusion

The sense of futility generated by activity designed to translate one's will into action is likely to be strongest, of course, when one has reason to believe that such action will never come to pass. When a party has no more than a theoretical chance of victory, when the election is a foregone conclusion, then the rather vague incentive of an "impressive defeat" is little spur to vigorous political activity.

The individual feels that no matter how hard he works, the candidate he supports will not be elected in any case. This is particularly likely to be the case when a state or local community has a well-established and virtually unchangeable tradition of electing candidates from one party. Many people prefer to remain inactive, or at least uninvolved, rather than to face the frustration stemming from the certain defeat of their candidates or principles. . . .

The gap between ideal and reality

Thus far we have focused on the individual's feeling of futility regarding the possibility of attaining some practical political goal. It is also possible, however, that if the goal itself is too remote or too difficult to attain, the individual will give up hope of trying to reach it. The level of social aspiration may be so very high that, rather than serving as an incentive to action, it may discourage and immobilize the individual.

For example, some people may sincerely embrace the social values of democracy, honesty in government, etc. We might thus expect them to be politically active in behalf of these principles. However, these values may be so high and pure, and the facts of political life so low and base, that they abandon any hope of bridging the gap between the normative and factual orders. Indeed it is often precisely the people who embrace the value of democracy most fervently who suffer the greatest disillusionment. . . . This gap between the factual and normative orders of society is expressed clearly in this respondent's pungent statement: "The United States is great on paper."

"Everyone who goes to the polls wants democracy. They all consider themselves democrats with a small d. By the time the idea is represented, it ends up far afield from the original ideals. . . . Unfortunately, in spite of the need to vote, not only in America but in any democratic country, very rarely is the democratic objective accomplished."

It is true, of course, that even where the ideal is very low, the reality may be considered so remote from it as to render an effort to bridge the gap futile. The wider this gap, however, the more discouraged the individual is likely to be. . . .

ABSENCE OF SPURS TO ACTION

In illustrating the fact that people may be reluctant to be political participants out of fear of the potential dangers of such activity or because they consider it futile, we have stressed the *deterrents* to participation. However, it is also relevant to examine the question of apathy in the light of the absence of influences, stimuli, or appeals which might encourage participation. Theoretically there is no limit to the number of factors which can *fail* to stimulate an individual to political activity. Nevertheless, it seems relevant to cite certain factors, as they appeared in the interviews, which might have been influential in stimulating participation.

It would appear appropriate to analyze this section in terms of the concept of *attributes* and *influences*. Under the heading of "attributes" would be included those reasons given by respondents which indicated that it was some characteristic of politics which lacked appeal or which did not seem to offer any gratification. Certain factors which appeared among some of our respondents are: (1) The fact that the subject-matter of politics is not psychologically compelling; (2) The act or process of

political activity lacks noninstrumental gratifications, fails to offer immediate satisfactions; and (3) the instrumental *results* of political activity do not appear to satisfy urgent and direct needs or provide important satisfactions. Under the heading of "influences," we refer to those cases in which people or groups fail, either by direct thrust or by shining example, to activate or inspire the respondent. Obviously these attributes and influences are not alternative determinants of apathy; for purposes of analysis, however, it is essential to consider them separately.

The subject matter of politics is often not psychologically compelling

Since the political institution deals with problems of the total society, involving subjects of general interest and concern, it tends to have an *abstract* or *impersonal* quality. However much the mass media seek to concretize and personalize political matters, they still remain, for many people, dull, remote and uninspiring.

One respondent mentioned that he did not pay much attention to national politics in the newspapers. When asked why, he replied:

"Well, I'm not interested enough. I don't take the time to read such matters. I like to read more exciting things, such as kidnap cases, and I also like the sports' section a lot." . . .

Absence of noninstrumental gratifications

The individual's incentive to political activity is often dulled by the absence of direct and immediate satisfactions to be derived from the activity itself. Just as people may engage in work not exclusively for the prestige and monetary rewards to be obtained from it but also because the work itself is satisfying, so people might conceivably engage in political activity because they enjoyed it, even if the goals they sought were not attained. Many people, however, find their current activities much more directly gratifying than political activity. . . .

One respondent was asked why she happened to miss the campaign speeches.

"I didn't have the time. If I had had the time, I would have been more interested. I work each day at the Community Center and it takes up most of my free time. I also devote many evenings to work there. I feel my work there is much more important than politics.". . .

Political results meet few direct and urgent needs

Most people, concerned with the immediate and imperative needs and exigencies of day-to-day life, do not conceive of political action as a vehicle for the satisfaction of these needs. Politics may be viewed as a moderately interesting spectacle, but one that is remote from the direct concerns of daily life. The man who wants an apartment usually does not attempt to get one by lobbying vigorously for federal housing projects; rather, he consults agents, newspapers or friends. A woman who wants lower food prices ordinarily does not attempt to achieve it by joining a citizens' committee striving to apply pressure on Congress to restore price controls; rather, she goes several blocks out of her way to shop at a super-market whose prices are lower than those of the neighborhood grocer. Lack of concern with politics is understandable when viewed in this light. . . .

People often lack a personal thrust to action

Empirical studies of politics have shown that personal influence may be of great importance in determining political attitudes and behavior.[2] Our data suggest that the interpersonal factor may operate in several different ways to promote apathy or discourage participation.

Potential participants may not be contacted by friends or party organizations.

One respondent claims that she would have been active had the stimulus been available. She was the friendly, cooperative type, always willing to lend a hand. When she was asked whether she had worked, she said:

"No, I wasn't asked to do anything. Many of my friends were asked to help — ring doorbells, stamp envelopes, and things like that. But I wasn't asked to do anything. Had I been asked, I would have been glad to help." . . .

Such respondents were certainly apathetic at the outset, but, as relatively compliant personalities, they might have been induced to participate. Such activity might in turn have led to increased interest. The absence of initial personal stimulation, however, ruled out the possibility that a start toward participation would be made.

Those who might consider it a social responsibility to participate politically may be reassured by the observation that most other people are apathetic. It also provides a very convenient rationalization for apathy.

"You can probably class me as apathetic, except when it's brought right to my attention, but I think most people are the same way. . . ."

Thus, many people are not motivated because of the absence of a shining example by others. Furthermore, whatever guilt they feel may be assuaged by the observation that others (including the most respectable) are equally apathetic. It is reasonable to speculate, incidentally, that an individual who might be ready for action would be discouraged by the spectacle of such wide-spread apathy; he might feel that he could not carry the burden with so little help. Thus apathy may become self-reinforcing. . . .

. . . A number of additional factors which our data suggest might contribute to political apathy [are] worth noting. . . . Some people are apathetic because they feel there is no need to do anything; they are contented with the social and political system, have faith in their representatives, and see no need for change. Their basic contentment tends to be linked with a confidence in the basic stability of the society. There are others who would favor change, but who feel that there is no real difference between the two major parties; the outcome of elections, therefore, lacks significance. Some people do not participate actively because of the incertitude of their political convictions; to them politics may be confused, complicated, contradictory; political communications may be rejected as propaganda; or the individuals may be uncertain regarding their own political activity. Others may be too exhausted by the pressure of other activities to pay much attention to it. Certain women express the attitude that political activity would be out of keeping with their social roles. Some people's reluctance to think about political matters ranges from a certain degree of mental laziness to a phobia toward serious thought which borders on the pathological. These and other factors would have to be examined before an adequate understanding of the determinants of political apathy could be achieved.

[2]Paul F. Lazarsfeld, Bernard Berelson, and Hazel Gaudet, *The People's Choice* (New York: Columbia, 1948), Second edition, Chaps. XV and XVI.

POLITICAL NEGATIVISM
Allen Schick

The stability of United States government points to the basic popular acceptance of its operation. Yet an impressive number of scholars has argued that a significant portion of the American citizenry does not share the majority's satisfaction. A variety of "signals"—particularly nonvoting and voting *against* rather than *for* candidates—have been interpreted as evidence of substantial popular alienation from politics. The term "alienation" suggests total rejection of the political system, not simply transient dissatisfaction with particular candidates, administration, or politicians. Alienation, defined this starkly, is a threat, and consequently a matter of highest concern, to an ongoing polity interested in maintaining its basic modes of operation. It is also of theoretical importance to the scholar interested in the viability of large-scale government undertaken with an intention to meet the requirements of democratic ideology.

Schick takes a close look at the nature of the data that are so often cited as evidence of alienation. He concludes that, for the most part, negative phenomena in American politics are misinterpreted as instances of alienation. Instead, he argues, much American negativism towards politics and government has a benign effect—may, in fact, be essential to a workable democracy. His discussion encompasses the totality of our political culture, but it also bears on the specific question of the significance of nonvoting.

"The world we have to deal with politically," Lippmann observed 40 years ago, "is out of reach, out of sight, out of mind. It has to be explored, reported, and imagined. Man is no Aristotelian god contemplating all existence at one glance."[1] In relation to the political world man stands in the position of the blind men describing the elephant in the famous fable. For each man, politics is that part of the political world with which he has some contact. There is little likelihood, however, that the fragment he experiences is a true sample of the total political world or an unambiguous picture of political reality. Ambivalence—the admixture of discontent and satisfaction—is nurtured by the way we experience political things.

Many of our cognizable contacts with government come about when something goes awry. The routine and conventional workings of government pass by without notice. It is when our routine or the government's is disrupted that we become aware of government. The mass media behave in much the same fashion. No newspaper, however comprehensive or unbiased it may be, can report all political matters. Newspapers often give special attention to questionable political practices and ignore the unexciting routines of political life. Because what we know about government is in many ways limited to those things the media select for us, there is a constant barrage of stimuli reinforcing political opprobrium. . . .

. . . The American political system furnishes many more opportunities for the expression of political discontent than for expressions of satisfaction; one must be careful not to take the standard indications of discontent as prima-facie evidence of alienation. . . . [To] collect commonplace reactions to politics and categorize them under the rubric of "alienation," [is to] neglect . . . the probability that these cynical reactions are expressed by persons who experience overriding satisfaction from, and loyalty to, the political system. . . .

Political attitudes are not expressed and cannot be interpreted *in vacuo*. The political style of a nation has a bearing on the way people respond to opinion surveys, and on the meaning of their responses. A conception of alienation must be framed in terms of the place of politics in American life. . . .

There is often a tendency to fit the pattern of American politics into prefabricated, "made in Europe" categories of analysis. Too many studies, steeped in classical sociology, start with the presumption that the American people must be alienated because they are living in a mass society and build up their evidence from this dubious premise. . . .

THE OPPROBRIUM OF POLITICS

In his study of *America as a Civilization*, Max Lerner observes that "the most characteristic trait of the American political style . . . is the belittling of politics."[2] Parties and politics

From "Alienation and Politics," a paper delivered before The American Political Science Association in Chicago, September 1964. Reprinted by permission of The American Political Science Association and Professor Schick.

[1] Walter Lippmann, *Public Opinion*, Macmillan Paperbacks Edition (New York, 1961) p. 29.
[2] Max Lerner, *America as a Civilization: Life and Thought in America Today* (New York, 1957) p. 356.

have never enjoyed high status in America. Charles Dickens detected this during his visit to America in 1842: "One great blemish in the popular mind of America, and the prolific parent of an innumerable brood of evils is Universal Distrust."[3] The sources of this mistrust can only be conjectured here. Various writers have attributed it to the emphasis on individualism; our revolutionary origins; the experiences of frontier life; negative images of government carried to these shores by immigrants; the depreciation of authority in family, school, and group; and the belief in free enterprise.

Expressions of political discontent thrive in such an environment. Politicians, Levin notes, "are one of the few culturally 'legitimate' objects of public scorn."[4] It is easier to condemn politics than to glorify it. Hence, much of what passes as political discontent may be commonplace and fashionable deprecation of politics. Moreover, every misstep of the political system confirms and reinforces the prevailing opprobrium, while laudable occurrences either produce skepticism or go unnoticed. What Herbert Gans found in Boston's West End probably applies to most Americans. ". . . they not only expect to find corruption and wrongdoings before the evidence is available, but may reject contrary evidence when it is available."[5]

In evaluating this *caveat emptor* attitude it is important to keep in mind a crucial dichotomy . . . : politics must be distinguished from the political system; the former designating the conventional meaning of politics as parties and politicians, the latter referring to the overall system of government including economic and social relationships and symbols of national identification. It is one thing to be alienated from politics in the first sense, but quite another thing to be alienated in the second sense.

THE PLACE OF POLITICS IN A DEMOCRACY

One of the great enigmas of American politics is the failure of the citizen to give more attention to public affairs. Government does more things, exercises greater controls, and impinges upon our lives in more ways than ever before. Yet the citizen is apathetic, indifferent and uninformed. "Political Institutions," Mills laments, have "become more objectively important to the course of American history, but because of mass alienation, less and less of subjective interest to the population at large."[6] Mass apathy, so the argument runs, stands as the outstanding demonstration of political alienation.

Yet there is another side to this ambivalent picture. In addition to the recent findings of Almond and Verba that Americans are better informed and more active politically than citizens of other democracies, and the impressive evidence gathered by William Andrews that Americans vote in much higher proportions than standard estimates indicate,[7] there is a need to understand the place of politics in American life. Unlike the politics of the Athenian *polis*, the politics of American democracy is not an autonomous sphere of life. Politics rarely is pursued for its own sake, but to achieve wants which cannot be satisfied by private means. Now the expansion of governmental activity has not made politics subjectively more important to the citizen because there has occurred simultaneously a vast expansion of the private sector. As the American people grow more affluent, they find it less necessary to rely on politics to satisfy their everyday wants. Such needs as housing, employment, recreation, and medical are, for most people, more readily met by private action rather than by political means. For the ordinary citizen, secure in job, home, and family, politics is therefore a minor and often remote concern. Politics, in short, is of marginal interest to most individuals because it is of marginal utility in their everyday lives.

[3]Charles Dickens, "It Would be Well If They Loved the Real Less and the Ideal More," in Henry S. Commager (ed.) *America in Perspective,* A Mentor Book (New York, 1962) p. 101.
[4]Murray Levin, *The Compleat Politician: Political Strategy in Massachusetts* (New York, 1962) p. 161.
[5]Herbert J. Gans and George Blackwood, *The Urban Villagers: Group and Class in the Life of Italian-Americans* (New York, 1962) p. 169.
[6]C. Wright Mills, *White Collar: American Middle Classes* (New York, 1951) p. 350.
[7]Gabriel A. Almond and Sidney Verba, *The Civic Culture* (Princeton, 1963); and William G. Andrews, "Don't Blame the American Voter," *The New York Times Magazine,* October 18, 1964.

DON'T BLAME THE AMERICAN VOTER
William G. Andrews

Americans excel at self-criticism. One index of the vitality of our system of government, in fact, is our willingness to identify our faults, broadcast them, and, of course, rectify them. Criticism of citizen apathy in elections is one of the most common instances of this general phenomenon. Alarm at low turnouts on election day is the predictable tone of the press and others who express public viewpoints after an election, particularly after off-year local elections.

Rosenberg's article gave some insight into several of the reasons people fail to vote (or otherwise participate in politics), but most of the reasons would not be accepted as valid excuses by people who are deeply concerned with low participation. The selection by Downs on pages 000-000 suggests explanations for nonvoting sufficiently novel as not likely even to be known, let alone accepted, by the deeply concerned. Andrews approaches the problem in an entirely different manner—by denying the basic conclusion that Americans are apathetic. He argues that comparisons of American voting turnout percentages with those of other Western democracies ignore the significant differences between the political systems involved and, moreover, that such comparisons juxtapose figures computed on very dissimilar bases. While readers will differ in their judgments about whether the facts presented justify the author's strong optimism, "Don't Blame the American Voter" is an important and challenging dissent from the dominant point of view on voting and nonvoting.

Every four years, the American voter is castigated for apathy, laziness, alienation, lack of civic virtue and a general unwillingness to keep himself informed on political affairs. His counterparts in other countries are held up as models to be emulated if American democracy is to be saved from collapse. . . .

But are the critics correct? . . . In voting participation, in the variety and volume of his electoral activity, in interest and knowledge, the American voter is, in fact, a much healthier creature than the diagnosticians are willing to admit. Indeed, I contend that his performance excels that of voters in other countries in most respects.

Let us look first at his allegedly inferior voting participation. In 1960, for instance, the voting-age population was 107 million and 68.8 million votes were counted in the Presidential election. This is described by the critics as a 64.3 per cent turnout and that figure is then compared unfavorably with the percentages posted by other Western democracies: Great Britain, 78.7 per cent in 1959; West Germany, 87.5 per cent in 1961; France, 68.7 per cent in 1962; Italy, 92.9 per cent in 1963; Switzerland, 66.1 per cent in 1963. . . .

But these foreign figures are based not on the voting-age population but on the number of *registered voters* in each country. If the American results in 1960 are computed on the same basis, therefore, we find that of *our* registered voters about 85.3 per cent cast their ballots.

The figures are still not strictly comparable, of course. Registration procedures vary enormously from state to state in America and from country to country in Europe. Even in those states with a system of permanent registration similar to European practice, registration lists are not cleared as often as in most such countries. Also, the American population is more mobile than that in Europe. For both these reasons, the number of persons who figure on registration lists but who have moved out of their districts or died is probably proportionately greater in the United States. On the other hand, it can be argued that many Americans who are eligible to vote do not take the trouble to register. But in any case, it can be seen that voting participation is far more nearly comparable to that in most Western democracies than is generally supposed.

But whether or not as many Americans go to the polls as do voters in most other democracies, they certainly go more often and do more when they get there.

They go more often because nowhere else, except in British local elections, are biennial elections common. Every two years the voter chooses his Congressman. Twice every six years he names a Senator. Sixty of our 99 state legislative chambers are elected biennially. Fifteen state governors serve for two-year terms as do many state administrative officers.

Over half (53.9 per cent) of America's Mayors hold office for one- or two-year terms, along with 39 per cent of our municipal councils. And since the overwhelming majority of municipal elections are not held concurrently with state and national elections, most Americans are called to the polls twice every two years — not allowing for primaries, special referenda, school-board elections, annual and special town meetings and so on.

The American voter also works harder at the polls because he is called upon to make a greater number of decisions than his counterparts abroad (with the possible exception of the voter in Switzerland). In most countries, the voter decides only who will represent him in local, national, and sometimes regional legislatures. In the United States, he may make as many as 11 additional political decisions.

(1) He decides who will be his chief executives. . . .

(2) The American voter decides who will head the principal state and local administrative agencies. . . .

(3) He chooses the members of second legislative chambers. . . .

(4) He names by ballot many specialized administrative or supervisory boards and commissions — school boards, university regents, public utility commissions, boards of assessors, finance committees, museum trustees, executive councils, traffic commissions and so on. Where such organizations exist abroad, they are usually appointed in the same way as other administrators.

(5) In all states, the American voter elects at least some judges and in most states all of them. In no other country is this done. Abroad, the judiciary is either appointive or a specialized branch of the civil service or a combination of the two.

(6) Some American voters have the privilege of being able to change their minds between elections and to decide by popular vote to remove a public official from office. In 12 states and many cities this may be done through recall petitions and elections. (In practice, this power is rarely used. Only one state Governor, two other state officers and about half a dozen Mayors of major cities have ever been recalled.)

(7) In eight states, the constitution requires that voters be asked at regular intervals if they wish a constitutional convention to be summoned. The revising convention is also fairly common in other states and, so far, more than 200 have been held. On each occasion the American voter must decide who shall be his delegate. In most other countries, constitutional conventions are held only to replace a regime that has collapsed.

(8) Americans also play a unique role in picking party candidates through direct primary elections and nominating conventions. And in many states even party officials are elected at the same time. Elsewhere, candidates are usually chosen by party constituency committees, sometimes subject to the approval of the national parties. Unless the voter abroad is a member of the party, he usually knows nothing of its proceedings and has no opportunity to take part in party decisions.

(9) The responsibilities of American voters also go beyond choosing their leaders. The popular referendum, by which they are called upon to decide constitutional and legislative issues by ballot, is more widely used in the United States than anywhere else except Switzerland.

. . . At the local level, literally tens of thousands of issues are passed on every biennium, so that a typical voter will probably answer four or five referendum questions each time he goes to the polls in a state and local election.

(10) Initiative, another device of direct democracy, enables American voters to petition for the inclusion of a question on the ballot despite opposition by the legislature. Although less widely used than the referendum, the right exists in 23 states, and again, only Switzerland has a comparable institution in frequent use.

(11) More than 1,400 towns, mostly in New England, practice town-meeting government whereby adult citizens are expected to meet at least once a year to deliberate public business and arrive at policy decisions. Only in certain cantons of Switzerland and in about 3,300 small English parishes does a comparable institution exist.

To this list of electoral responsibilities one might also add the American voter's responsibility to register. In other countries, the state itself takes the initiative in preparing lists of eligible voters; here, it falls to the individual.

When confronted by the reality of this massive participation of the American voter in the affairs of state and nation, some critics retreat to the argument that his participation is ill-informed and grudging. They quote the studies showing that from 15 to 30 per cent of the American public is unaware of even the most important foreign policy issues, and that only about

25 per cent is consistently well-informed. (The performance is usually somewhat better in the area of domestic policy.)

Admittedly, these figures should send shivers down the spines of idealists, but they seem a little less distressing when compared with the results of studies among the electorates of other Western democracies.

It is not very heartening, for instance, to learn that only about 60 per cent of Americans had "heard or read anything about" NATO at the time the treaty was signed in 1949, but this doesn't look so bad against the fact that only 37 per cent of Frenchmen and 40 per cent of Germans knew about the organization as late as 1955, or that only 38 per cent of Britons knew about it in 1957. . . .

But the most reliable comparative study of the American voter and his foreign counterpart is a recent survey of political attitudes made by Gabriel Almond and Sidney Verba in their book "The Civic Culture." Key questions were put to samples of voters in America, Great Britain, West Germany and Italy, with these results (expressed as percentages): Citizens who could

name four or more party leaders: United States, 65; Great Britain, 42; Germany, 69; Italy, 36. Citizens who believed they could not influence the government: United States, 15; Great Britain, 19; Germany, 34; Italy, 47. Citizens who were poorly informed on politics: United States, 13; Great Britain, 13; Germany, 8; Italy, 33. Citizens who felt satisfaction when voting: United States, 71; Great Britain, 43; Germany, 35; Italy, 30. Citizens who identified themselves with a party: United States, 82; Great Britain, 61; Germany, 44; Italy, 14.

On the evidence, therefore, it is clear not only that Americans go to the polls in numbers comparable to those in other countries, but that they are probably better prepared and show greater interest than most. . . .

American democracy is no fragile plant. It is a sturdy oak—and still growing as the Southern Negro is assimilated into the political community. It serves no useful purpose, therefore, to nag the voter with often unfounded complaints. His performance may fall short of perfection, but it is the best the world has yet known—and it is still improving.

THE CAUSES AND EFFECTS OF RATIONAL ABSTENTION
Anthony Downs

The traditional American concern about nonparticipation, expressed behaviorally by such events as "get-out-the-vote" campaigns in the mass media, usually sounds a moral theme: in a democracy, it is a citizen's duty to vote. One such campaign, however, conducted in 1964 by the American Heritage Foundation, appealed to rational self-interest:

"Vote . . . and the choice is *yours!*
Don't vote . . . and the choice is *theirs!*"

Downs also treats the matter of political participation in terms of individual self-interest—but he does so with much greater sophistication. In *An Economic Theory of Democracy* he does not rely on questionnaires, election results, census figures, or other empirical material. Instead, he asks what the politically rational individual would do in a democracy. By deduction from basic propositions concerning the nature of democracy and political rationality, he arrives at a set of sometimes startling conclusions.

Downs' tightly reasoned deductive theory is not intended to portray American political activity as it

actually occurs. Rather, it is meant to illuminate the extent to which real politics incorporates rational action, as narrowly defined: ". . . action which is efficiently designed to achieve the consciously selected political or economic ends of the actor."*

Central to Downs' reasoning is the assertion that casting a vote "is of small significance." This means that each person's vote contributes only $\frac{1}{nth}$ to an election outcome, where n is the total number of voters. The voter's psychological evaluation of his vote's worth involves a further calculation of how evenly the total vote is likely to split. If the election contest appears to be close, this calculation makes the individual's vote seem somewhat more valuable—but still miniscule in impact. In reading the following excerpt, it will be important to consider what other psychological considerations Downs intentionally omitted from his definition of political rationality.

The title of Downs' book is misleading, partly because of its similarity to Charles Beard's *An Economic Interpretation of the Constitution of the United States* (1935). Whereas Beard attempted to establish the primacy of financial motives in politics, Downs by no means implies that a desire for money is the sole or even the most important consideration of people in politics. His theory of democracy is "economic" only in the sense that he has borrowed from the social science of economics such concepts as *expenditures, income,* and *utility* in order to explain political behavior; in the same way a more traditional political theory might be called "physical" if it borrowed from physics such concepts as *force, line of least resistance, power,* and *equilibrium.*

Citizens who are eligible to vote in democratic elections often fail to do so. In fact, some citizens never vote, and in some elections abstainers outnumber voters. In this [selection] we examine the conditions under which abstention is rational and attempt to appraise its impact upon the distribution of political power.

Throughout this analysis, we assume that every rational man decides whether to vote just as he makes all other decisions: if the returns outweigh the costs, he votes; if not, he abstains.

. . . We attempt to prove the following propositions:

1. When voting is costless, every citizen who is indifferent abstains and every citizen who has any preference whatsoever votes.
2. If voting is costly, it is rational for some indifferent citizens to vote and for some citizens with preferences to abstain.
3. When voting costs exist, small changes in their size may radically affect the distribution of political power.
4. The cost of information acts in effect to disenfranchise low-income groups relative to high-income groups when voting is costly.
5. Voting costs may also disenfranchise low-income citizens relative to wealthier citizens.
6. It is sometimes rational for a citizen to vote even when his short-run costs exceed his short-run returns, because social responsibility produces a long-run return.

PARTICIPATION IN ELECTIONS WHEN VOTING IS COSTLESS

When the cost of voting is zero, any return whatsoever, no matter how small, makes it rational to vote and irrational to abstain. Therefore, whether abstention is rational depends entirely on the nature of the returns from voting.

Why only those citizens who are indifferent abstain

. . . A citizen's reward for voting correctly consists of his vote value, i.e., his party differential discounted to allow for the influence of other voters upon the election's outcome. If the citizen is indifferent among parties, his party differential is zero, so his vote value must also be zero. It appears that he obtains no return from voting unless he prefers one party over the others; hence indifferent citizens always abstain.

However, this conclusion is false, because the return from voting *per se* is not the same thing as the return from voting correctly. The alternative to voting *per se* is abstaining; whereas the alternative to voting correctly is voting incorrectly—at least so we have viewed it in our analysis. But an incorrect vote is still a vote; so if there is any gain from voting *per se,* a man who votes incorrectly procures it, though a man who abstains does not.

The advantage of voting *per se* is that it makes democracy possible. If no one votes, then the system collapses because no government is chosen. We assume that the citizens of a democracy subscribe to its principles and therefore derive benefits from its continuance; hence they do not want it to collapse. For this reason they attach value to the act of voting *per se* and receive a return from it.

Paradoxically, the size of this return depends upon the cost of voting. When voting costs are zero, the return from voting *per se* is also zero, but when voting is costly, the return from voting *per se* is positive. The second of these assertions we discuss later; now let us examine the first one.

Democracy cannot operate rationally if everyone is indifferent about who wins each election. Of course, not everyone has to have a party preference, but someone must if the election is to be a meaningful act of choice. Therefore we assume throughout this [selection] that (1) at least one citizen is not indifferent, (2) no tie votes occur, and (3) indifference does not reflect equal disgust with the candidates but rather equal satisfaction with them.

When the cost of voting is zero, everyone who is not indifferent votes, because his return from doing so, though small, is larger than zero. Therefore citizens who are indifferent know that the election will work and democracy will continue to function even if they abstain. This conclusion holds even when the vast majority of the electorate is indifferent; in fact, only one man need vote. The parties running still must cater to the interests of the whole electorate, because (1) they do not know in advance who will be indifferent and (2) once elected, they know that the citizens who were indifferent may vote in the future. Thus parties compete with each other to attract the potential votes of men who previously abstained as well as the actual votes of those who voted.

As a result, men who are indifferent about who wins have nothing to gain from voting, so they abstain. Hence when the cost of voting is zero, every citizen who is perfectly indifferent abstains. However, the above reasoning does not apply when voting is costly, as we shall see later.

The nature of indifference

In our model, indifferent voters never influence the outcome of elections. Yet their interests are still catered to by each party, because competition forces parties to seek potential as well as actual votes. This fact raises the question of whether indifference has any political significance at all.

Indifferent voters are those who cannot see any net difference in the utility incomes they expect from each party if it is elected. Therefore it seems reasonable *a priori* that they should have no influence on who wins. However, this conclusion can be questioned on two counts.

First, are indifferent voters equally pleased by all parties or equally repelled by them? When a large portion of the electorate is indifferent—as often seems to be the case in reality—the rationality of elections as government-selectors depends upon the answer to this question. If indifference reflects equal disgust with all candidates and a strong preference for some noncandidate, the election is bound to produce a government repugnant to many citizens. On the other hand, if indifference indicates high but equal satisfaction with those running, only the citizens who vote against the winner will be displeased by the outcome.

Essentially, [the] argument raises [this] issue . . . : How are the candidates for each election chosen? [For the purposes of this analysis,] we assume that every political viewpoint which

has a significant number of supporters is represented by some party running in the election. Thus indifference in our model is not caused by equal loathing for all the candidates but reflects ambivalence of a less pejorative nature.

The second question raised by indifference is whether indifferent voters really have zero party differentials or merely lack information. . . . Most voters do not acquire enough information to discover their true preferences, since each knows his vote is of small significance. Perhaps a great many voters who are indifferent would cease to be so if they found out their true views. However, the cost of information makes further research irrational. Since this cost is harder to bear for low-income citizens than for high-income ones, the incidence of falsely indifferent voters may be higher among the former than among the latter. If so, uncertainty imposes a bias on the distribution of political power. It causes a disproportionate number of low-income citizens to refrain from influencing election outcomes.

The validity of this argument rests upon the following proposition: the more information a citizen receives about the policies of each party, the less likely he is to be indifferent. Unless this proposition is true, there is no reason to believe that men who know their true preferences are less likely to be indifferent than those who do not.

In our opinion, the proposition is false. The amount of information a man has necessarily affects the confidence with which he holds his decisions, but it does not necessarily affect their nature. If everyone had 100 percent information, some citizens might still be indifferent. Therefore indifference is not merely an illusion caused by lack of data; so we cannot argue *a priori* that increases in data will tend to eliminate it. However, more information does raise the confidence of each citizen in his decision, *ceteris paribus*, because it moves him closer to being 100 percent informed. For this reason, the more data a man has, the less he must discount his estimated return from voting correctly.

When the cost of voting is zero, it makes no difference how much each citizen discounts his estimated party differential as long as the rate is less than 100 percent, since even a tiny net return causes him to vote. Thus information costs do not increase abstention among low-income groups relative to high-income groups. But when voting is costly, the fact that poorer citizens cannot afford as much information as their wealthier neighbors does create a bias. . . .

PARTICIPATION IN ELECTIONS WHEN VOTING IS COSTLY

Voting costs and their behavioral effects

Heretofore we have assumed that voting is a costless act, but this assumption is self-contradictory because every act takes time. In fact, time is the principal cost of voting: time to register, to discover what parties are running, to deliberate, to go to the polls, and to mark the ballot. Since time is a scarce resource, voting is inherently costly.

This fact alters our previous conclusion that everyone votes if he has any party preference at all. When there are costs to voting, they may outweigh the returns thereof; hence rational abstention becomes possible even for citizens who want a particular party to win. In fact, since the returns from voting are often miniscule, even low voting costs may cause many partisan citizens to abstain.

The importance of their abstention depends on the effects it has upon the distribution of political power. Such effects can stem from two sources: (1) biases in the distribution of ability to bear the costs of voting, and (2) biases in the distribution of high returns from voting.

The only direct money costs connected with registering to vote and voting are any poll taxes extant and the cost of transportation. Ability to bear these costs varies inversely with income, so upper-income citizens have an advantage. Where poll taxes do not exist, the principal cost of voting is usually the utility income lost by devoting time to it rather than something else. If the time must be taken out of working hours, this cost can be quite high, in which case high-income groups again have an advantage. But if the time comes during leisure hours, there is no reason to suppose any such income-correlated disparity exists.

At first glance, all of these costs may appear trivial, and biases in ability to bear them seem irrelevant. However, the returns from voting are usually so low that tiny variations in its cost may have tremendous effects on the distribution of political power. This fact explains why such simple practices as holding elections on holidays, keeping polls open late, repealing small poll taxes, and providing free rides to the polls may strikingly affect election results.

The nature, size, and impact of the returns from voting

The return a citizen receives from voting is compounded of several factors. The first is the strength of his desire to see one party win instead of the others, i.e., the size of his party differential. . . . Party policies determine this factor. A second factor is the degree to which he discounts his party differential to allow for the influence of other voters. . . . [and] this depends upon how close he thinks the election will be. These two factors together constitute his vote value.

The third factor is independent of the other two; it is the value of voting *per se*. Although we discussed it briefly earlier in [this selection], we must examine it more carefully here because of the vital role it plays when voting is costly.

We assume that everyone in our model world derives utility from living in a democracy, as stated previously. When the cost of voting is zero, receipt of this utility is not jeopardized by abstention, because only those who are indifferent abstain. But positive voting costs alter this situation by causing some men who have definite preferences to abstain also. In fact, since each citizen's vote value is usually quite small, any cost at all may threaten the political system with collapse through lack of participation.

Further analysis is complicated by an oligopoly problem. . . . If each partisan voter expects many others to vote, his own vote value is tiny; hence it is outweighed by a very small cost of voting. The more voters there are who feel this way, the smaller is the total vote. But a small total vote raises the probability that any one ballot will be decisive; hence the vote value of each citizen may rise to a point where it outweighs the cost of voting. Therefore citizens who think others expect many to vote will themselves expect few to vote, and they will want to be among those few.

Each citizen is thus trapped in a maze of conjectural variation. The importance of his own vote depends upon how important other people think their votes are, which in turn depends on how important he thinks his vote is. He can conclude either that (1) since so many others are going to vote, his ballot is not worth casting or (2) since most others reason this way, they will abstain and therefore he should vote. If everyone arrives at the first conclusion, no one votes; whereas if everyone arrives at the second conclusion, every citizen votes unless he is indifferent.

Both these outcomes are self-defeating. When no one votes, democracy collapses. Yet if everyone who is not indifferent votes, in the next election each will abstain, since his ballot had so little effect previously (i.e., when everyone voted). Thus if we assume all men think alike, democracy seems unable to function rationally. What rule can we posit within the framework of our model to show how rational men can arrive at different conclusions though viewing the same situation?

The answer consists of two parts:

1. Rational men in a democracy are motivated to some extent by a sense of social responsibility relatively independent of their own short-run gains and losses.

2. If we view such responsibility as one part of the return from voting, it is possible that the cost of voting is outweighed by its returns for some but not all rational men.

Let us examine these propositions in order.

One thing that all citizens in our model have in common is the desire to see democracy work. Yet if voting costs exist, pursuit of short-run rationality can conceivably cause democracy to break down. However improbable this outcome may seem, it is so disastrous that every citizen is willing to bear at least some cost in order to insure himself against it. The more probable it appears, the more cost he is willing to bear.

Since voting is one form of insurance against this catastrophe, every rational citizen receives some return from voting *per se* when voting is costly. Its magnitude (1) is never zero, (2) varies directly with the benefits he gains from democracy, and (3) varies inversely with the number of others he expects to vote. The last of these factors depends upon the cost of voting and the returns he thinks others get from it. Thus we have not completely eliminated the oligopoly problem, but we have introduced another factor which tends to offset its importance.

To show how this factor works, let us approach it from another angle. Implicit throughout our study is the following assumption: rational men accept limitations on their ability to make short-run gains in order to procure greater gains in the long run. . . . The limitations men accept are usually "rules of the game" without which no game can be played. Each individual knows he can gain at some moments by violating the rules of the game, but he also knows that consistent violation by many citizens will destroy the game and introduce social chaos. Since he himself would be a loser if chaos prevailed, he resists the momentary temptation to let short-run individual rationality triumph over long-run individual rationality. Surely, such resistance is rational.

However, it is not uniform for three reasons: (1) the connection between a particular violation of the rules and eventual chaos is not equally obvious in all cases, (2) some violations lead to disorders worse than those caused by other violations, and (3) the immediate gains from violation are not always the same. For example, the deleterious effects of universal failure to vote are both clearer and worse than those of universal failure to become well-informed before voting. Similarly, the cost avoided by not paying income tax is much larger than that avoided by not voting. For these reasons, men can rely on each other to abide by the rules voluntarily to different degrees for different rules. In some cases, they have to back up the rules with force in order to insure observance.

Participation in elections is one of the rules of the game in a democracy, because without it democracy cannot work. Since the consequences of universal failure to vote are both obvious and disastrous, and since the cost of voting is small, at least some men can rationally be motivated to vote even when their personal gains in the short run are outweighed by their personal costs. However, this conclusion raises two problems.

The first is the arbitrary nature of assuming that such motivation operates in regard to voting but not in regard to other political actions. Why, for instance, are rational men not willing to find their true preferences before voting, since they will benefit in the long run from doing so? We can only answer by pointing to the factors mentioned previously: (1) the potential ill effects of not voting are worse than those of not becoming informed, (2) the connection between failure to vote and its ill effects is much clearer than that between failure to become informed and its ill effects, and (3) the cost of voting is lower than the cost of becoming informed.[1]. . .

A second difficulty is explaining why some abstain even though all favor democracy and benefit from its continuance. Solving this problem requires the second proposition mentioned earlier: the returns in fact outweigh the costs for some but not for all.

Although the benefits each citizen derives from living in a democracy actually accrue to him continuously over time, he can view them as a capital sum which pays interest at each election. This procedure is rational because voting is a necessary prerequisite for democracy; hence democracy is in one sense a reward for voting. We call the part of this reward the citizen receives at each election his *long-run participation value*.

Of course, he will actually get this reward even if he himself does not vote as long as a sufficient number of other citizens do. But we have already shown that he is willing to bear certain short-run costs he could avoid in order to do his share in providing long-run benefits. The maximum cost he will bear for this reason in any given election is that which just offsets his long-run participation value.

Thus the total return which a rational citizen receives from voting in a given election consists of his long-run participation value plus his vote value. In other words, the reward a man obtains for voting depends upon (1) how much he values living in a democracy, (2) how much he cares which party wins, (3) how close he thinks the election will be, and (4) how many other citizens he thinks will vote. These four variables insure a relatively wide range of possible returns from voting for different individuals. The range of possible costs is also wide, as we saw before. Therefore a matching of returns and costs can easily result in a mixed outcome—i.e., a large number of voters whose returns exceed their costs and a large number of abstainers whose costs exceed their returns.

Without abandoning our assumption that all men are rational, we can thus explain the following phenomena by means of our model:

1. Some men abstain all the time, others abstain sometimes, and others never abstain.
2. The percentage of the electorate abstaining varies from election to election.
3. Many men who vote do not become well-informed before voting.

4. Only a few men who become well-informed do not vote.

Furthermore, our analysis has isolated several factors upon which the incidence of rational abstention depends. Hence it may be useful in designing methods of predicting how many voters will abstain in a given election.

A revised summary of how rational citizens decide how to vote

. . . In an uncertain world, each rational citizen makes his voting decision in the following manner:[2]

1. He makes preliminary estimates of his expected party differential, the cost of voting, his long-run participation value, and the number of other citizens he believes will vote.
2. If his party differential is zero because all party policies and platforms appear identical to him, he weighs his long-run participation value plus the expected value of "change" as opposed to "no change" (or vice versa) against the cost of voting.
    a. If returns outweigh costs and he favors "change," he votes for the opposition party. . . .
    b. If returns outweigh costs and he favors "no change," he votes for the incumbent party. . . .
    c. If costs outweigh returns, he abstains.
3. If his party differential is zero because he expects identical utility incomes from all parties even though their policies and platforms differ, he weighs only his long-run participation value against the cost of voting.
    a. If returns outweigh costs, he votes for a party chosen at random.
    b. If costs outweigh returns, he abstains.
4. If his party differential is not zero, he estimates how close the election will be and discounts his party differential accordingly. (In a multiparty system he also must decide whether his favorite party is hopeless. . . .
    a. If the discounted party differential plus the long-run participation value exceed the cost of voting, he votes for his favorite party. . . .

[1] In this case, another fact is relevant: voting is a discrete and clearly identifiable act, whereas "being well-informed" is a vague state of mind which even the individual himself has a hard time recognizing.
[2] Certain of the statements require modification if the voter has more than two parties to choose from—*Ed.*

b. If the sum of these quantities is smaller than the cost of voting, he abstains.

5. Throughout the above processes he procures more information about all the entities involved whenever its expected pay-off exceeds its cost. Since this information may alter his estimate of any entity, he may shift from one category to another in the midst of his delibera-tions. He votes according to the rules applicable to the category he is in on election day.[3]

[3]This exceedingly complicated method of deciding how to vote seems to bear little resemblance to how men act in the real world. However, except for one step, the entire process is necessarily implicit in the behavior of any rational voter, even if casual observation fails to confirm this fact.

CHAPTER 2

TAKING SIDES

The origins of political opinion and behavior lie in the earliest experiences of childhood. The early age at which an individual begins to develop political awareness, attachments, and behavior is a matter of considerable surprise to most laymen and is of high interest to those political scientists who have studied the process of political learning usually referred to as *political socialization.*

Political learning can be thought of as involving one or more of three processes: *accretion, stage development,* and *transfer.* Accretion refers simply to the accumulation over time of political information and attitudes. If accretion were the only process, it could be assumed that political facts, concepts, and beliefs are learned in any order and that the particular sequence in which an individual learns them depends only on when he happens to encounter them.

The stage developmental theory of learning observes that perhaps adults, and certainly children, seem to be capable of assimilating certain types of information and acquiring certain types of feelings only after they have reached a sufficient stage of mental development. That the more complex concepts of polit-

ical science are not comprehended and used by elementary school children is not due to lack of exposure, it is argued, for no greater amount of exposure would be likely to effect any greater amount of learning.

The transfer theory attempts to explain how people cope with situations for which they have been prepared neither by previous experience nor by directly relevant training (reading or being told about such situations, for example). The standard response of someone confronting such a novel situation is to search for some past experience or training that seems to be *analogous* and to behave in the new situation in whatever way would be appropriate to the analogous one. A simple illustration of this process is the young child's development of feelings towards the President. According to Robert Hess and David Easton the child's feelings are likely to be markedly similar to those he has for his father, or at least similar to those that fall within the range of appropriateness in children's perspectives of fathers.[1] In other words, if a

[1]Robert D. Hess and David Easton, "The Child's Image of the President," *Public Opinion Quarterly,* XXIV (Winter 1960), 632-644.

child happens to hate his father, it does not follow that he will also hate the President; his feelings may reflect his sense that the President is a "better father" than his own.

At first glance the accretion theory and the stage developmental theory should appear to be contradictory. But it is plausible to imagine reaching certain temporary plateaus of mental capacity, and at a given plateau learning one set of political facts rather than another simply for accidental or traditional reasons. That fifth-graders typically absorb substantial amounts of American history is not likely to be related to newly achieved mental capacity. It is more a function of conventional curriculum decisions in American elementary schools.

Not only facts but also emotional states are learned through these three processes of political socialization. Information about politics and government is usually acquired in conjunction with emotional drives. Typically, the first emotions a child develops about a political system are feelings of unquestioning affection and loyalty. Cognitive recognition of such symbols of that system as the flag, a President's face, and the name of the country is quickly if not simultaneously "enriched" with affective overtones. Partisanship is also a matter of affection and loyalty but involves discrimination as well. Most Americans begin to develop a sense of partisan attachment to one of the major political parties in the late elementary grades, at ages nine to eleven or so, the exact time depending on such factors as the individual's cognitive and emotional development, the extent of his parents' political interest, his school curriculum, and the scheduling of Presidential elections.

The fact that the scheduling of Presidential elections is probably relevant underscores the primacy of national politics in the political socialization of children and adults alike. States-rights or local home-rule advocates are usually the ones who extol "government close to the people"; yet psychologically — in terms of familiarity, scrutiny, and emotional involvement — national politics are unquestionably "closer" to the people.

Contrary to what might seem to be a rational sequence — rational in Downs' terms, for example — attachment to a particular political party is, to a large extent, developed prior to any understanding of why the attachment is felt. This is because partisan attachment usu-

ally is acquired through the child's psychological desire to imitate his parents. The panoply of social and economic facts that determine party identification among adults is at this early stage almost totally irrelevant. Only later is a rationale developed in terms of such considerations as socio-economic status.

Adherence to parents' political attachments is one of the dominant facts about American politics. To some extent it is simply a function of social and economic immobility — that is, when children grow up, they tend to attain approximately the same economic and social status as that of their parents. But there is more to it than that. In those instances in which a person's party allegiance and his social and/or economic standing do not coincide, the incongruence can often be explained by examining his family's partisan affiliation. These observations do not mean, however, that American political opinion is totally static. Because there are only two major parties to choose between, each encompassing a broad diversity of opinion, an individual can rather easily shift his point of view while still comfortably maintaining allegiance to the same political party. He can move from extreme conservatism to "the-middle-of-the-road" while still remaining a Republican, for example.

The tenaciousness of this form of family loyalty may seem surprising to the many college students for whom young adulthood is a time of rejection of parents. This rejection may include rebellion against family political beliefs, but because rebellion is often intended to hurt parents, it must take place in "arenas" of activity in which the parents have high concern. The arena of sex qualifies easily, but politics often is not of enough importance to Americans to merit rebellion by offspring. Rejection of the political affiliation of one's parents, then, occurs mainly among the small segment of Americans (primarily the well educated) for whom politics is of relatively high concern. Herbert H. Hyman and Fred I. Greenstein, in the first two selections of this chapter, explore further the subject of political socialization in childhood and adolescence.

The persistence of party loyalty between generations is an important aspect of our politics, but it does not adequately explain the crucial question of the causes of allegiances to one party or another. If we can see a Tennessee mountaineer's Republicanism as related to his father's and grandfather's partisan stance, we have a demonstration of the possible power of loyalty to family political tradition, in the face of what would seem to be the "rational" position for someone of very low income to take. But what made this man's grandfather a Republican? By going back into a family's history, one comes sooner or later to an establishment of family partisanship that was probably based on social and economic considerations, not prior family tradition. The mountaineer's grandfather was probably a Republican not because of loyalty to *his* father or grandfather, but because of his own opposition—as a small farmer who owned no slaves—to Tennessee's fighting on the side of the Confederacy to preserve slavery in the Civil War.

As this illustration demonstrates, family political loyalty can be strong; but when it clearly conflicts with a person's contemporary social or economic status, change in party allegiance is likely to occur over the long run. Even the most fierce instances of apparently incongruous party loyalty based on family tradition, those traceable to the trauma of the Civil War—rich Democrats throughout the South, and impoverished Republicans in the Southern Appalachians and in Northern New England—now show signs of giving way to current socio-economic considerations.

The generalized strength of socio-economic status in determining party choice is widely recognized today. A quarter of a century ago, this was not necessarily as clearly understood. One of the classic studies of voting, undertaken by Paul F. Lazarsfeld and others in 1940, was designed anticipating that election outcomes were substantially affected by the mass media and other sources of persuasion. The results of the study, however, demonstrated the extraordinary immobility of voters' party preferences, and identified the source of that inertia as largely socio-economic.[2] From the perspective of the 1960's, Robert R. Alford reviews the relationships between socio-economic class and political behavior and examines what changes are occurring in them over time.

A full understanding of the forces and influences that create and maintain partisan loyalties requires some linkage between social and economic background and an individual's operating mental processes. Early psychological and sociological investigations of voting behavior and party allegiance too often treated this linkage too casually, or not at all. A major contribution of the University of Michigan's Survey Research Center has been its attention to the psychological correlates of political behavior. Their interest in psychological determinants is best exemplified by another classic study, *The Voter Decides*, published in 1954.[3] Their concern with the linkages between social background, psychological states, and voting, however, is better represented in the more comprehensive and recent volume, *The American Voter*, excerpted here.

For purposes of organization, this chapter focuses on partisanship, as Chapter One focused on participation. But, as Lazarsfeld and his associates pointed out in *The People's Choice*, the two are not necessarily independent. There are many possible causes of nonparticipation, one of which may be the presence within the individual of "cross pressures"—internally contradictory partisan feelings—and the most favorable condition for political participation is partisanship unencumbered by cross pressures. Since children and adolescents learn more or less simultaneously both that they ought to participate and that they ought to take sides, it is important in reading this chapter to try from time to time to extrapolate the influence of partisanship on participation and nonparticipation.

Underlying any consideration of partisanship is its psychological "legitimacy." Partisanship has had its ups and downs of popularity. Legislated provisions for "nonpartisan" elections (usually at the local level) indicate one extreme. In recent decades political scientists have moved in the other direction, trying to restore partisanship—and specifically party allegiance—as a virtue. Between these positions lies the contention that too much partisan feeling is a symptom of a sick polity. The authors of *The Civic Culture*, quoted in the Preface, view American culture as one in which political interest and activity—including partisanship—are not central; the selection by Schick in Chapter One presents a concurring opinion. Others believe that this low salience of politics is indicative of a society that is constructively stable. That interpretation remains open to question. Clearly, the relationships among partisanship, participation, stability, and constructive change need further investigation and thought.

[2]Paul F. Lazarsfeld, Bernard Berelson, and Hazel Gaudet, *The People's Choice* (New York: Columbia University Press, 1948).
[3]Angus Campbell, Gerald Gurin, and Warren E. Miller, *The Voter Decides* (Evanston, Ill.: Row, Peterson & Company, 1954).

POLITICAL SOCIALIZATION

Herbert H. Hyman

Americans voting for the first time enter the voting booth after eighteen or twenty-one years of training for that act. Some of the training has been conscious, undertaken by adults in order to render the young person a "good citizen." Virtually all of this formal training takes place in school. Other agencies of political socialization—the family and the church, to cite two major ones—rarely allocate time specifically for informing children and adolescents about government and politics (although churches and synagogues do, of course, consciously attempt to teach basic moral stances, most of which have relevance to political decisions).

It is likely that most of what is learned through formal schooling is cognitive—that is, consists more of learning facts about politics than of acquiring preferences for types of policy, political parties, and so forth. Most affective political learning—the acquiring of political likes, dislikes, and feelings of obligation—is picked up informally, through agencies other than the school. Loyalty to country is frequently taught formally in school, but other types of loyalty or dislike are usually absorbed by the child or adolescent from overheard conversations, unspoken pressures to conform to peer groups, and many other sources.

The following selection documents the acquisition of political affect prior to adulthood. Writing in 1959, Hyman noted not only that adolescents develop increasingly polarized political feelings as they proceed through high school—polarized roughly according to their social class position—but also that by the time they have reached ninth grade, the starting point for his study, there is already considerable division of political opinion.

It is clear that there is a gradual, increasing absorption of some ideological point of view with progress through high school. . . . [By the last year in high school] the absorption of political orientation has progressed close to its maximum level [that is, the proportion of students with no opinions on issues is no greater than in the case of adults]. . . . It is also clear that even in the first year of high school, absorption of an orientation has gone quite far. [See Table I.]

. . . Variations in the presence or absence of a view are dependent on the ideological area examined. Thus, for example . . . Remmer's data in Table I demonstrate that the area of class conflict has the highest undecided level. Pre-

TABLE I THE DEVELOPMENT OF POLITICAL ORIENTATIONS AS INDICATED BY THE ABSENCE OF VIEWS AMONG YOUTH OF DIFFERENT AGES[1]

	Per Cent Undecided Among Youths In Grades			
	Nine	*Ten*	*Eleven*	*Twelve*
Government should control railroads	17	17	15	11
Mining and manufacturing should be owned by government	16	13	12	11
Banks and credit mechanisms should be run by government	15	14	12	9
Government should abolish rights of inheritance	20	21	16	16
Modern society moved chiefly by desire for profit	30	27	20	18
History essentially involves class conflicts	21	18	12	12
Right to strike should be abolished	26	24	18	16
Relative self-interest of businessmen vs. workers	53	52	45	43

[1]All questions except the last are taken from Poll #30 of H. H. Remmers. The last question is taken from Poll #32.

sumably, with additional data one could establish different developmental rates for given ideological areas.

. . . If one contemplates the crazy quilt of institutions, educational and socializing agencies impinging on children at different points in time, each communicating only a piece of the whole constellation of political ideas, it is understandable that the various aspects develop at different points in time and in different ways. Naturally, when one studies adults, at late stages of development, all of the components will

WHERE MOTHER COMPLETED →	AGE OF YOUTH → NINTH GRADE			TWELFTH GRADE		
	Grade School	College	Diff.	Grade School	College	Diff.
Favor Eisenhower in the 1952 elections	54.6	71.4	16.8	52.9	71.4	18.5
In politics would back business ideas	59.3	69.2	9.9	61.4	69.7	8.3
Workers would have better chance if they didn't support unions	40.0	39.7	−.3	19.0	21.6	2.6
Businessmen more interested in general welfare of people	19.0	21.3	2.3	15.3	31.5	16.2
Identify self with working class	40.2	19.4	−20.8	44.7	14.6	−30.1

PERCENTAGE OF YOUTH EXPRESSING A PARTICULAR ORIENTATION ACCORDING TO AGE AND PARENTAL INCOME

PARENTAL INCOME →	AGE OF YOUTH → NINTH GRADE			TWELFTH GRADE		
	Low	High	Diff.	Low	High	Diff.
Favor Eisenhower in the 1952 elections	51.3	69.4	18.1	43.9	70.3	26.4
In politics would back business ideas	56.9	72.7	15.8	67.0	67.6	.6
Workers would have better chance if they didn't support unions	35.1	34.8	−.3	27.0	27.4	.4
Businessmen more interested in general welfare	23.0	23.3	.3	14.8	22.6	7.8
Identify self with working class	41.3	14.1	−27.2	51.4	25.7	−25.7

[2]Data are taken from Polls #32 and #33 of H. H. Remmers.

already be present and ideology will have had time to become integrated. . . .

PROGRESSIVE DIFFERENTIATION OF THE POLITICAL PROFILE OF SUB-GROUPS WITH AGE

Thus far, we have shown that for youth taken in the *aggregate*, there is a progressive development of positive political orientations with age or year in school. . . . We did not describe orientations with particular contents for the total youth group. However, if we now examine youth *from different classes* at different stages of development we should expect the polarity of points of view . . . to increase with age. In Table II below we express such findings.

It can be seen that the *difference* in the orientation of contrasted sub-groups of youth increases with year in school. The finding is particularly compelling, if one recalls the fact of differential drop-out from school among the poorer children. Given this fact, the lower-class child remaining in school till Grade 12 is so-to-speak in less economic need and therefore would not exhibit the lower-class pattern in as extreme a form. Nevertheless, the difference is enhanced. While there is an accentuation of the respective orientations of groups with age, it should be noted that the difference at the earliest age level is quite striking, suggesting that the beginnings of the phenomenon are earlier in childhood and that further changes are gradual and small.

CHILDREN AND POLITICS

Fred I. Greenstein

Recognition by Hyman and others that a great deal of political socialization precedes the high school years led in the 1960's to extensive study of how younger children learn their politics. Greenstein pushes inquiry back into the elementary grade level. The reader may find it useful to try to reconstruct his own sense of political awareness at that age, and to speculate about the extent to which the Greenstein findings may suggest a need for even earlier exploration.

. . . From an early age, beginning with the parents' characterization of the child himself as good or bad, and continuing, for example, through the distinctions made between good guys and bad guys in the entertainment media, the child learns to judge figures in both the remote and immediate environments. Yet . . . children seem more aware of the positive than of the negative aspects of public figures. They evidently are reluctant to evaluate leaders unfavorably. This suggests an "immature" pattern of candidate orientation: immature in the strictly statistical sense of being a pattern which is typical of childhood and disappears with increasing age, and evidently also in the sense of indicating an unformed critical capacity. . . .

[In the author's study of 9—13-year-olds in New Haven, he found that] children's issue orientations are so underdeveloped that by eighth grade only about four tenths of the middle-class children could describe issue difference between the parties and only slightly more than half could describe any differences at all. We might therefore suspect that party identification is uncommon among children.

. . . This is *not* the case. By fourth grade more than six out of ten of the New Haven children were able to state whether their party preference was Republican or Democratic: this although little more than a third of the fourth graders could name even one public representative from either of the two major parties and less than a fifth could name a leader of each of the parties. The prevalence of party identifications among nine-year-olds is especially striking when we realize that the proportion of adult Americans who identify with parties (75 per cent) is not much greater. In fact, in the 21—24-year-old segment of the adult population the frequency of party identification is identical to that of New Haven fourth graders.[1]

Here, as in children's assessments of the importance of political roles, we find that political feelings, evaluations, and attachments form well before the child learns the relevant supporting information. It is not until fifth grade that the modal child can name at least one party leader, and not until eighth grade that children typically name leaders of both parties.

The prevalence of party identifications among New Haven children cannot be attributed to "response errors," such as guessing, or the arbitrary checking of alternatives on the questionnaire. Children's party preferences correlate appropriately with the demographic patterns of partisanship in New Haven. They also are positively associated with favorable evaluations of leaders of the same parties.

The source of these preferences is, as often has been noted in the voting literature, the family. Only a handful of children in the entire sample indicated that their own party preferences differed from those of their parents. In interviews children explicitly speak of party as an attribute of the family. . . . Party identifications probably develop without much explicit teaching on the part of parents, more or less in the form of a gradual awareness by the child of something which is part of him. The process doubtless is similar to the development of ethnic and religious identifications.

That party identifications are so common among young New Haven children lends support to Hyman's assertion that "the adult pattern that seems established in most complete form in earlier life is that of party affiliation."[2] More specifically, it seems to be the *direction of*

From "Theoretical Orientation," in *Children and Politics* (New Haven: Yale University Press, 1965), pp. 66-84.

[1] The frequency of party identification in the adult population is reported in various of the Survey Research Center studies; for example, Angus Campbell, Gerald Gurin, and Warren E. Miller, *The Voter Decides* (Evanston, Ill.: Row, Peterson & Company, 1954). I am indebted to Angus Campbell for informing me of the frequency of party identification among young voters. For a tabulation of party identification by age, which does not include the small proportion of the electorate classified as "apolitical" and which therefore indicates a somewhat larger proportion of identifiers, especially in the younger age groups, see Angus Campbell, Philip E. Converse, Warren E. Miller, and Donald E. Stokes, *The American Voter* (New York, John Wiley & Sons, Inc., 1960), p. 162.

[2] Herbert H. Hyman, *Political Socialization* (Glencoe, Ill.: The Free Press, 1958), p. 46.

party affiliation which is set early in life. We have already seen that it is some years until the party preference becomes grounded in such elementary information as whether the president is a Republican or a Democrat. We may also assume that children's party identifications are not as *intense* as they will be in later years, since even in adult life party attachments become stronger with age.[3]

. . . A general factor in children's cognitive development—the inability of young children to think in abstract terms—may impede the formation of issue orientations. A fundamental psychological process, identification, may be at work to assist the formation of party loyalty. Although the process of identification is not well understood, and knowledge is especially sparse about secondary identifications (such as those with religious denomination, ethnic group, and party), identifications seem to be a vital part of the individual's development. They make it possible for him to both relate himself to, and distinguish himself from, others. Therefore one element in the earliness of party identifications, and in their subsequent stability, may be that they help maintain a sense of personal identity, as well as a link between the child, his parents, and other significant individuals and groups. . . .

What children are exposed to . . . may help explain the earlier acquisition of party identification than of issue orientation. The parties are mentioned with at least moderate frequency in the child's face-to-face environment and in the media. Specific issues are presented largely during the brief period of the election campaign (and then the dominant impression probably is of the candidates themselves and not their utterances); broad ideologies are rarely presented at all, especially in the child's face-to-face environment, since these are of little significance to the adult population.

Such environmental influences are reinforced by children's own predispositions: what they are able to learn and interested in learning. It often has been pointed out that single executives are more easily dramatized, perceived, and understood than are such complex institutions as legislative assemblies. . . . It is relatively simple to become aware of individual executives; legislators are easily lost in the crowd of their colleagues, and the legislative process is complex and difficult to follow.

Similarly, the parties are simple perceptual objects. They are stable, there are only two of them, and children often are aware of their personified symbols, the donkey and the elephant. Furthermore, children readily form identifications at an early age. In contrast, issue orientation does not form easily or simply. . . .

My argument so far can be briefly summarized: the political orientations which are most important in the behavior of adults arise earliest in the childhood learning sequence; this is so partly because these are the orientations adults are most likely to display before children; but the sequence of learning is also affected by what children are able to absorb at various ages. . . .

The preschool years and the early school years are a time of great plasticity and receptivity: nothing in later life can compare with this period for the sheer volume of learning that takes place. The most commonly accepted assumptions of a culture—for example, assumptions about the structure of the family and kinship—are typically acquired during this period. And there is evidence that the culture content which is taught first to young children is least likely to change in the face of contact with other cultures. . . .

There are a number of reasons why we would expect this to be the case. First, the immature child is likely to learn uncritically: he is not conscious of alternatives and he lacks standards for judging information. Secondly, much of early learning takes place at a nonconscious level, through processes such as imitation and identification. What we learn without being conscious that we *are* learning is likely to be accepted as a given—a "fact of nature." In addition, as Bruner notes,[4] the agents of the young child's learning—his parents—are highly authoritative. Finally, early learning takes place at a time when fundamental personality characteristics are being formed. Social and political learning which takes place at this point can become a part of the individual's basic psychic equipment. (As I have suggested, a case in point may be party identification.)

For all of these reasons, it would not be surprising if the age at which learning takes place, *in and of itself,* were significant in explaining the later importance of orientations which are learned early. . . .

Even if early learning were not independently

[3]Campbell, *The American Voter,* pp. 161-167.
[4]Edward M. Bruner, "Cultural Transmission and Cultural Change," *Southwestern Journal of Anthropology,* XII (1956), 191-199.

significant, it would be important because it begins the learning sequence. As Irvin Child points out, "tendencies first acquired can shape later learning."[5] Learning invariably is selective and early learning can determine which segments of reality are selected and incorporated into the individual's frame of reference at later stages of his development. "Once a concept develops," O. J. Harvey and his associates comment, "it serves as an experiential filter through which impinging events are screened, gauged, and evaluated, a process which determines in large part what responses can and will occur. . . ."[6]

The likelihood that early learning will have a vital effect on later learning seems to be especially great in the case of partisan motivations. Party identification, learned as it is uncritically and at an early age, can readily become "an experiential filter." It has been well documented that adult party identifiers evaluate new political developments in terms of their party preference, and that they may even selectively perceive the information most favorable to their own party position.[7] In early childhood, party preferences undoubtedly are an imperfect filter, since the child has not added to his identification the minimum degree of supporting information necessary to use it: for example, knowledge of who the public representatives of his party are. At this age, children probably acquire party-related be-

liefs (such as candidate evaluations) directly from their parents. By eighth grade, however, most children can identify the party leaders, and therefore are capable of using their party preferences as tools of choice. . . .

"The early family socialization process," Almond has commented, "is . . . one of the most important factors making for the resistance to social and political change."[8] The New Haven findings on the sequence of children's political development serve as something of a gloss on this assertion, for . . . early political learning seems to maintain, perhaps even reinforce, adult political priorities. . . .

. . . The stable attachments of a large proportion of the American electorate to the existing major political parties provide something of a balance wheel to the political system by impeding the rise of new political movements. The stability of voters' party preferences . . . has the further effect of fostering the long periods in American political history during which one or the other party is generally dominant. Our analysis of the development of partisan motivations helps to provide insight into why generations of voters coming of age in the affluent 1950s and 1960s might be expected faithfully to reproduce voting patterns which have their roots in the experiences of earlier generations with the vicissitudes of the 1930s.

THE FUNNEL OF CAUSALITY
Angus Campbell, Philip E. Converse, Warren E. Miller, and Donald E. Stokes

The contributions of the Survey Research Center of the University of Michigan to an understanding of mass political behavior are numerous. The Center's basic voting studies, of which *The Voter Decides* is the archetype, deal particularly with psychological analyses of voter preference, an emphasis that is perhaps its foremost contribution to political explanation. Also important in the Center's work are longitudinal studies (surveys repeated over time); methodological innovation and refinement, including the use of attitude scales and sampling techniques; and survey sampling on a national scale.

The Center's concentration on psychological correlates of voting behavior has been, some would argue, at the expense of sufficient attention to sociological correlates. Recently, however, the Center has moved toward a more encompassing approach to voting analysis, and in doing so it has made important con-

tributions to the theory of political process. The reading reprinted here is taken from the Center's most ambitious work to date, *The American Voter*, in which the authors attempt to integrate social and economic background factors, personality characteristics, attitudes, and opinions into a viable model of choice de-

[5]Irvin Child, "Socialization," in Gardner Lindzey, ed., *Handbook of Social Psychology* (Cambridge, Mass.: Addison-Wesley, 1954), Vol. 2. pp. 678-679.
[6]O. J. Harvey et al., *Conceptual Systems and Personality Organization* (New York: John Wiley & Sons, Inc., 1961), pp. 2-3.
[7]See, for example, Campbell, *The American Voter*, pp. 120-145, especially p. 135. Also Bernard Berelson et al., *Voting* (Chicago: University of Chicago Press, 1954), pp. 215-233.
[8]Gabriel A. Almond, "A Functional Approach to Comparative Politics," in Gabriel A. Almond and James S. Coleman, eds., *The Politics of Developing Areas* (Princeton: Princeton University Press, 1960), p. 27.
From "Theoretical Orientation," in *The American Voter* (New York: John Wiley & Sons, Inc., 1960), pp. 24-32.

termination that takes into consideration time sequence and levels of probability. In reading this selection, it might be helpful to check the description of process against personal experience and against the sequence of political socialization summarized in the introduction to this chapter and discussed by Greenstein.

Making allowance for the authors' warning not to push analogies too far, the reader may find it helpful to diagram the "funnel of causality" described in the excerpt.

A STRUCTURE FOR THEORY: THE FUNNEL OF CAUSALITY

. . . We wish to account for a single behavior at a fixed point in time. But it is behavior that stems from a multitude of prior factors. We can visualize the chain of events with which we wish to deal as contained in a *funnel of causality.*

The notion of a funnel is intended merely as a metaphor that we find helpful up to a certain point. That is, like all physical analogies for complex and intangible processes, it becomes more misleading than clarifying if pressed too far. With these cautions in mind, then, let us imagine that the axis of the funnel represents a time dimension. Events are conceived to follow each other in a converging sequence of causal chains, moving from the mouth to the stem of the funnel. The funnel shape is a logical product of the explanatory task chosen. Most of the complex events in the funnel occur as a result of multiple prior causes. Each such event is, in its turn, responsible for multiple effects as well, but our focus of interest narrows as we approach the dependent behavior. We progressively eliminate those effects that do not continue to have relevance for the political act. Since we are forced to take all partial causes as relevant at any juncture, relevant effects are therefore many fewer in number than relevant causes. The result is a convergence effect.

Now let us take a cross section of the cone of the funnel at any point, erecting a plane at right angles to the axis. Let us imagine that we can measure all events and states as they stand at the moment they flow through this plane. We would expect two results. First, we would have a congeries of variables that would be, in a peculiar and limited sense, of the same "conceptual order," that is, owing to their simultaneity. Second, this array of variables should be able to predict the dependent behavior perfectly, provided that we know the necessary combining laws.

One way of maintaining conceptual clarity, therefore, is to restrict our measurements to states as they exist at one "slice of time.". . .

We do not wish to preserve conceptual order at the price of restriction in the scope of our theory. We want a theory that will help us assess the current political effects of remote events like the depression or the Civil War. Now the funnel is bounded at its narrow end by the event that we are trying to explain. If we are dealing with the 1956 election, then we think in terms of a funnel terminating on Election Day, 1956. If we wish instead to study the 1960 election, we think of a new funnel that narrows to a point in 1960; events and states of Election Day, 1956, now represent one cross section of time four years prior to the dependent behavior. Yet, there is no fixed boundary for the funnel earlier in time. In effect, we can range freely in time back through the funnel.

To think of a funnel in this way greatly enlarges our explanatory chore, for in the ideal case we want to take measurements that refer to states not at one cross section alone, but at a greater number. Each cross section contains all the elements that will successfully predict the next, and so on, until we have arrived at the final political act. Nevertheless, in such an expanded theory, we must remain cognizant of the temporal area in the funnel to which any particular measurement refers. The "conceptual status" of each measurement of an independent variable involves, as one element, location on a time dimension.

But time alone is not sufficient as an ordering dimension. The states that must be measured at any cross section in time to permit perfect prediction would be extremely heterogeneous. Since qualitative differences in content are involved, a great number of ordering dimensions could be established. Let us take note of three important ones.

Exogenous factors *versus* relevant conditions

First, any single cross section will be divisible into (1) exogenous factors and (2) relevant conditions. Exogenous factors are those eliminated from consideration by fiat at the outset. They include all those conditions that are so remote in nature from the content interest of the investigator that their inclusion in a system of variables, even if possible, would be undesirable. A potential voter who has a flat tire on the way to the polls may fail in his intention to vote. In this instance, failure to vote would be due to certain accidental circumstances. Sufficient motivation was present and effort was expended that would normally have led to the casting of a ballot. The immediate cause of non-voting involved a flat tire. Once we have located this circumstance, we do not wish to pursue the matter further, tracing out the chain of events in the funnel that led to the mishap with the tire. We shall have no difficulty agreeing that such concerns are alien to our interest.

We will be obliged to understand what happens within our system of relevant conditions when exogenous factors impinge upon it. If "accidental" obstacles such as flat tires and bad weather block the way to the polls, we would like to be able to specify how much motivation will be required to surmount obstacles of varying magnitude, as well as the general incidence of such obstacles in the election situation. At the same time, we are not obliged to construct a theory that will indicate when and where flat tires will occur, or make long-range predictions about the weather on Election Day.

This relegation of some factors to an exogenous status, even though they affect the system at a time close to the dependent behavior, stands in sharp contrast to treatment of other forms of non-voting. In many cases, for example, the immediate cause of failure to vote may be a low motivational state readily linked to general indifference toward political matters. Here we are interested in seeking determinants of apathy that lie deeper in the funnel. A flat tire may be as efficient in preventing a vote as apathy, but the causes of apathy remain within our content interest. The causes of the flat tire do not.

The distinction between exogenous factors and relevant conditions is quite relative; that which is an exogenous factor for a narrow conceptual system may become a relevant condition within the terms of a more inclusive system. Ordinarily, the boundary is dictated by the level at which units of analysis are chosen and by the subject matter of the discipline in which investigation is conducted. But there is always room for choice on the breadth of the system that is to be employed.

Hence we may imagine that an outer ring of conditions within the funnel is left unobserved as exogenous. This fact has an important implication. As long as every cross section in the funnel has some exogenous factors, our predictions will never be perfect. *How* excellent they

will be depends upon the proportion of the total cross section that such factors occupy. We can presume that this proportion increases the deeper we recede in the funnel, away from the dependent behavior.

The distinction between exogenous and relevant factors, though left to the discretion of the investigator, can be maintained with clarity under all circumstances. A given factor, if measured and treated within the conceptual system applied to the phenomenon, is thereby defined as relevant. We may make some other distinctions as well, which, if less clear-cut, will be of value in thinking about the nature of events in the funnel.

Personal *versus* external conditions

For some purposes it is convenient to subdivide relevant and exogenous factors according to whether or not they enjoy a subjective reality for the individual at a given point in time. We shall call *personal conditions* those events or states within the funnel of which the individual is aware, although he need not conceptualize them as the investigator does. *External conditions* are those that warrant a place in the funnel because they are causally significant for later behavior, yet which currently lie beyond the awareness of the actor.

This distinction is most useful in a consideration of the political stimuli that can affect behavior only when perceived by the actor. Suppose, for example, that we were to trace events backward in time through the funnel conceptualized for a given election. We would soon encounter a point at which the individual is unaware of the existence of the candidate-to-be, although events that will lead to that candidate's nomination and that ultimately will exert profound influence on the individual's behavior are crystallizing rapidly. At such a point in the funnel, the conceptual status of the candidate as potential stimulus object is that of an external condition. When the individual knows who the candidate is, the conceptual status shifts to that of a personal condition. . . .

Responses toward most objects are prefaced by attitudes toward those objects, which, in a proximal sense, determine the response. Therefore, the understanding of external conditions becomes more and more important as we attempt to anticipate behavior over longer and longer intervals. When we predict at short range, few events or conditions not already personal can intervene to deflect behavior to a new course. The deeper we range into the funnel, the larger the proportion of external factors with which we must cope.

Political versus non-political conditions

Finally, conditions in the funnel may in a rough way be classified into those that are political and those that are not. If we may locate factors as central or peripheral within any cross section, according to our interest in them and their presumed importance as determinants of ultimate behavior, then conditions that are political form the core, or central artery, running longitudinally through the funnel. This central position of the political in the funnel follows quite naturally from the fact that the subject of inquiry is political. The non-political relevant conditions form a shell around this political core. What portion of non-political conditions shall also be considered relevant depends again on the scope of the investigation.

When is a specified condition political, and when is it not? In everyday thinking we readily categorize events and objects in this fashion. Various individuals, groups, public problems, and current happenings are considered to be more or less political. And the relationship of such objects to politics can be seen to change in time. A person may decide to "go into politics"; a public controversy is "made a political issue"; a group should "get out of politics.". . .

We have said that at each juncture in the flow of events, effects that are not relevant for understanding the voting act are eliminated, thus creating the shape of a funnel. This fact now has a further implication; the proportion of events that are political (objectively or subjectively) increases as we take our cross sections closer and closer to the final behavior. Relevant measurements just prior to the act will be almost completely political. At a greater distance we will have to consider a larger proportion of other social and economic factors, unless we eliminate them by definition at the outset.

Process variables: communication and "political translation"

Enough of the composition of the funnel has been outlined to suggest that as events approach the narrow end of the funnel, they are more completely relevant, personal, and political. Now the boundary line between the exogenous and the relevant is drawn at the discretion of the theorist. But when we use a phenomenological approach, the way in which external events become personal, and the way in which non-political events become political, depend on processes that operate within the funnel itself. The analyst does not intervene to make a citizen aware of an external condition. Nor does he point out the political implications of objects or events that the subject perceives as non-political. These are perceptual and cognitive changes that occur naturally as events unfold. Their timing and scope depend on individual conditions and hence must be predicted within the terms of the theory itself.

Figure 1 shows the four possible ways in which events may be categorized according to these two distinctions. An event may at some point in time be external and non-political

FIGURE 1   CHANGE IN STATUS OVER TIME OF EVENTS AFFECTING BEHAVIOR

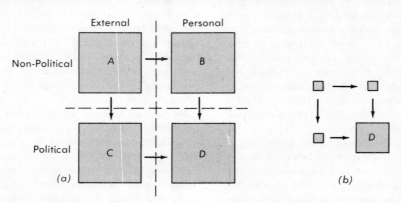

(a) The situation at a point in time remote from the behavior; (b) the situation at a point in time close to the behavior.

(A); personal and non-political (B); external and political (C); or personal and political (D). The second portion of the figure provides a schematic indication of the situation just before the vote to be predicted is cast. By this point in time, personal and political elements predominate: most events and conditions that are going to affect the behavior have come into the voter's awareness and have acquired political meaning.

The mechanisms involved in these categoric changes of elements over time are critical to our understanding of events in the funnel. If the vote to be predicted is that occurring in 1956, an example of an external, non-political sequence of events (A) lying within the funnel at a point early in the 1940's would be the emergence of Dwight D. Eisenhower as a major military figure. As we move forward in time, the consequences of these events can proceed from A toward D by one of two routes. In this case, the normal route was $A \rightarrow B \rightarrow D$. Early in the war few voters were aware of the rise of Eisenhower or would have attributed to it any political significance. By 1945, most Americans were aware of General Eisenhower. But for very few was this a fact of even potential political significance (B). During the mid-1940's, awareness led to some emotional content; for most Americans in this case the affect was positive. If we were measuring a cross section in time in 1947, it is likely that we could find a relationship between affect toward General Eisenhower shown at that time, and the individual's 1956 vote, even if traditional party preference were held constant. As Eisenhower began to receive mention as a possible presidential candidate, processes leading from B to D were set in motion. The object, Eisenhower, began to take on political coloration. This was faint, until his announcement that he would run for the Republican nomination. The affect that the individual felt for Eisenhower now was placed in contact with all the political cognitions and predispositions that had been formed independently in the core area of the funnel.

The second possible route from A to D lies through C (Fig. 1). In the illustration under discussion, this route was more rare. But there were undoubtedly a number of Americans who were personally unaware of the figure of Eisenhower until the point at which he broke into their consciousness as a political candidate. In this case, Eisenhower's movement into politics was an external event.

The major process by which an external event becomes personal is that of communication. That part of our theory that deals with the conditions under which an object or condition moves from a non-political area of the funnel to a political area will depend upon examination of communication vehicles such as the mass media and interpersonal communication. There are other more direct processes that can effect this transformation: loss of a job in 1930 may have turned the depression from an external to a personal event without mediation of a communication system in the normal sense. But most of the beliefs that come to affect political behavior are probably developed by way of communication processes.

A non-political event becomes political by . . . *political translation*. As Fig. 1 suggests, political translation may occur externally; it also may occur within the individual himself. For some people, the fact of a depression in the 1930's immediately took on political meaning, with a minimum of outside suggestion. It was perceived directly as something that the government could and should do something about. The role of the Hoover Administration was evaluated accordingly. For others, with a different set of existing perceptions regarding the potential of governmental activity, the translation was made outside, by other agents in the society. The labor unions contended that the depression was subject to governmental control; during the Hoover Administration, Democratic Party spokesmen bore down hard on the same point. Thus the fact of depression was presented to many Americans with a political meaning already attached.

THE POLITICS OF DIVERSITY
Robert R. Alford

As we have observed, one of the major services performed by the pioneering voting studies was to demonstrate the basic associations between fundamental population characteristics and election behavior in the United States. But the relationships between social class and party preference, for example, or between age and likelihood of voting, while statistically significant and politically meaningful, certainly do not paint a complete picture. Single factors such as social class go a long way toward explaining broad patterns of voting behavior but still leave a great deal unexplained. There is only a modest probability that accurate prediction of election results can be based on only a few population characteristics.

Alford carries the exploration of relationships between population characteristics and voting choice a step beyond the classic studies by introducing two elements of comparison. First, in the initial paragraph of this selection, he compares voting along social-class lines in the United States with class-based voting in several other countries. And second, he attempts to trace changes in the relationships between certain population characteristics and voting behavior over time, in the United States. Alford is mainly interested in "class voting"—the tendency for voters' party preferences to reflect their social class (defined here in terms of occupation: manual or nonmanual). He has structured his consideration of other variables such as region and religion to make them auxiliary modifiers of his basic variable, class. Because Alford's book was published in 1963, it does not include data from the 1964 and 1966 elections; the reader may wish to speculate about the continuity of the results of those elections with the trends Alford sees as evident through 1960.

Social class and political behavior are not as closely associated in the United States as they are in Australia and Great Britain. In several surveys of the national electorate taken from 1952 to 1960, the average level of class voting (the difference in Democratic voting between manual and non-manual occupational strata) was 16 percentage points. This contrasts with average figures of 40 percentage points for Great Britain, 33 for Australia, and 8 for Canada. . . .

DIVERSITY IN THE UNITED STATES

. . . The parties in the United States are not explicitly linked to class organizations and do not appeal for support on the basis of class. However, voters do see the parties as linked to specific class interests, and probably many people vote in accordance with an image of the parties as representing their economic interests. These are perhaps the most important reasons why class voting is relatively low and yet still exists.

A number of characteristics of American society and its political system undoubtedly reduce the level of class voting further. The enormous size of the country, its division into fifty states with real degrees of sovereignty, tremendous ethnic and religious diversity, and a decentralized party structure, all reduce the salience of *national* class divisions as the main bases for party cleavages. The decentralized, undisciplined character of American parties makes them difficult to distinguish from pressure groups or from combinations of interest groups. The party system thus reflects the federal, plural character of both American society and the governmental system. As the author of a recent study of American federalism put it, "a powerful 'pressure group' at the national level may be very closely identified with a State or local party in one or more States, yet prefer to remain aloof from the national party battle in order to maintain freedom to exert pressure upon both parties when tactics require it."[1] That national class divisions exist and divide the parties even as distinctly as they do, is a measure of the degree of economic and political integration the United States has achieved.

The diversity of support for the political parties has been shown by a series of studies of voting. . . . The initial study, which set a pattern for subsequent research in both the United States and Great Britain, was *The People's Choice;* this was a survey of voting behavior in Erie County, Ohio, in the 1940 presidential election.[2] Since it embraced only one northern city and its environs, the regional economic and political diversity of the United States presumably did not affect voting behavior. Still, social class, religion, and rural-urban differences were found crucially to affect

"The United States: The Politics of Diversity," Chapter 8 in *Party and Society* (Chicago: Rand McNally & Company, 1963), pp. 219-247.
[1] M. J. C. Vile, *The Structure of American Federalism* (London: Oxford University Press, 1961), p. 92.
[2] P. Lazarsfeld, B. Berelson, and H. Gaudet, *The People's Choice* (New York: Columbia University Press, 1948).

the political loyalties of voters. Having a low income, being a Catholic, or living in an urban environment, all predisposed voters toward the Democrats: having a high income, being a Protestant, or living in a rural environment predisposed voters toward the Republicans. The study focused on the consequences of "contradictory" social characteristics that presumably pushed people in opposite political directions—the now classic notion of "cross-pressures." A relatively high proportion of persons in Erie County was under cross-pressures, indicating that the diversity of sources of political loyalties is great in the United States. . . .

Despite their diversity of support and their ambiguous class base (compared to the British and Australian parties), American political parties are both perceived as supported by, and actually are supported by, persons at different occupational, educational, and income levels, although, as in the other countries, a sizable minority votes for the "other" party. . . .

But, regardless of the current situations, has the association of class and vote declined since the 1930's? It is by now a commonplace notion that the salience of class for voting was less in the prosperous 1950's than it was in the depressed 1930's. A recent study found a decline of class voting in the period 1948 to 1956, which appears to document the decreasing importance of social class for voting behavior. The authors of *The American Voter* computed an index of "status polarization" which showed that the correlation between the occupational status of respondents and their partisan vote in three separate national surveys in 1948, 1952, and 1956 dropped from 0.44 to 0.26 to 0.12.[3] According to the authors:

"The most striking feature of the polarization trend in the recent past has been the steady and rapid depolarization between 1948 and 1956. This decline occurred in a post-war period when the nation was enjoying a striking ascent to prosperity and a consequent release from the pressing economic concerns that had characterized the Depression."[4]

The way that this decline of "status polarization" is explained is also relevant here, because the authors infer that changes have taken place since the 1930's, although they have no specific evidence of such changes. A substitute for this is evidence on the status polarization (or class voting, the term which will be used henceforth to avoid confusion) among different age-groups. In their 1948 and 1952 surveys, a marked "depression-effect" was found. Persons in their twenties and thirties during the depression of the 1930's (presumably those most affected by it) exhibited the highest level of class voting. In 1956, this was not evident, and the authors conclude that this illustrates the "fading effects of the Depression."[5]

This finding of highest class voting among the depression generation does not contradict the usual inference that persons in such a generation should be more similar in their political attitudes and behavior than persons not sharing this common experience. Another study of American voting behavior which specifically focused upon the problem of generational differences found that the depression generation (those who were born in the period 1913-1922) was likely to be more Democratic—regardless of sex, occupation, income, or other social differences.[6] In spite of the Michigan finding that manual and non-manual strata in the depression generation are farther apart in their voting patterns than any other age groups, political consensus is still present. Both strata were affected similarly by the Democratic political currents. These two findings reflect the relative independence of the absolute level of vote for a party from the level of class cleavage. . . .

The decline of class voting between 1948 and 1956 is linked by the authors of *The American Voter* to "increasing prosperity and fading memories of the Great Depression of the 1930's." These two factors should imply a continuing decrease of class voting since the 1930's. But the authors must account for another of their own empirical findings—that class-voting was lower in 1944 than in 1948, after which it dropped almost linearly. They suggest that variations in the importance of domestic economic versus foreign policy issues account for this change: When economic issues are important, class voting tends to rise; when non-economic issues, such as foreign policy, are important, class voting tends to drop. ". . . war is a basic public concern

[3]A. Campbell, Philip E. Converse, Warren E. Miller, and Donald E. Stokes, *The American Voter* (New York: John Wiley & Sons, Inc., 1960), p. 347.
[4]*Ibid.*, p. 357.
[5]*Ibid.*, p. 359.
[6]Jane O'Grady, "Political Generations: An Empirical Analysis" (Master's thesis, Department of Sociology, University of California, 1960).

that may eclipse those problems of domestic economics leading to cleavage among status interest groups."[7] The authors thus infer what the patterns of class voting *might* have been during the 1930's. Presumably class voting should have been high in the elections of 1932 and 1936, when class issues were dominant. With World War II, "national" issues superseded class ones, and class voting should have been lower in 1940 and 1944. As Campbell *et al.* put it, "Polarization tendencies carrying over from the Great Depression may have been dampened as a result of the national crisis posed by the Second World War, rebounding upward after that conflict was concluded." Domestic economic issues again became important, resulting in the rise of class voting in 1948. After this peak, "the renewal of the threat of global war and the outbreak of hostilities in Korea may have acted, in concert with increasing prosperity, to depress the level of status polarization [class voting] once again."[8] . . .

. . . These inferences as to declining class voting certainly imply that a long-term decline of the importance of social class in the support of the American parties has taken place. But has it?

TRENDS IN CLASS VOTING SINCE THE 1930'S

Although fluctuations in the level of class voting have occurred in the period 1936 to 1960, there is some evidence that no consistent decline has taken place. Before the evidence for this conclusion is presented, a brief recapitulation of the assumptions upon which the measure of class voting is based is in order.

In estimating the importance of the class bases of politics, shifts to the Right or to the Left should be minimized because they blur the differences between social strata. In such political systems as the Anglo-American ones, shifts usually occur in the same direction in all politically relevant social groups. A shift to the Right such as the Eisenhower victories in 1952 and 1956 could conceivably be regarded as a decline in the importance of social class as a determinant of political behavior. It is probably true that a large vote for Eisenhower among workers meant that class identifications were less important in those elections than in that of 1948, for example. But it is contended here that only if the *gap* between manual and non-manual support of a party has lessened can one speak meaningfully of a decline of class voting. The data

presented in *The American Voter* show without question that not only did all social groups vote more Republican in 1952 and 1956 than they did in 1948, but that *in addition* social classes moved closer together. But, was this part of a long-term decline of the importance of the class bases of politics? Or . . . was this only a fluctuation within the "normal range" of change of the class bases of American politics, given the social and political structure of American society in this historical period? . . .

No pattern of consistent decline of class voting is evident, and its level reached that of Britain and Australia only in the 1948 election. Nor has the level of class voting dropped to the average Canadian level in any election. It may be concluded . . . that there has been no substantial shift in the class bases of American politics since the 1930's, despite the prosperity since World War II and despite the shifts to the Right in the Eisenhower era. . . .

Before we can accept the conclusion that class voting has not declined, it is important to consider where it may have declined or where it may have actually increased. Trends in various regions of the United States, as well as among various religious groups, may offer a clue as to the future role of social class in American politics. It is not at all clear, for example, that class voting will remain as low as it is. The disappearance of the loyalties of middle-class southerners to the Democratic party, when and if it occurs, may mean a rise of class voting and therefore a realignment of the social bases of the parties more upon class lines. And the possible dwindling of special religious and ethnic loyalties to the parties may have similar consequences. American political scientist Clinton Rossiter has suggested that in the future:

"the influence of class on political behavior and allegiance may become even more visible than it is today, especially as the influences of ethnology and religion fade ever so slowly but steadily from view. . . . we are still a long way from the class struggle in American politics, but that does not mean that class consciousness is a negligible factor. To the contrary, it must inevitably become a more important factor as Americans become ever more alert to the rewards and symbols of status."[9]

[7]Campbell et al., The American Voter, pp. 360-361.
[8]*Ibid.*, p. 361.
[9]Clinton Rossiter, *Parties and Politics in America* (Ithaca: Cornell University Press, 1960), p. 166.

... We might expect that if any trend toward the political re-integration of the South is evident, class voting might have increased in that region since the early 1940's. On the other hand, in the most urbanized and older regions, such as New England or the Middle Atlantic states, class voting might have declined from a formerly high level, somewhat like the pattern in the London metropolitan area of Great Britain. These two trends—in the South and East—might cancel each other out to produce the overall lack of change of class voting. Or we might find that class voting is higher in the urban South than in the rest of the South and infer that this is a sign of impending change of the social bases of southern politics and an omen of a future national realignment more along class lines.

Similarly, trends in the class voting patterns of Protestants and Catholics may foreshadow the future. It is possible that class voting has dropped among Protestants but increased among Catholics to cancel each other out as far as an over-all index is concerned. The diversity of politics in the United States implies that a single measure of the importance of a single factor for voting behavior is almost meaningless unless the relationship is examined in various other subgroups of the population.

REGIONALISM AND CLASS VOTING

... Many states, not only in the South, have had a traditional alignment with one of the major parties. This has meant that each of the parties has long cherished a sectional strong-hold within which the other party had little chance of winning legislative representation ... As V. O. Key puts it:

"Sectionalism ... contributes to the multiclass composition of each of the major parties, a characteristic bewildering to those who regard only a class politics as 'natural'. A politics that arrays the people of one section against those of another pulls into one party men of all social strata. A common interest bound the southern banker, merchant, cotton farmer, and wage earner together against the northern combination of finance, manufacturing, and segments of industrial labor."[10]

One major question which can be answered by survey data, but which is not as readily answerable from ecological studies of the voting patterns of social areas, is whether class voting is actually substantially lower in areas such as the South. The second major question of concern here is, of course, whether class voting has declined in any major regions or whether it has increased, particularly in the South. ...

... The political diversity of America remains great in this respect—that the degree of variation of class voting over time within and between the major regions of the country is considerable. The Eisenhower elections marked not a dwindling of this difference, but an intensification of it. ...

[There appears to be] no dwindling of the political diversity of America's regions ... and no apparent trend toward the reintegration of the South. ... There is also little evidence that the more urbanized regions such as New England or the Middle Atlantic states have high levels of class voting. ... It seemed plausible to predict that class voting would be higher rather than lower in the regions both older and more urbanized in the United States, unlike Great Britain, because of the disappearance in urban and long-settled areas of various parochial political loyalties interfering with the emergence of class-based politics. No pattern of that kind seems to exist in the United States as yet.

No detailed exploration of the regional regularities can be undertaken. It seems probable, however, that they are not accidental, and that certain historical and structural features of these regions could be found to account for the differences. The consistently low level of class voting in the South is no surprise and easily explained. But why does the West North Central region exhibit almost the highest consistent pattern of class voting? These are the midwest agrarian states, which are largely Republican: Minnesota, Iowa, Missouri, North and South Dakota, Nebraska, and Kansas. Clearly this is not a "regionalism" like that of the South, because both [social class] strata are not pulled over to a single party. On the contrary, ... the Democratic vote of manual workers is usually above the average; that of non-manuals, usually below. For some of these states, the high level of class voting may reflect the historical patterns of agrarian revolts, expressed through the Nonpartisan League in North

[10]V. O. Key, Jr., *Politics, Parties, and Pressure Groups* (4th ed.; New York: Thomas Y. Crowell Co., 1958), p. 267.

Dakota and the socialist traditions of Minnesota.[11] But, whatever the cause, class voting in this midwest region is usually high. . . .

The vacillations of the mountain region (the strip along the Rocky Mountains from Montana to New Mexico) are not so easily laid to a particular historical tradition and may merely reflect the small numbers of cases (the fewest in any region) or the heterogeneity of the region. . . . Part of this vacillation may be due to the frontier character of the region. Further research might be able to pin down some of the reasons for this and other regional regularities of political behavior.

Although national surveys offer no evidence that the South, at least, is becoming more like other regions in its level of class voting — and is therefore losing its special regional allegiance to the Democratic party — other studies indicate that such a change may be imminent. The Republican vote has steadily climbed in the South and may be derived from middle-class more than from working-class persons. . . .

The authors of *The American Voter* note that "generally speaking, [status] polarization is lower in the South than in other regions of the nation," but their data show that "Between 1952 and 1956 . . . when levels [of status polarization] were declining elsewhere, there was an actual increase of polarization in the South, from a coefficient not much above zero to a point of clear significance in 1956."[12] In a footnote, they suggest that "this trend may reflect growing industrialization and urbanization in the South, processes that are likely in the long run to blur traditional differences in political behavior generally." This suggestion reflects a hypothesis which the present author shares: Class voting should increase if and when the influence of the traditional regional, ethnic, and religious loyalties to party dwindles. . . .

. . . The national two-party split between Left and Right is repeated in the South, the main difference being that *both* party elites are further to the Right than their northern counterparts. This indicates that changes tending to bring the South into two-party competition will not result in a liberal Republican party and a conservative Democratic party, but rather the same alignment as the rest of the nation. . . .

RELIGION AND CLASS VOTING

The continuing diversity of American politics is also shown by religious differences in class voting. . . . Has class voting dropped among either Protestants or Catholics, and what possible significance do shifts by either grouping have for a future trend in class voting?

Evidence from six surveys in five different presidential elections indicates that class voting may be declining slightly among Protestants, but that non-class factors affect the voting behavior of Catholics so much that no clear trend exists. . . .

The decline found among Protestants is not sharp, and the margin for error is such that we must conclude that for Protestants as well as for the total electorate in the United States, there is no evidence of any change in class voting. . . .

Protestants have exhibited a higher level of class voting than Catholics in each election except in 1952. The general pattern is consistent with the presumed ethnic and minority sentiments among Catholics which override class sentiments as bases for political loyalties. If only the 1944, 1948, and 1952 data were available, it would appear that Protestants and Catholics were becoming just alike in their levels of class voting, since a pattern of convergence culminated in actually higher class voting among Catholics than among Protestants in 1952. This change was due to a rise of Catholic class voting — not to a drop of Protestant class voting. More specifically, it was due to a pull of the Catholic middle class to the Republican nominee. . . .

. . . [In 1960] the association of religion and voting went up sharply, undoubtedly because of the candidacy of a Catholic for President . . . Even manual Protestants did not give the Democratic candidate a majority. Whether the victory of a Catholic candidate will finally end Catholic minority consciousness is an open question. American political scientist Peter H. Odegard suggests that "minority" consciousness may be the chief cause of the Catholic deviation:

"As consciousness of 'minority' status declines for any religious group, one may assume that other factors than religion will play a larger and larger role in determining voting behavior. That is to say, as intensity of religious identity or distinction declines, economic and social

[11]It must be noted that these data do not include farmers, but only manual and non-manual occupations.
[12]Campbell et al., The American Voter, pp. 367-368.

status may be expected to increase in importance in explaining voting behavior. As this occurs among American Catholics and Jews, their party preferences will be less and less influenced by religion and more by other factors. They should then become indistinguishable from the preferences of others of the same or similar economic and social status, regardless of religious affiliation."[13]

Although certainly this argument is plausible and should hold for the regional as well as the religious deviations from class voting in the United States, no evidence of a consistent increase of class voting or a decline of the religious deviation is as yet manifest. It might be noted that only among non-manual persons identifying themselves as middle-class did the religious difference in voting behavior disappear. . . . Not only objectively higher status but a subjective sense of being part of the "great middle class" is required to rid Catholics of their sense of minority consciousness and, as a consequence, of their Democratic loyalties.

[13]Peter H. Odegard, "Catholicism and Elections in the United States," in P. H. Odegard, ed., *Religion and Politics* (Published for the Eagleton Institute of Politics at Rutgers, the State University, by Oceana Publications, Inc., 1960), pp. 120-121.

CHAPTER 3

INTEREST GROUPS AS A CHANNEL

It is sometimes important to view politics from the perspective of the individual, but most political studies find it more useful to discuss similarities and differences between and among agglomerations of individuals—not random agglomerations, but meaningful ones, *groups.* The basis upon which a political analyst categorizes people into groups is related to his training and interests, the analytical task at hand, the availability of sufficient data upon which to assign individuals to groups, and his own theoretical clarity and competence. Such grouping of individuals (or, to be more precise, of information about individuals) opens the door to a substantial advance in political analysis: quantification and statistical interpretation.

It is useful to think of politically relevant groups as falling into two broad classifications, which in turn can be subdivided. The major division is between *interactional* groups and *categorical* groups. Interactional groups are those in which the members communicate with one another by such means as face-to-face meetings and written or oral correspondence.

Interactional groups can be subclassified into *formal* and *informal* groups, depending on whether or not they abide by a formal constitution, laws, rules, and so forth. Cliques, for example, clearly meet the interaction criterion but lack formal signs of organization; gangs may or may not be formal groups, depending on the members' inclination toward formalizing operations by creating rules.

Categorical groups lack interaction. They can be subdivided into *identificational* and *analytical* groups. Identificational groups are composed of persons who, although never communicating with one another, nevertheless have a sense of being "members" of those groups. For instance, when a political figure addresses an appeal to "the idealistic and restless youth of the country," those persons who assume that *they* are being addressed can be considered "members" of an identificational group called "idealistic and restless youth." Whether these people are in fact idealistic and restless is beside the point, as long as they consider themselves so.

Finally, social scientists often recognize meaningful agglomerations of people who, because of some trait or common history, appear to respond similarly to political stimuli. For analytical purposes it makes sense to treat these people as a group, even though the "members" are unaware of both the existence of such a group and their own membership in it. These groups are called analytical groups. Most investigations of the relationships between personality types and political behavior involve comparisons among analytical groups. This is because a respondent in a survey can relatively easily classify himself by income level, age, religion, and so forth, but is seldom able to classify himself overtly in personality terms.

In Chapters One and Two we dealt primarily with the broad social, economic, and psychological variables that generally define categorical groups—identificational at best, but often analytical. The Rosenberg selection and parts of other excerpts related the dynamics of informal group interaction—with friends, family, coworkers, and so forth—to political actions. Chapter Three is concerned with a significant type of formal group: the interest group.

As David B. Truman indicates, interest groups are one of the most important and most misunderstood components of the American political scene. The more common phrase "pressure group" conveys the tone of opprobrium that many people use when referring to organized expressions of personal interest. Yet it is unrealistic to think of an operative democracy without a complement of interest groups. Since there is no prospect of eliminating such groups from the political life of a free society—even if it were desirable to do so—an alternative would seem to be to encourage their proliferation and their scope in the aggregate, in order to achieve broader representation of the range of interests that bear on politics and government. But even this position is essentially defensive; a contemporary political scientist, Lewis A. Froman, chooses to view group political action more sanguinely, as performing a necessary and positive function in a democracy.

Regardless of how people feel about interest groups, they have in fact grown in number, specialization, inclusiveness, and possibly importance in policy determination. Harmon Zeigler explores their present role and modes of operation.

Interest groups differ from one another in many ways. Their substantive emphases—tariffs, peace, civil rights, farm subsidies, and so forth—constitute one basis of distinction. Another basis is the kinds and extent of resources they command; among the possible resources are number of members, money, leisure time for group activities, expertise in a subject area and/or in legislative procedures, and the ability to use potent popular symbols. Spatial dispersion or concentration of members can affect the ultimate effectiveness of a particular interest group, as can such organizational matters as frequency and competitiveness of leader elections, extent of structural control over branches and chapters, and number of years in existence as an organization. The number of other *organizations* its members belong to also bears on the ability of an interest group to convert member commitment into specific pressures on a legislative body. Although access to decision-makers might be considered a group resource, it is better viewed as the desired output, the consequence of resource utilization. "Getting a legislator's ear" by no means insures success, but it is so important a first step as to be considered a prime objective of interest groups.

Because interest groups rely on so many types of resources, they modify or distort democratic equality to the extent that resources other than number of members are unevenly distributed throughout the population as a whole. This distortion is ameliorated by the existence in substantial numbers of the so-called "mass membership" interest groups—those whose major source of influence *is* their membership size (and their attendant possession of large amounts of money in the aggregate). These interest groups represent a relatively recent involvement in pressure politics by lower-middle- and lower-class persons (and/or persons who have the interests of those social classes at heart).

There remain, however, vast numbers of Americans—most of them lower class—who would be hard put to name any organized pressure group that acts on their behalf. A further flaw in the total picture is the dearth of groups representing the interests of consumers; most interest groups concentrate on winning objectives for producers (including laborers). Anthony Downs suggests an explanation for this phenomenon.

It is difficult to assess the full impact of interest

groups, whether considered as a whole or individually, on the course of American politics. Journals and magazines such as the *Congressional Quarterly* diligently record their activities, including their income and expenditures, and much is inferred about the efficacy of their activities when final policy emerges. Lester W. Milbrath looks at lobbying, one of many interest group activities, and finds it both relatively "clean" and relatively ineffective. The selection by Bauer, Pool, and Dexter suggests why interest groups are less potent than popularly imagined. E. E. Schattschneider agrees that lobbying and all other interest group activities are ineffective, at least in comparison with a specific alternative use of time, money, and effort. That alternative, he argues, is involvement in party activity. Thus normative reservations about interest groups, held by much of the population at large, are supported by professional reservations based on sheer utility.

GROUPS AND SOCIETY
David B. Truman

Arthur F. Bentley's *The Process of Government,* published in 1908, was a remarkably advanced herald of the movement of political science away from study of formal governmental institutions towards the greater complexities of informal political processes. It foreshadowed, among other things, a wealth of documentation of interest group activity and influence. More than forty years later, David Truman, expressing explicitly and implicitly the profession's debt to Bentley's vision, wrote *The Governmental Process,* an attempt to synthesize the body of findings and speculations about the operations of interest groups that Bentley had begun and to which many others had later contributed.

The primary focus of Truman's work was the years following World War II. These were years of heightened interest group activity. Fear of economic recession as war production ceased, eagerness to push for wage and price gains with the termination of wartime freezes, and determination on the part of some to regenerate the social welfare momentum of the New Deal — all contributed to renewed intensity of legislative and interest group enterprise. The spirit of the times was ably caught and skillfully analyzed by a number of political scientists. Attention was early focussed on the Full Employment Bill of 1946, an intended commitment on the part of the federal government to use its powers to offset the adverse consequences of conversion to a peacetime economy. The struggle over this legislation between liberal and conservative interest groups was extensively documented, especially by Stephen K. Bailey in *Congress Makes a Law.** The re-election of President Truman in 1948 gave further impetus to welfare legislation, centering especially on a bitter fight for health insurance in 1950, when the monumental — and successful — effort of the American Medical Association to defeat "socialized medicine" again drew the attention of social scientists (and many others, of course) to interest groups.

Much of the academic study of pressure groups in that postwar period took the form of individualistic case studies. By the mid-1950's, however, the time was ripe for someone to take the longer view, to make the leap from case studies to more comprehensive theoretical work. David Truman filled this need with *The Governmental Process.* Although the book is now rather dated — its illustrations are necessarily timebound — Truman's concepts and insights apply as well to present-day interest group activities as they did to the then-current activities he analyzed.

. . . Any society is composed of groups, the habitual interactions of men. Any society, even one employing the simplest and most primitive techniques, is a mosaic of overlapping groups of various specialized sorts. Through these formations a society is experienced by its members, and in this way it must be observed and understood by its students. These group affiliations, with varying degrees of completeness and finality, form and guide the attitudes and therefore the behavior of their participants. How completely and finally a particular group controls the attitudes and behavior of its members is a matter to be determined through observation of the degree to which habitual patterns of interaction persist. The

Reprinted with omissions by permission of the publisher from "Groups and Society," in *The Governmental Process* by David B. Truman, pp. 43-44, 32, 39. Copyright 1951 by Alfred A. Knopf, Inc.
*Stephen K. Bailey, *Congress Makes a Law* (New York: Columbia University Press, 1950).

frequency and persistence of interactions within a group will determine its strength. . . . The moving pattern of a complex society such as the one in which we live is one of changes and disturbances in the habitual subpatterns of interaction, followed by a return to the previous state of equilibrium or, if the disturbances are intense or prolonged, by the emergence of new groups whose specialized function it is to facilitate the establishment of a new balance, a new adjustment in the habitual interactions of individuals. . . .

When one views any society as a sort of mosaic of groups, one is confronted with a bewildering array of groups that may be classified in different ways. Thus various characteristic activities seem to be carried on in one group that make it different from another in that particular respect. . . . Similarly, although it is an observable fact that all groups involve the same fundamental process, the interaction of individuals, they seem to differ from one another in the form that this process takes—for example, in the degree of formality. In the pursuit of meaning and understanding, students of society, particularly sociologists, have classified groups on these and other bases, distinguishing and defining classes of groups. . . . In addition to the category "institution,". . . various sub-categories have been designated on the basis of fairly obvious differences of function—the family, economic groups, political groups, and religious groups. On somewhat different bases distinctions are drawn among crowds, publics, assemblies, organizations, mobs, primary groups, secondary groups, in-groups, out-groups, and a host of others.

INTEREST GROUPS

. . . [The term "interest group"] has been used for the purposes of polemics so freely that it has acquired certain emotional connotations which may render it ambiguous when used in analysis. *Political, partisan,* and even the word *politics* itself share with *interest, vested interest, special interest,* and *interest group,* among others, a connotation of impropriety and selfishness that almost denies them the neutral precision requisite to careful discussion.

As used here "interest group" refers to any group that, on the basis of one or more shared attitudes, makes certain claims upon other groups in the society for the establishment, maintenance, or enhancement of forms of behavior that are implied by the shared attitudes. . . . From interaction in groups arise certain common habits of response, which may be called norms, or shared attitudes. These afford the participants frames of reference for interpreting and evaluating events and behaviors. In this respect all groups are interest groups because they are shared-attitude groups. In some groups at various points in time, however, a second kind of common response emerges, in addition to the frames of reference. These are shared attitudes toward what is needed or wanted in a given situation, observable as demands or claims upon other groups in the society. The term "interest group" will be reserved here for those groups that exhibit both aspects of the shared attitudes. . . .

Definition of the interest group in this fashion has a number of distinct advantages in the task of political analysis. In the first place, it permits the identification of various potential as well as existing interest groups. That is, it invites examination of an interest whether or not it is found at the moment as one of the characteristics of a particular organized group. Although no group that makes claims upon other groups in the society will be found without an interest or interests, it is possible to examine interests that are not at a particular point in time the basis of interactions among individuals, but that may become such. Without the modern techniques for the measurement of attitude and opinion, this position would indeed be risky, since it would invite the error of ascribing an interest to individuals quite apart from any overt behavior that they might display. In the scientific study of society only frustration and defeat are likely to follow an attempt to deal with data that are not directly observable. Even the most insistent defenders of the scientific position, however, admit that, although activity is the basic datum of social science, a "becoming" stage of activity must be recognized as a phase of activity if any segment of a moving social situation is to be understood. There are, in other words, potential activities, or "tendencies of activity." These tendencies are the central feature of the most widely accepted social psychological definition of attitude. Gordon W. Allport, after examining a series of definitions, arrived at his own generally used statement: "An attitude is a mental and neutral *state of readiness,* organized through experience, exerting a directive or dynamic influence upon the individual's response to all objects and situations with which it is related."[1] On the basis of widely held attitudes that are not expressed in interaction, therefore, it is possible to talk of potential interest groups.

In the second place, as these statements suggest, this concept of interest group permits attention to what Lundberg calls the "degree of integrative interaction."[2] The frequency, or rate, of interaction will in part determine the primacy of a particular group affiliation in the behavior of an individual, and . . . it will be of major importance in determining the relative effectiveness with which a group asserts its claims upon other groups. This approach affords all the advantages and none of the disadvantages that once accrued to the sociologists' concepts of "primary groups" and "secondary groups," meaning by the former face-to-face interaction as opposed to indirect contacts such as those made through the media of mass communication. Before the enormous expansion and development of the latter techniques, and still in societies where they have not penetrated, it was a verifiable fact that solidarity of group behavior depended largely upon physical proximity. Frequent face-to-face contact in no small measure accounted for the influence of such primary groups as the family, the neighborhood, and the like. As the social functions performed by the family institution in our society have declined, some of these secondary groups, such as labor unions, have achieved a rate of interaction that equals or surpasses that of certain of the primary groups. This shift in importance has been facilitated largely by the development of means of communication that permit frequent interaction among individuals not in face-to-face contact or not continuously so. . . .

In the third place, this concept of the interest group permits us to evaluate the significance of formal organization. The existence of neither the group nor the interest is dependent upon formal organization, although that feature has significance, particularly in the context of politics. Organization indicates merely a stage or degree of interaction. The fact that one interest group is highly organized whereas another is not or is merely a potential group—whether the interest involved is that of affording more protection to consumers, greater privileges for brunettes, or more vigorous enforcement of civil rights—is a matter of great significance at any particular moment. It does not mean, however, that the momentarily weaker group, or interest, will inevitably remain so. Events may easily produce an increased rate of interaction among the affected individuals to the point where formal organization or a significant interest group will emerge and greater influence will ensue. The point may be illustrated by noting that this increased rate of interaction is usually what is meant when the journalists speak of "an aroused public opinion."

Finally, this use of the concept also gives a proper perspective to the political activities of many interest groups. . . .Claims upon other groups in the society . . . may be asserted or enforced by means of a variety of techniques and through any of the institutions of the society, not merely the government. An interest group concentrating upon replacing the valuable shade trees in a village adjacent to a large gentleman's farm may achieve its objective by prevailing upon the baronial family to purchase the trees and pay for their planting. A group interested in the protection of certain moralities among the younger generation may secure the behaviors they desire in part through inducing motion picture producers to permit its officers to censor films before they are released. Whether a group operates in such fashions as these or attempts to work through governmental institutions, thereby becoming a political interest group, may be a function of circumstances; the government may have primary or exclusive responsibility in the area involved, as in the war-time allocation of scarce materials. Or the choice between political and other modes of operation may be a function of technique; it may be easier or more effective to achieve temperance objectives through the government than by prevailing upon people to sign pledges. The process is essentially the same whether the interest group operates through other institutions or becomes political.

To summarize briefly, an interest group is a shared-attitude group that makes certain claims upon other groups in the society. If and when it makes its claims through or upon any of the institutions of government, it becomes a political interest group. . . .

[1]Gordon W. Allport, "Attitudes," in Carl Murchison, ed., A Handbook of Social Psychology (Worcester, Mass.: Clark University Press, 1935), chap. 17.
[2]George Andrew Lundberg, Foundations of Sociology (New York: Macmillan, 1939), p. 310.

It follows that any group in the society may function as an interest group and that any of them may function as political interest groups, that is, those that make their claims through or upon governmental institutions. An economic group, such as a corporation, that seeks a special tax ruling is in that respect functioning as a political interest group. Trade associations, labor unions, philatelic societies, world government societies, political parties, professional organizations, and a host of others can and do seek to achieve all or a portion of their objectives by operating through or upon the institutions of government. Even a family group, whose prestige or financial interests approach imperial proportions, may make such claims. It will be useful and significant to identify or classify such groups according to the regularity or the success with which such claims are advanced through these channels. Even the casual observer will give somewhat different places to the philatelic society that prevails upon the Postmaster General to provide special handling for letters bearing a new stamp issue and a trade association that seeks legislation to protect it against its competitors. These may sensibly be placed in separate subcategories, but they both display the fundamental characteristics of such groups.

Seen in these terms, is an interest group inherently "selfish"? In the first place, such judgments have no value for a scientific understanding of government or the operation of society. Schematically, they represent nothing more than the existence of a conflicting interest, possibly, but not necessarily, involving another group or groups. Judgments of this kind are and must be made by all citizens in their everyday life, but they are not properly a part of the systematic analysis of the social process. Secondly, many such political interest groups are from almost any point of view highly altruistic. One need only recall those groups that have consistently risen to defend the basic guarantees of the American Constitution, to improve the lot of the underprivileged, or to diffuse the advantages stemming from scientific advance. Evaluations such as these may be made of particular groups, depending on the observer's own attitudes, but . . . they will not facilitate one's understanding of the social system of which the groups are a part.

Where does the term "pressure group" fit into this scheme? This expression, perhaps more than any other, has been absorbed into the language of political abuse. It carries a load of emotional connotations indicating selfish, irresponsible insistence upon special privileges. Any group that regards itself as disinterested and altruistic will usually repudiate with vigor any attempt to attach this label to it, a fact that suggests that the term has little use except to indicate a value judgment concerning those groups of which one disapproves. Some writers, however, in a courageous effort to reclaim for the term a core of neutral meaning, use it as a synonym for "political interest group." This usage has certain disadvantages aside from the obvious possibility that many readers will be unable to accept the suggestion that "the objectives of the pressure group may be good or bad; the group may be animated by the highest moral purpose or it may be driving for the 'narrowest kind of class gain."[3] If the word "pressure" has more than a simply figurative meaning, it suggests a method or a category of methods that may be used by an interest group to achieve its objectives. . . .

INTEREST GROUPS

Lewis A. Froman, Jr.

Democratic political systems generally attempt to "build in" to the formal structure of government some method of reflecting group interests. Despite an ideological bias that tends to picture democracy as the sum of atomistic individual preferences, in fact the United States government, the state governments, and many local polities provide an indirect means of embodying subgroup points of view in the process of deciding public policy.

That means is the system of electing legislators from geographic areas rather than "at large." The election of legislators from states to the national Congress, from districts to state legislatures, or from wards to city councils is based in part on the assumption that people in different areas have different

[3]V. O. Key, Jr., *Politics, Parties, and Pressure Groups*, 2nd ed. (New York: Thomas Y. Crowell Company, 1947), pp. 16-17. From Lewis A. Froman, Jr., Some Descriptions and Generalizations," in *People and Politics* (Englewood Cliffs, N. J.: Prentice-Hall, Inc., 1962), pp. 100-101.

policy interests. To a great extent this is a valid assumption. But the use of geographic boundaries to demarcate interest groups is a clumsy way of getting at the actual syndromes of interest in American society; no geographic boundaries can be drawn around groups of citizens with extensively similar policy preferences.

Therefore, political systems must provide some way for persons with common interests to have an appropriate effect on government, even when they happen not to reside in a common geographic area. The only formal governmental device that most effectively achieves this objective — functional representation of interests — is the election procedure called *proportional representation*. But it is a complex and controversial device, used currently in only one United States locality.

As Froman argues, organized interest groups informally provide for functional representation, in the absence of suitable formal methods. In doing so, they contribute a valuable service that the political parties, and the people as individuals, are unable or unwilling to perform — they lend cohesion and direction to the aggregate of millions of individual policy preferences.

Organized political interest groups are the outgrowth of similar needs arising from common frustrations among people in similar situations. For example, factory workers live and work in common environments and meet common problems. They are faced with a certain level of income with no guarantee that it will increase. They (like most other people) want more money, better working conditions, and so forth. The use of group tactics, such as strikes, pooling financial resources for propaganda purposes, and other maneuvers that are possible only in a group effort, eventually are seen as ways in which they will better be able to meet their needs. Joining into larger groups for the purpose of petitioning their government for help in meeting their demands soon follows.

Since these groups represent not only votes but financial aid to political office-seekers, interest groups can expect at least a minimal amount of access to those engaged in the formation of public policy.

This kind of reasoning applies to other groups as well. Just as labor unions were the result of workers joining together to better their lot, so it is with farmers, veterans, and ethnic, racial, and religious groupings and manufacturers and business interests of all kinds. And, as groups grow in size and make more demands, it becomes necessary for those with competing demands to organize for the purpose of exerting pressures of their own. Organization breeds organization; largeness begets largeness.

Interest groups provide a vital function for democratic politics. That is, not only do they help to promote the interests of their members, but they also serve as an important link between government officials and the public at large. . . . Parties in the United States are not issue-oriented. The primary purpose of American political parties is to make nominations and staff the government with people who are able to win more votes than their opponents. Parties, in this sense, provide for geographical representation. Since candidates are elected from particular constituencies (congressional districts or states), congressional representation helps to insure that sectional and local interests will be considered in the formation of public policy. Interest groups, on the other hand, provide for functional representation within the populace. They insure that a certain segment of the public is heard with respect to economic, social, and political issues. Such issues often cut across geographically defined districts. Interest groups, then, provide another link between the public and its representatives, a link which is concerned with outcomes on particular issues, and which is very often national in scope.

THE GROUP, ITS MEMBERSHIP, AND THE PUBLIC

Harmon Zeigler

The first two selections in this chapter have approached the phenomenon of interest groups rather benignly. In theory, functional representation of the significant interests in a society sounds worthwhile. But when Americans begin to probe the specific means by which interest groups try to translate their members' interests into public policy, the mood shifts. "Lobbying," "bloc voting," and "propagandizing" refer to three major modes of interest group activity designed to affect policy decisions. Each term carries negative connotations. The connotations may or may not be fair, but they accurately convey public sentiment, and that sentiment is not much affected by changes in terminology (e.g., when "propaganda" is called "education" by union or manufacturers' "representatives"—that is lobbyists). Part of the negative response is traceable to uneasiness about the consequence of unequal resources—especially money—available to different interest groups representing equal numbers of people. Another part involves a sense that many interests in society are not represented at all in the daily tugging and pulling that occurs in governmental decision-making.

In this selection, Zeigler does not attempt to deal with the moral implications of these negative sentiments. Instead, he recounts in detail the actual modes of interest group activity and distinguishes between the courses of action chosen by interest groups with different characteristics. The most fundamental of these differences, of course, is size of membership.

A popular conception of lobbying techniques is that, for the most part, lobbyists indulge in providing elaborate entertainment for legislators, offering bribes, and, if all else fails, threatening retaliation by defeating the recalcitrant legislator in his next effort at re-election. This notion of the unscrupulous lobbyist is almost entirely without foundation. What may have been true of days gone by has been made impossible by, among other things, the rapid development of the mass communications media. Indeed, instead of devoting most of their efforts exclusively toward cultivating direct channels of access to governmental decision makers, it has become a steady trend for interest groups to expend more of their energy and resources in the hopes of creating a more generally favorable climate of opinion in the society as a whole. Presumably, the goal of an interest group would be not to influence a wider public but rather to use widespread support in order to extract favorable reactions from those in a position to make authoritative decisions. Further, all interest groups do not rely on public relations techniques to the same extent. In some instances, the cause of a particular group is furthered by the avoidance of publicity and the utilization of the advantage of surprise. The Army, for example, in seeking to establish military control over the creation of atomic energy, worked in absolute secrecy in close cooperation with the War Department to draft legislation before the atomic scientists, who were anxious to impose civilian control, were even aware that legislation was being contemplated. Consequently, when a bill assuring military control was introduced in the House, those who opposed the legislation had to work at a feverish pace to try to recoup what had been lost because of lack of access to information about the opposition's activities.[1]

PUBLIC RELATIONS: ASPIRATIONS AND EFFECTS

The use of extensive public relations may also vary considerably according to the degree to which a group is subjected to unusually hostile publicity. Thus, the AFL-CIO spent more than a million dollars to try to counter the unfavorable image which it believed organized labor was creating due to the exposure by the McClellan Committee of some rather unsavory aspects of the labor movement. Finally, one might suspect that the use of mass propaganda might vary with the size of the organization. Key has suggested that smaller groups, such as business organizations, would be more attracted to extensive reliance upon public relations since "they command directly the support of only a few people, and they can readily subscribe to the doctrine that they must carry their cause by the generous support of propaganda to shape the opinions of the general public."[2] However, Lester Milbrath's research based upon interviews with lobbyists

Harmon Zeigler, "The Group, Its Membership, and the Public," Chapter 8 in *Interest Groups in American Society*, pp. 233-247. © 1964. Reprinted by permission of Prentice-Hall, Inc., Englewood Cliffs, N. J.

[1] Byron S. Miller, "A Law Is Passed—The Atomic Energy Act of 1946," *University of Chicago Law Review*, XV (Summer 1948), 804.

[2] V. O. Key, Jr., *Public Opinion and American Democracy* (New York: Alfred A. Knopf, Inc., 1961), p. 515.

reveals that mass membership organizations, particularly farm and labor, rated public relations campaigns highest in comparison with other groups.[3] Since these mass organizations also ranked letter-writing campaigns higher than other types of groups, Milbrath suggests that the assumption of the lobbyist from the large organization that he has a greater potential audience produces the higher rating. The obvious assumption is that the mass membership organizations apparently look upon public relations as a device to mobilize *membership* behind the position of the organization, while the smaller organizations are aiming toward "general" public opinion. As Monypenny argues, the smaller group can expect more internal cohesion than the larger group, and hence would expend more of its energy outward.[4] Indeed, business groups such as the National Association of Manufacturers, place primary reliance upon public relations.[5]

If we consider the techniques of mass propaganda, we should not be victimized by the vast amount of attention given to the idea that private groups can control or even shape opinions. Although the effects of a public relations campaign are difficult to measure, a body of firm generalizations developed in the social sciences state that it is very likely that the consequences of propaganda efforts are negligible. It is one thing to sell a particular brand of soap through advertising; it is quite another matter to sell a candidate or a legislative proposal by the same techniques. In the case of soap, most Americans are sufficiently convinced that personal cleanliness is a desirable attribute; the particular brand they use is of no great importance. On the other hand, propaganda which deals with more complex situations comes into contact with more deeply rooted values. In the case of ethnic prejudices, for example, propaganda would not reshape basic attitudes to any appreciable extent. Further, the attempts of organized labor to show that "union workers are nice people" would have little impact unless the recipients of the propaganda were already inclined to accept this premise. It is the function of propaganda, whether recognized by practitioners of the art or not, to mobilize, reinforce, or channel pre-existing, but possibly latent, attitudes. It is interesting to note Milbrath's comments upon the lobbyists' perception of the effect of propaganda in view of these conclusions. Some

lobbyists, while they were not convinced that the message of their organization was penetrating very deeply, rationalized that governmental decision makers might believe that a particular campaign was persuasive and might possibly alter their position in order to conform to an expected reaction from the "outside world."

Propaganda techniques

Generally, the propaganda campaigns of organized groups are of two types: defensive efforts to ward off some immediate threat, such as the campaign of the American Medical Association to defeat the King-Anderson bill; and generalized, long-range programs to create a favorable image of the organization without reference to any immediate objectives. In both types of campaigns there are similarities, one of the most obvious being the use of symbols. If the group is trying to establish its legitimacy, or its conformity to generally held societal norms, it will utilize "good" symbols. Organized labor, to illustrate, seeks to create an association of the words "labor" and "America," an identification of unions with "freedom" and "neighbors." The AFL-CIO Industrial Union Department's brochure entitled "The All Union Family" describes a family as living at "99 Shady Lane, Anytown, U.S.A." The members of the union family are "Mr. and Mrs. John Q. America and their two wonderful kids." Labor, . . . essentially a protest movement, has to try to integrate itself more fully into the mainstream of American life. Its program is, of course, long-term. It begins with the assumption that labor has to carve out a niche for itself and, in so doing, faces an uphill struggle. . . . By contrast, an association such as the American Bar Association, whose membership operates with less of a handicap, sees its job to be one of *restoring* confidence.

If the goals of an organization are to prevent the establishment of a program judged to be detrimental to its organizational interests, the technique is to identify the proponents of the program with "evil" symbols. No symbol is more exhausted by constant usage than the old

[3]Lester Milbrath, "Lobbying as a Communications Process," *Public Opinion Quarterly*, XXIV (Spring 1960), 45.
[4]Philip Monypenny, "Political Science and the Study of Groups: Notes to Guide a Research Project," *Western Political Quarterly*, VII (June 1954), 197.
[5]Joseph G. La Palombara, "Pressure, Propaganda, and Political Action in the Election of 1950," *Journal of Politics*, XIV (May 1952), 305.

reliable, "socialism." This symbol, made famous by its repeated use by the American Medical Association, has become almost standard in the operating procedure of nearly all organizations whose objectives can, without a thoroughly implausible stretching of the imagination, be associated with free enterprise. Real estate organizations, such as the National Association of Real Estate Boards and National Association of Home Builders, played heavily upon the theme of socialism in their efforts to defeat public housing legislation. Electing to concentrate propaganda dissemination at the local level, where the impact of public housing would be apparent, the Realtors' Washington Committee (which served as coordinator) distributed "kits" to local realtors which spelled out in some detail the approach to be taken. The advice was to equate public housing with "statism," "socialism," or any other "scarism," and "wherever possible stir up religious and racial prejudice."[6]

These instructions did result in advertisements in local papers stressing the drastically simplified alternative: "Do you believe in socialism? No! Is public housing socialism? Yes!"[7] However, there were organizations equally concerned with supporting public housing. If there had been little counterpropaganda there would have been, theoretically, a greater possibility that the symbolism of the realtors could have effected at least a mobilization of opposition. Monopolization of media for the promulgation of specified objectives is a rarity, and, with the existence of opposing propaganda, the probable result of the entire effort was neutralization.

Organizations using propaganda techniques often feel that they can do a more effective job if some other organization, not directly identifiable with the primary antagonist, can be persuaded to do most of the arguing. Key notes that ". . . any group that feels itself to be in the doghouse will tend to hide behind false fronts when it propagandizes the public."[8] The exact rationale for this assumption is difficult to locate. Perhaps the most readily understandable explanation is the fear that a public relations campaign might succeed in stimulating opposition which then could be transferred to the source of the propaganda. The extent to which this occurs is, like the effects of public relations activities, difficult to ascertain. However, Stokes' analysis of the 1958 right to work

referendum in Ohio is suggestive of the possibilities of unanticipated consequences in propaganda campaigns. Stokes notes that the beginning of the campaign found little more than half of the electorate even familiar with the issue, with about half of this aware group in favor of adoption of a right to work law. However, as the efforts for and against the law grew more intense, awareness spread to three-quarters of the electorate. As interest spread, support for right to work held firm only in the business community. In every other segment of the population, right to work declined in popularity until, at the conclusion of the campaign, only businessmen gave majority approval. What was the basic contributing factor to this growth of opposition? Stokes offers the following explanation:

". . . the primary source of the rising tide against right to work was the connection the public drew between the issue and the recession. Responsibility for the economic distress of 1957-1958 was not at first charged to the business community. The recession *had* reinforced the public's belief that the Republicans, as the party of business, would not prevent unemployment. But it was not until right to work was brought before the public that the economic distress was given a forceful political translation. To many people in Ohio, placing right to work on the ballot looked like an effort by business to kick the working man when he was down. With this idea planted in the public's mind, labor was able to rally the opposition to the issue successfully, leaving business isolated in support of the law."[9]

The Ohio experience suggests that the more business propagandized, the more it became identified with circumstances over which it had no control. Perhaps, then, there is wisdom in the use of "front groups."

The American Bar Association has stated that

[6]Lee F. Johnson, "Housing: A 1950 Tragedy," *The Survey*, December 1950, p. 553. See also House Select Committee on Lobbying Activities, *Hearings*, Housing Lobby, 81st Congress, 2nd session, 1950 (Washington, D.C.: Government Printing Office, 1950).
[7]House Select Committee on Lobbying Activities, *Hearings*, Housing Lobby, 81st Congress, 2nd session, 1950 (Washington, D.C.: Government Printing Office, 1950) p. 370.
[8]Key, *op. cit.*, p. 517.
[9]Donald E. Stokes, *Voting Research and the Businessman in Politics* (Ann Arbor: The Foundation for Research on Human Behavior, 1960) p. 23.

"... the most effective way to tell the lawyer's story is to have someone else tell it." In this case, the lawyers have a ready-made proponent in insurance companies and related financial institutions. Lawyers, as the ABA observes, "are in a position to control the appointment of many fiduciaries — executors, trustees, escrow agents and the like [and] are in a position to advise a client that he should have more insurance because of estate and inheritance tax problems, and may even recommend an insurance company if requested to do so by a client."[10]

Whether or not as a result of this none too subtle suggestion, the organized bar has enjoyed the cooperation of banks and insurance companies ranging from the very large, such as John Hancock and the Guaranty Trust Company of New York, to the smaller local institutions of considerable regional prestige. Other groups are less fortunate and have to resort to the deliberate creation of auxiliary organizations. The railroad interests in Pennsylvania, in opposing a law to raise the long haul truck weight limit, not only used established associations like the Pennsylvania State Grange to disseminate their literature, but also relied upon some very obvious artificial fronts. One of the public relations specialists directing the railroads program was quoted as saying: "Of course we release some stories under direct attribution, but they will be of less propaganda value than those we can generate from motorists, property owners, taxpayers, farmers or women's groups. In sum, we not only have to create publicity ideas; we also have to go out into the field and create the groups and occasions so that these ideas will become realities."[11]

This technique is different from the alliance formation operations often indulged in by groups with similar aspirations, such as the American Jewish Congress and the National Association for the Advancement of Colored People. It also differs from the more direct infiltration methods of the John Birch Society. The Society does seek to establish fronts, but also hopes to infiltrate established community organizations without incurring overt identification. This semisecret association would be less inclined to rely on the shotgun type propaganda effort in the expectation that it would be able to exert a more subtle influence upon opinion leaders within a community. Most of its activity is local, although coordinated from its national headquarters. Loss of the element of secrecy — the ability to catch an opponent by surprise — might also mean public disapproval and loss of support.

PRESSURE GROUPS AND ELECTIONS: MYTHS AND REALITIES OF GROUP VOTING

Many of the propaganda activities of organized groups become most intense when they are given personification by means of the electoral process. This is the time when non-member opinion is more easily accessible to the pleadings of organizations, and it is also the time when membership opinion might be more readily unified. Interest groups also reason that, if the "right" man can be elected, their task of persuasion will be simplified. Finally, we cannot neglect the most widely publicized aspect of electoral activity by interest groups — the threat of retaliation against a candidate for public office whose record is displeasing. When the NAM declares "we have endeavored ... to elect congressmen whom we have known to possess the courage of their convictions ... and who fearlessly oppose the legislation we have been opposing" and countless other organizations inform legislators that their record will be remembered in November, the student of group politics might indeed tremble at such awesome displays of power.[12] However, as in the case of public relations campaigns, the hard facts of political life do not coincide with a simplified model of human motivations.

It is beyond the abilities of an organized group to guarantee, with any degree of certainty, that its members will automatically respond to the suggestions of the leaders. It is, however, true that group affiliations are an important variable in the reaching of an electoral decision. We know that, with varying degrees of consistency, people with similar group memberships tend to vote as a unit or, to use an expression popular among southern politicians, a "bloc." Jews, Negroes, Catholics, and members of labor unions are predominately Democratic in preference; professional or managerial people are more inclined to identify with the Republican Party. Yet it would hardly

[10]American Bar Association, Standing Committee on Public Relations, *Public Relations for Bar Associations* (1953) p. 61.
[11]Robert Bendiner, "The Engineering of Consent — A Case Study," *The Reporter*, August 11, 1955, p. 17.
[12]Quoted in La Palombara, op. cit., 306.

be accurate to assume that relatively consistent voting patterns can be equated with a simple delivery of a group's votes by leaders of organizations formally representing that group. Few groups will fail to reveal a minority who do not conform to the preponderant group mood. The basic exception to this statement is the Jews. Unlike most ethnic groups, the pro-Democratic inclinations of the Jews do not vary with class or status lines within the group. Wealthier and more educated Jews are, if anything, more Democratic than lower income Jews. However, with Catholics and Negroes, such homogeneity is lacking. While Negroes have been principally Democratic, there has been some defection of Negro leadership to the Republican Party. Catholics are slightly more Democratic than the total population, but, when the voting of Catholics is compared with Protestants of similar social and economic circumstances, the Democratic bias tends to disappear.

Intragroup differences become greater if we consider not merely voting but also attitudes. Again the Jews exhibit a strong awareness of group-oriented political goals. There are apparently well defined standards on contemporary questions, stemming from the application of traditional Jewish values to current problems. Fuchs notes that "no matter what criteria have been used to define liberalism and conservatism, Jews have invariably been rated overwhelmingly more liberal than Christians."[13] Catholics, while responding to group norms on some issues, do not seem to have developed a unique position on most political problems. In the case of the Negroes, there is conspicuous absence of any distinct combination of attitudes beyond the vote. Negroes are less politically involved and considerably less sophisticated than other ethnic groups and are therefore less likely to respond cohesively on the basis of a commonly perceived external stimulus.

These differences suggest that there should be a distinction between examples of people with the same backgrounds and environments taking a position in response to the overt political "line" of a group, and situations in which people of similar circumstances react in the same way independent of actual group pressure. The latter case is probably the rule. Individual values, to the extent that they reflect group norms, are sufficiently established to resist any sudden or capricious reversal of

position by a formal organization. It would be absurd to suppose that the American Jewish Congress, if for some reason it chose to do so, could hope to accomplish even the slightest reduction of the Democratic leanings of the Jewish community. On the other hand, it is not always necessary for an organization to inform its clientele of the need for activity to redress a wrong. As Stokes says, ". . . wheat farmers may respond in unison to a drop in the price of their crop, without needing a farm organization to tell them that their pocketbook nerve has been touched."[14]

Group techniques in the electoral process

Having examined limitations upon the electoral activity of political associations, we can now approach their electoral techniques with greater perspective. Pressure groups seek to achieve the election of favorable candidates by two basic methods: financial contributions and voter mobilization. In spite of the frequently cited folksaying that "money talks," lobbyists do not put much stock in this technique as a means of establishing a channel of communication with a politican. Naturally, contributions flow into the campaign chests of candidates whose public record or personal inclinations coincide with the views of the contributing group. Most of labor's contributions go to Democratic candidates and most corporate contributions are made Republicans. Heard points out that the two sources of contributions balanced approximately equally in 1956.[15] In some cases, where an organization takes part in electoral activity only sporadically, its campaign contributions will be more carefully placed. Thus, while the AFL-CIO's Committee on Political Education ranks candidates on the basis of their votes on a series of issues, and makes contributions accordingly, the American Medical Association's Political Action Committee, organized in 1961, concerned itself only with the defeat of the King-Anderson Bill. Labor's money is usually sent into every state where a favorable candidate is contesting an election, while the AMA's contributions went into far fewer campaigns. Contributions were offered to the five Democratic and three Republican

[13]Lawrence Fuchs, "American Jews and the Presidential Vote," American Political Science Review, XLIX (June 1955), 392.
[14]Stokes, op. cit., p. 15.
[15]Alexander Heard, The Costs of Democracy (Chapel Hill: University of North Carolina Press, 1960), p. 196.

members of the House Ways and Means Committee who were regarded as doubtful on the medicare issue.

Regardless of the way money is spent, one cannot argue that the candidate who has the most money will invariably win, although this argument was once fashionable. There are, of course, basic campaign costs to be met, and the organization which provides money for the distribution of literature, appeals through mass media, and the various types of appeal to the voters might hope to gain the favor of the recipient of such funds. Perhaps more important to a candidate's campaign is the willingness of an organization to undertake a sustained effort to increase the voting of people who are in agreement with the candidate's position. The very large organizations, such as the AFL-CIO, that like to think they have substantial strength at the polls, engage quite heavily in the publication of voting records and personal solicitation of votes among their own members. But the smaller organizations, such as business or professional groups, can make no claims of a deliverable body of voters and can only offer their services as proselytizers of a larger public. However, while the target of the efforts of the two types of groups varies, their techniques are similar. There is general recognition of the very basic fact that, while the nonpersonal appeals of mass communication should not be neglected, success will depend more upon informal and personal contacts. Examples drawn from divergent sources will illustrate this technique.

Studies of United Automobile Workers Unions in Detroit and Chicago note that the leadership of both unions is actively engaged in the support of Democratic candidates through personal contacts with members. In Chicago, the local union president spent considerable amounts of time in supplementing an organizational postcard campaign. Each member of the union was given one of these cards by leadership within the place of employment and "if you got one of these Poles or Bohunks who couldn't read or write, we'd get somebody to do it for them and make them sign their X [indicating a pledge of support] on it."[16] In Detroit, similar efforts were more coordinated. The membership of the union was divided according to congressional district, and neighborhood meetings were sponsored, giving workers the opportunity to discuss the issues. At the

plants, "lists of endorsed slates are passed out to the workers, and lunch hour and coffee breaks at election time are punctuated with political discussion."[17] Although both unions were equally vociferous in their efforts, the results were not the same. The majority of Detroit union members "trust the voting recommendations of labor groups," but in Chicago there is greater distrust and apathy.[18] What explains this difference? We know that the more active members of an organization tend to conform more readily to group norms.[19] The Detroit union has developed an elaborate plan of formal endorsement of candidates in which the individual member, while not participating directly, does not necessarily feel that a candidate is being "shoved down his throat." Further, there is very close collaboration between the union and the state Democratic party. This proximity between the union and the political process enables the organization to establish a "natural" connection with politics. The establishing of union membership is frequently an automatic process, and since there is an inclination of union members to look upon political activity as a secondary aspect of the union's proper sphere of activities, the methods of the Detroit union are a good remedy for this situation. However, the Detroit case is hardly typical.

What of the smaller organization that must work with nonmember opinions? Even if their own members are ready and willing to toe the mark, this is of little consequence. However, if the organization or its members enjoy considerable community prestige, a candidate may believe that his campaign will be augmented by its participation. In political contests in which the issue of compulsory health insurance is being debated, various "medical arts committees" have arranged for doctors to write personal letters urging their patients' opposi-

[16]Harold Wilensky, "The Labor Vote: A Local Union's Impact on the Political Conduct of Its Members," Social Forces, XXXV (December 1956), 114.
[17]Nicholas A. Masters, "The Politics of Union Endorsement of Candidates in the Detroit Area," Midwest Journal of Political Science, I (August 1957), 146.
[18]Harold L. Sheppard and Nicholas A. Masters, "The Political Attitudes and Preferences of Union Members: The Case of the Detroit Auto Workers," American Political Science Review, LIII (June 1959), 447.
[19]James G. March, "Group Norms and the Active Minority," American Sociological Review, XVIV (December 1954), 733-741.

tion to "forces at work in this nation today which replace the health and medical care you have always enjoyed under the truly American system of private medicine."[20] In most cases, such letters urged the patient to vote for lists of endorsed candidates who, according to the physicians, could be expected to vote "right" if elected. In Ohio, a small group of trade association executives, using virtually no publicity, worked on behalf of the candidacy of Senator Robert Taft by singling out opinion leaders in every county of the state. Each of these local influentials was urged to arrange meetings, to register Taft supporters and get them to the polls, and to have voters visited by members of their professions. These programs roughly parallel the standard political party operations. To attribute unusual success to them would be to overlook the many other variables contributing to victory or defeat. In Ohio, for example, the substitution of the office-block for the party column ballot was estimated by Taft to have been responsible for more than one-fourth of his majority. The fact that physicians in Florida supported George Smathers in his successful attempt to unseat Senator Claude Pepper in the 1950 Democratic primaries can hardly be regarded as any sort of first cause. The threat of an organization that it will punish politicians for poor voting records simply cannot be made good.

A concluding evaluation

A more plausible assessment of the role of pressure groups in the electoral process can be made if we consider them as allies of the regular political organizations. The cooperation between the AFL-CIO and the Democratic party well illustrates the nature of this alliance. Labor support is not a unified and reliable basis of support for the Democratic party. E. E. Schattschneider estimates that the Democrats can be expected to get about 5,600,000 votes from among the membership of the AFL-CIO, which is about one-third of the total membership.[21] While this is not a great many votes in a Presidential election, for example, some consideration should be given to the geographical distribution of these votes. Nicholas Masters, drawing our attention to the tiny smattering of votes that meant victory for Kennedy, maintains that labor support has become crucial in the urban areas of states having large electoral votes. Candidates in these areas of labor concentration need the active support of unions, not because union leaders control a bloc of votes, but because they may be able to increase the magnitude of urban majorities for the Democrats. However, this does not mean that the Democratic party is in a position of dependence for "... the AFL-CIO must remain Democratic in order to maintain a strong and viable bargaining position in politics."[22] If one tries to assess the relative dependence of the two organizations upon each other, a good beginning can be made with Key's labeling of the pressure group as the "junior partner."[23] If the pressure group has no choice but to support party candidates, then the party clearly assumes the position of dominance. . . .

PRODUCERS, CONSUMERS, AND INTEREST GROUPS
Anthony Downs

Although large segments of the American population may in some sense be "represented" by one or several interest groups, actual *involvement* in interest group activities is characteristic of a very small cadre of persons. Downs explains why, in this second selection from *An Economic Theory of Democracy*. But more importantly, perhaps, his discussion leads to another fundamental attribute of interest group behavior — the dearth of organizations representing the interests of consumers, as against producers, and the weakness of those few that do exist. In introducing the preceding selection by Zeigler, we observed that part of the negative feeling of citizens toward interest group politics stems from "a sense

[20]"New Power at the Polls," *Medical Economics*, January 1951, p.77.
[21]E. E. Schattschneider, *The Semisovereign People* (New York: Holt, Rinehart & Winston, 1960), p. 50. [Schattschneider's calculations are reprinted on pages 71-72 of this text—Ed.]
[22]Nicholas A. Masters, "Organized Labor as a Base of Support for the Democratic Party," *Law and Contemporary Problems*, XXVII (Spring 1962), 256.
[23]V. O. Key, Jr., *op. cit.*, p. 524.
From "The Returns from Information and Their Diminution," pp. 253-256 of *An Economic Theory of Democracy* by Anthony Downs. Copyright © 1957 by Harper & Brothers. Reprinted by permission of Harper & Row, Publishers.

that many interests in society are not represented at all." Upon analysis, it appears that much of the frustration comes from an apparent inability to counteract, as consumers, price increases and other producer-favoring decisions made within and outside of government.

Since Downs writes in a highly compressed fashion, and since so much of what he writes is constructed on previously discussed propositions, some key points in this excerpt may require elaboration. Downs begins by stating that "A voter's party differential is subject to heavy discounting because of the great number of other voters"; he described the mental process of discounting the importance of that differential in the excerpt on pages 21-28, and he repeats in this selection the basic message that, even with high personal stakes in an election, a citizen may feel little compulsion to vote.

Stakes can also be high for lobbyists, but they persist in their intense activities because each feels that his activity ("intervention") will produce a noticeable effect. That optimism relies in part on the realization that there are only a few other lobbyists in competition with him (as opposed to the millions of individuals with whom a voter is in competition). That there are only a few is due to "the great cost of obtaining enough information to exert effective influence."

This high cost (of time and energy, as well as money) forces lobbyists to concentrate on a narrow field of legislation. Because men earn their incomes in a narrow field of endeavor and spend their incomes in a broad range of areas, they tend to lobby as producers rather than as consumers. That is, faced with a desire to improve their buying power, they are pushed toward trying to raise their incomes (lobbying in their role as producers) rather than toward trying to lower prices (lobbying in their role as consumers). This principle applies not only to professional lobbyists but to any citizen interested in trying to influence legislation by participating in an interest group, and it explains the failure of consumer-oriented interest groups to achieve much following or influence.

Remember that Downs is dealing with a deductive model of rational political behavior that corresponds to but does not directly portray reality. His hope is that his analysis will provide strong leads for an understanding of the real world, that his model is to a significant degree correlated with actual experience.

. . . Almost everyone at least considers voting, but relatively few citizens ever consider exerting influence in any particular area of policy. . . . A voter's party differential is subject to heavy discounting because of the great number of other voters. In contrast, an influencer's intervention value may suffer hardly any discount because only a small number of others are interested in the policy he wants to influence. Perhaps many people are affected by this policy, but since most of them do not realize in advance the source of these effects, they cannot seek to alter policy pursued at that source.

Such ignorance is not the result of mere apathy; rather it stems from the great cost of obtaining enough information to exert effective influence. Each influencer must be acquainted with the situation at least well enough to be in favor of a specific policy. True, many people voice strong policy preferences without benefit of much information, and the ballots these people cast are just as potent as those of the well-informed. Nevertheless, the government knows that its behavior in a given policy area will affect many people who show no immediate interest in that area. Consequently, it must be persuaded that these presently passive citizens will not react against whatever policy an influencer is promoting. A would-be influencer has to be knowledgeable enough to carry out this persuasion. . . .

. . . Influencers are specialists in whatever policy areas they wish to influence; whereas voters are generalizers trying to draw an overall comparison between parties. Specialization demands expert knowledge and information, especially if competition is keen, but most men cannot afford to become expert in many fields simultaneously. Therefore influencers usually operate in only one or two policy areas at once. This means that in each area, only a small number of specialists are trying to influence the government.

Naturally, the men who stand most to gain from exerting influence in a policy area are the ones who can best afford the expense of becoming expert about it. Their potential returns from influence are high enough to justify a large investment of information. In almost every policy area, those who stand the most to gain are the men who earn their incomes there. This is true because most men earn their incomes in one area but spend them in many; hence the area of earning is much more vital to them than any one area of spending. Furthermore, the cost of data purchased in order to influence government policy in an area of production can often be charged to a business firm or labor union. These corporate units can, in turn, deduct the cost from their taxable incomes. Also they may be large enough to gain economies of scale in data consumption through intensive specialization in relevant policy areas.

For all these reasons, producers are much more likely to become influencers than consumers. The former can better afford both to invest in the specialized information needed for influencing and to pay the cost of communicating their views to the government. . . . However, almost every man is both a producer and a consumer at different moments of his life. Therefore we must rephrase the above conclusion as follows: men are more likely to exert political influence in their roles as income-receivers than in their roles as income-spenders, whether acting as private citizens or as members of a corporate entity.

This conclusion is of great importance because from it we can deduce (1) the pattern of information investment which any particular citizen is likely to make, (2) which citizens are likely to be well-informed on any given policy area, and (3) what pressures upon government are likely to be strongest in any area. Clearly, the cost of acquiring information and communicating opinions to government determines the structure of political influence. Only those who can afford to bear this cost are in a position to be influential.

A striking example of this fact is the failure of consumers-at-large to exercise any cogent influence over government decisions affecting them. For instance, legislators are notorious for writing tariff laws which favor a few producers in each field at the expense of thousands of consumers. On the basis of votes alone, this practice is hardly compatible with our central hypothesis about government behavior. But once we introduce the cost of information, the explanation springs full-armed from our theory. Each producer can afford to bring great influence to bear upon that section of the tariff law affecting his product. Conversely, few consumers can bring any influence to bear upon any parts of the law, since each consumer's interests are spread over so many products. In fact, most consumers cannot even afford to find out whether tariffs are raising the price they pay for any given product. Yet without such knowledge they cannot have policy preferences for the government to pay attention to.

Under these conditions, government is bound to be more attentive to producers than consumers when it creates policy. This is true even though (1) government formulates policy so as to maximize votes and (2) more voting consumers are affected by any given policy than voting producers. As a result, such devices as tripartite industrial control boards with representatives from labor, management, and consumers are doomed to failure. The consumer representative never has effective forces behind him comparable to those of labor and management. Hence these boards practically always seize any opportunities for labor and management jointly to exploit consumers. Even giant labor unions acting for their members' interests as consumers have to spread their influence across too many products to be truly effective as counterweights to producers in each field. Economically speaking, government policy in a democracy almost always exhibits an anti-consumer, proproducer bias. And this bias in our model exists not because the various agents concerned are irrational but because they behave rationally. . . .

Actually, all of these deductions follow directly from the role of information in the division of labor. In a specialized society, every man is naturally better informed about the area of his specialty than about other areas. This has two effects: (1) because his income derives from this area, the returns to him on information useful for influencing policy in it are high, and (2) because he is already familiar with the area, the cost to him of becoming well-informed about it is low. Thus by its very nature, the division of labor creates a few men in each policy area who can rationally afford to influence government policy there, and makes it irrational for most men to do so. This outcome occurs even if all men are equal in intelligence, wealth, income, and interest in government activity.

AMERICAN BUSINESS AND PUBLIC POLICY

Raymond A. Bauer, Ithiel de Sola Pool, and Lewis A. Dexter

That lobbying activities tend to be conducted mainly by producers has been demonstrated over and over again during periodic legislative revisions of tariffs. One of the most intensive studies of the lobbying process was undertaken by Bauer, Pool, and Dexter, who focused on renewal of the Reciprocal Trade Act in 1953 through 1955. The following excerpts from that study are important in providing a picture of the types of organizations that become involved in such struggles and in disclosing some sharp insights into the actual ineffectiveness of those lobby groups that the public at large views as among the most powerful.

DRAMATIS PERSONAE

Lobbying and related activities

Historically, the tariff has been a favorite concern of lobbies. Its story has more than once been written as a history of lobbying tricks, stratagems, and propaganda devices. The classic picture of a pack of wolves descending on Capitol Hill and buying, bullying, or cajoling congressmen is given in Schattschneider's excellent study.[1]

If one approached the history of the 1954-1955 debate with a naïve faith in classic democratic theory, expecting to find a group of statesmen on Capitol Hill who had been selected by their constituents for their superior wisdom and who were expected to deliberate seriously and freely about national interest, it would come as a shock to discover some of the things that occurred alongside such deliberations. It would be a shock to find a series of hired spokesmen for special interests enjoining congressmen to do favors for toy-marble-makers, bicycle manufacturers, cherry-growers, fishermen, importers, and others. It would come as an even greater shock to discover that a significant number of congressmen might act on the basis of such representations. If our starting point were naïveté, we might describe this set of facts by saying that lobbies had a colossal influence.

But our starting point was not naïveté. We follow several generations of muckraking exposés and of the "group approach" to politics. Our initial expectation was that, the façade once penetrated, we would find the decisive events in tariff legislation to be a series of deals worked out between subtle and richly financed interest groups and congressmen pressured by

them. It thus came as a surprise to discover that the lobbies were on the whole poorly financed, ill-managed, out of contact with Congress, and at best only marginally effective in supporting tendencies and measures which already had behind them considerable Congressional impetus from other sources. We do not deny that there were large numbers of pressure groups. We are certain that, whatever the outcome, it would have been quite different if all the organized interest groups on one side had been silenced while all those on the other had remained vocal. However, it is in the nature of the democratic struggle that that does not happen. When we look at a typical lobby, we find that its opportunities for maneuver are sharply limited, its staff mediocre, and its major problem not the influencing of Congressional votes but the finding of clients and contributors to enable it to survive at all.

Lobbying also proved unimportant compared to other functions of pressure groups. Lobbying and pressure groups have become so identified with each other that it is often forgotten that pressure, or interest, groups also have other functions and programs. In 1953-1955, their effect in buttonholing, cajoling, and persuading congressmen was far less than their effect in organizing and channeling communications. The predominant influence which a group like the Committee for a National Trade Policy had was as the recognized spokesman for the freer-trade point of view. Whether it functioned well or badly, aggressively or with restraint, it was the place to which a newsman would turn if he wished a statement from that side about a legislative event. It was the source to which a congressman would turn for facts he needed or to which his assistant would telephone to line up witnesses for a hearing. It was the place where a businessman would expect staff-type thinking to be done for him. The arguments it used would become the arguments all on that side would repeat. And, just as the CNTP in that way dominated and set the tone of much

Raymond A. Bauer, Ithiel de Sola Pool, and Lewis A. Dexter, "Dramatis Personae," Chapter 21, "Quasiunanimity—Premise of Action," Chapter 22, and "Further Difficulties of the Pressure Groups," Chapter 23, in American Business and Public Policy (New York: Atherton Press, 1963) pp. 323-349.
[1]E. E. Schattschneider, Politics, Pressures, and the Tariff (Hamden, Conn.: Shoe String Press, Inc., 1935).

of the communications process for the side of freer trade, so the Nationwide Committee of Industry, Agriculture, and Labor on Import-Export Policy did for the side of protection, the National Coal Association for the coal industry, the Manufacturing Chemists Association for the chemical industry, and so on. These associations became nodes in the communications process. What they knew or failed to learn, what they heard or did not hear, what they said or failed to say, had a profound effect on what other people learned, heard, or said. These other people were not merely the general public, but, more importantly, their own members, the press, the administration, and congressmen.

Thus, although lobbying by any given pressure group was relatively limited in effectiveness, the presence of pressure associations astride the communications process was important indeed.

The organizations

We shall not try to list all the interest groups that were active around the issue of Reciprocal Trade renewal but merely to convey an impression of the types of organizations aligned on either side. They fall easily into four groups:

1. Special associations formed for the exclusive purpose of promoting or opposing protection.

2. Large, multipurpose associations, such as the Chamber of Commerce, National Association of Manufacturers, and League of Women Voters, all of which played some role in this, as in many other, legislative controversies.

3. Trade associations of manufacturers or dealers in particular products.

4. Law and public-relations firms which worked for any of the above types of groups or for individual firms.

QUASIUNANIMITY — PREMISE OF ACTION

. . . The usual pattern in American business and trade associations is one of unanimity, or, more accurately, quasiunanimity.

Sometimes the minority preserves the façade of such unanimity if it does not feel that it has too much at stake. It then keeps its peace and does not obstruct. . . . Thus, there can be dissent when the minority is relatively indifferent. The dissenters maintain the appearance of unanimity by self-restraint.

At other times, when the minority feels strongly on the issue, restraint is imposed on the majority. In this common situation, multipurpose organizations duck the controversial issues. . . .

The problem becomes especially crucial in such catchall, multipurpose organizations as the Chamber of Commerce and the National Association of Manufacturers. Since such organizations are supposed to represent a wide range of interests in a wide range of business, special efforts are taken to avoid generating any avoidable internal conflict. Cautious procedures are employed for reaching a policy position, and spokesmen are confined to stating that position without elaboration, for fear that even the most cautious elaboration may produce dissension. . . .

The NAM and the Chamber of Commerce are constrained by the fact that they must try to speak for the full range of American business. They necessarily take positions only when business is relatively united.

But are specific industry associations more daring? Yes, but only to a degree. Here, too, we generally find the controlling principle to be quasiunanimity.

For example, the National Electrical Manufacturers Association had on the surface been one of the most active of the trade associations on the issue of protection; yet a close view reveals that it had taken no position. In July, 1953, the association decided to have a study of foreign-trade policies made. The occasion was the one-year extension of the Reciprocal Trade Act and creation of the Randall Commission. Accordingly, it had Donovan, Leisure, Newton, and Irvine make an analysis of legislation, treaties, and regulations affecting the ability of American manufacturers to compete with foreign producers, and it commissioned the National Industrial Conference Board to make a study called "United States and its Foreign Trade Position," which actually deals with electrical machinery. The more controversial phase of this, "The United States Electrical Manufacturing Industry in its Relation to the Security, Health, Safety and Welfare of the Country," was in turn subcontracted to Stone and Webster, an engineering corporation. To quote the NEMA,

"All three organizations participating in the study were instructed to present factual conclusions only and to make no attempt at analysis, evaluation, or recommendation. In view of this objective and factual approach, O. Glen Saxon, Professor of Economics at Yale University, was asked to make an analysis and evaluation of the three documents and to prepare his own conclusions and recommendations as to foreign economic policy."

Note that nowhere had the association taken a stand. In April, 1954, however, a group of manufacturers in their own name issued some "Recommendations of Electrical Manufacturers on Foreign Trade Policy." The signatories included manufacturers representing $3⅓ billion of annual sales and more than 235,000 employees. They included Westinghouse and eight departments of General Electric, but not General Electric as such. Sensitivity to conflicting interests reached down even below the corporate level. The chairman of the board of G.E. testified before the House committee supporting the Trade Agreements Act "in broad effect."

Many trade associations and also many major companies adopted this permissive pattern, evading an official position while permitting action which smacked of one. . . .

A variant way of avoiding internal friction is for a parent body to have a policy but not to enforce it on its members. The best example of this was the labor movement. . . . The national CIO leadership strongly favored a more liberal trade policy, but many member unions and even the United Auto Workers locals associated with bicycle manufacturing favored protection for their industries. National officials of the CIO and UAW were extremely anxious to avoid putting any appreciable pressure on their locals. The only difference between the stance of the CIO leaders and that of typical trade-association executives is that the CIO leadership did view itself as a policy-forming unit, whereas trade-association executives typically view themselves as arbitrators between forces in the organization and as the members' mouthpiece. National labor leaders have more freedom in setting policies than do trade-association executives because AFL-CIO affiliates and locals are unlikely to secede if in disagreement with a national policy. But the labor leadership, too, felt impotent to prevent dissenting members from expressing their points of view.

Thus, throughout, there is a pattern of avoidance of issues, suppression of controversy, and at least the pretense of unanimity.

Sometimes issues cannot be avoided. What happens when there are sharp differences of opinion in American trade associations? Here, the pattern is one of multiplication of associations. Most business firms belong to several associations, and large firms belong to scores. An industry is apt to have many associations covering the variety of interests represented within it. . . .

Partial coalition and partial conflict of interests is the pattern throughout. Woolen manufacturers share with wool-growers an interest in research and in the promotion of the use of wool, but they are at odds on whether these be American or British woolens. The manufacturers' and growers' interests converge in wanting protection against woolen fabric imports, but they find themselves in conflict regarding imports of raw wool. Cheap raw-wool imports help the American manufacturer compete with his British rivals, but hurt the American grower. In conflict with both the manufacturers and the growers, importers want free trade in general. Thus, a multiplicity of associations is called into being to reflect these varied interests. Alongside the National Association of Woolen Manufacturers, the American Wool Council unites the producers and the dealers with the manufacturers. For purposes of wool promotion, the Wool Bureau unites the entire American industry. It is represented in the American Wool Council with the British International Wool Secretariat. Separated from these associations to represent special interests are the American Trade Association for British Woolens and, for the fabric wholesalers, the Woolen Jobbers Association.

This pattern of multiplication and division permits each association to follow the rule of quasiunanimity within its range of issues and to permit those of its own members who have a different viewpoint to express it through another and more appropriate association. Often, these divergent bodies actually operate from the same headquarters and share personnel. There are some business firms in the field of association management which provide staff and offices for a large number of very small associations. For the larger associations, which have their own staffs and offices, it is also convenient to have several faces for different purposes. . . .

To summarize, it is difficult to get multipurpose business associations to take stands on controversial issues. The broader and more heterogeneous the organization, the greater the probability that some subgroups will dissent on a given issue. In a sense this means that, the more an organization represents the business community as a whole, the more unlikely it is to become committed on such an issue as foreign-trade policy. . . .

FURTHER DIFFICULTIES OF THE PRESSURE GROUPS

The efforts of business and trade associations to avoid disintegration over controversial issues lead to a proliferation of organizations and particularly to the formation of specialized pressure groups designed to deal with specific issues. Even such single-minded groups had difficulties we did not anticipate. They suffered from shortages of money, skilled personnel, information, and time.

"All that money being thrown around"

The image of lobbyists wallowing in ill-gotten and ill-spent lucre is one of the great myths of our time. There are few very-well-paid lobbyists even at the peak of the profession. However, there have been legislative issues on which a great deal of money has been spent. . . .

The reciprocal-trade controversy . . . was one on the outcome of which many people stood to gain or lose large sums of money. Despite that, the men we observed were not overfed lobbyists with lush bankrolls throwing swank cocktail parties, but rather hard-working organizers devoting an excessive portion of their time to raising enough money to keep their organizations going and constantly skimping on obvious things to do because the money was not available.

The lobbyists themselves are the source of part of the false public image of men with unbounded resources. Each side vastly overestimates the other. Each pictures the other as having an unlimited budget, an enormous staff, and all the operational possibilities which they themselves wish they had but feel frustrated because they have not. Each side sees itself as David against Goliath. . . .

We have no reason to believe that any one of the pressure groups on the trade issue wanted to buy votes. We know that Congressional votes were in general not available to be bought. But even if a group wished to turn from propaganda to corruption, no one of the organizations had the discretionary funds to undertake such an enterprise. . . .

The failure to recognize the multiplicity and diversity of spending bodies, each with its individual goals, leads to a false image of pressure group processes. The total sums spent somehow leave the impression of plutocratic giants, able by their wealth to totally distort the public process. Clearly, if one takes the few instances concerning which we have reasonably reliable figures and projects those figures over the total number of organizations operating in this field and if one then adds to these organizational expenditures the amounts spent by business firms and individuals in their own contributed time and effort—for example, arranging meetings, making speeches, writing letters—one cannot escape the conclusion that the reciprocal-trade controversy cost the participants many millions of dollars a year. Yet, wherever one looked at the persons actually spending that money, one saw only harassed men with tight budgets and limited campaign funds, once their essential organizational overheads had been met.

Lack of skilled personnel

A profession needs an ideology to justify itself. Without a proud self-image, it will not attract its full potential in personnel. A man and his family are proud of the practice of law. Most mothers would say, "I didn't raise my boy to be a lobbyist." As long as that situation prevails, the best talent will not be found in pressure politics. One of our respondents described legislative work as a young man's game. A family man moves from it to more stable occupations. Many lobbyists were in fact older, but those were not generally the most gifted men. This is a difficult point to document. We have no evidence on intrinsic ability; yet it is our distinct impression that, except for a few highly capable men at the top of the heap, the best men leave the field.

Lack of knowledge

The lack of money and personnel is compounded by such other problems as inadequate information. It takes able men and much money to do good research, and research is one thing every lobby needs. Facts are their stock in trade. Research is needed to write speeches, to put out pamphlets, to prepare testimony, to find the arguments which will convince doubters. It may not be research as the academician conceives it, but, such as it is, it takes much of the organizer's time.

At one level, if one asked what these association organizers did, we would answer in these terms: they produced publicity; they arranged meetings; they stimulated letters, articles, and speeches. In so doing, they raised the level of public discussion and awareness of public policy. We do not mean for a moment to suggest that they were educators in intent or that their products would meet the normal standards of scholarship. We suggest only that the net effect of all this discussion, counterdiscussion, statement, and correction is a certain degree of enlightenment.

The scholarly researcher may be both intrigued and disturbed as he observes the research activity conducted by interest groups and the standards of integrity in it. The prevailing attitude was least self-consciously expressed by one public-relations man from whose interview we quote:

"He said: 'We did a survey recently which showed 300,000 unemployed as a result of foreign imports. That's probably about right, although no one can prove it one way or the other. . . .' I asked if some of the protectionists whom he dealt with who responded to particular injuries didn't have some trouble rationalizing their view in terms of the big picture. He said, 'No, it doesn't bother them for long. They convince themselves that theirs is the national interest.' He then cited himself as an example. He said: 'Often I have doubts when I take a job, but after a while I find I am convinced. I like to tell myself that it is because I know more about the subject, but that is not really it. If that were it, why would I always find I am convinced of the side I am working on?' I suggested to him that there might be limits to this process. He said: 'That's right. You don't get into a job in the first place if you don't like the looks of it. . . .' He said that he did a job on the oil cartel. 'There are seven companies that divide up the world between them. We publicized that, and it is probably true.' "

In short, the job of an operator is to seek those facts which build his case. The operator here, as in psychological warfare, as in law cases, as in all fields except pure research, is balancing three standards. He wants the facts that will support his case, that will not kick back by exposing him

as deceitful, and that are reliable because he himself objects in principle to lying. His assumption is that, since he is on the right side, there must be some facts that will help, not hurt. His job is to find them. He has no taboo against stating with great certitude something that is only probable or against stating broadly something that is only partially true; but he does not want to make his case out of whole cloth, nor does he believe that he can successfully do so. As one respondent put it:

"He said that they tried to get informational bulletins out, and then he said half-apologetically, 'We call them informational bulletins, but some people don't think they are just information. . . . You know, we may slant the data a little bit our way, but it has to be sound; we see to it that it is sound because we cannot get caught off base.' "

Thus, a large part of the activity of the organizers consists of research, and one of the reasons for their relative ineffectiveness is the lack of good research on both sides. Congressmen frequently said that they would talk to anybody who would bring them really fresh information. Bored to death by hearing the same old stories, they often expressed a real craving for some solid facts that they could believe. One may wonder whether this was not to some extent a search for a *deus ex machina*, a wistful feeling on the part of congressmen that there must be some objective answer that would get them out of difficult decisions. Yet, receptive to facts they were, whatever the reason.

Thus, information is often power. A complex example is provided by the petroleum industry. For good and sufficient reasons, major oil companies are afraid to be overtly politically aggressive. They collided with the antitrust laws once, and they have been a symbol of big business in the public mind. They hesitate to lobby, and they would probably never dream of organizing their employees in a letter-writing campaign. Their time-perspective is a long one, and they recognize that self-restraint on a momentary issue will in the end pay off in public acceptance of the industry. It is therefore somewhat of a mystery how these few large firms succeeded in holding off oil-import quotas as long as they did against the much more vigorous demands of the American independent producers for protection. The answer lies in part in the fund of expertise and knowledge which they have accumulated. . . . When one needs facts about the world petroleum situation, he is likely to find them in the excellent library organized by Standard Oil of New Jersey. Indeed, in their fight against Standard and the other major producers, the independents turned to Standard Oil to get the basic data with which to fight them. The sensitivity of the big companies to public relations, their unwillingness to be aggressive, and the power that knowledge gives them are all illustrated by the fact that, when the independents went to Standard to get the data with which to fight Standard, the latter helped them and asked no questions. Standard thus won the respect and the frustrated awe which . . . was felt by those who opposed it, but on the basis of imperfect knowledge.

Though information can be power, it is a power usually untapped by the pressure groups we studied. The amount of factual information most of them had assembled was limited indeed. Neither side budgeted much for research. . . .

Lack of time

The harassment we observed was not only financial. The life of a Washington pressure-group organizer is not a leisurely one. That is both its charm and its agony. In working for any legislative cause, whether as a lobbyist or as a congressman, there is just too much to do. An executive of a trade association has to concern himself, not only with national policies, but also with organization finances, membership, meetings, bulletins and magazines, correspondence, inquiries, staffing, and the like. He must follow legislative and administrative developments, not only on tariffs, but also on government contracts, taxes, and regulations of all sorts. He has to collect economic statistics,

business news, and scientific and legislative reports. If he is in a single-issue organization . . . he is concerned with changes in tariff rates and regulations for each of the products listed in the tariff rules. He is concerned, not only with the Reciprocal Trade Bill and all its ramifications, but also with customs simplification, GATT, OTC, Buy-American legislation, agricultural legislation, and such administrative proceedings as Tariff Commission escape-clause proceedings and State Department reciprocal-trade negotiations. In this day of big government, there is never enough time to do more than select from among its complexities what to cope with, or else to drift, pushed by events into a few of the many things one might do. Most pressure-group activity is emergency fire-fighting. There is seldom time to do much more. Long-range planning goes by default.

Summary

We have noted some difficulties which pressure groups face in attempting to do an effective job: lack of funds, adequate personnel, knowledge, and time. A close look at the pressure groups revealed them as something far short of the omnipotent, well-oiled machines that are portrayed in political literature. Most surprising to us was the lack of money. We have not contended that all pressure campaigns are similarly impoverished, but most are. The heart of the matter lies in the number of organizations among which the available funds are divided. The statement that "millions of dollars were spent on each side" proves to be meaningless until one has ascertained what proportion of these "vast sums" has gone into the overhead of the organizations. The balance available for external spending is what counts if the pressure groups are to have any appreciable effect.

THE DANGERS AND CONTRIBUTIONS OF LOBBYING

Lester W. Milbrath

In this excerpt from the most rigorous empirical study of lobbying to appear in recent years, Milbrath in effect suggests that consumers have a considerably stronger voice in the interplay of pressures than Downs' analysis would allow. His comments are directed particularly toward assessing the net impact of lobbying on governmental policy. As Bauer and his colleagues reminded us, that impact is not the same as the impact of pressure group activity as a whole. Although popular myth holds that lobbying is highly influential, Milbrath, like the Bauer group, finds little data to support the myth. However, what impact lobbyists do have is generally beneficial, in his opinion, and his reasons can by extension be applied also to pressure group activity in its totality. Some of the contributions Milbrath attributes to interest groups are contrasted with those of political parties; this aspect of his analysis — assessing the relative roles and contributions of interest groups and parties — should be kept in mind when you read the selection by Schatt-schneider on pages 69-75.

THE DANGERS OF LOBBYING

. . . There is relatively little influence or power in lobbying per se. There are many forces in addition to lobbying which influence public policy; in most cases these other forces clearly outweigh the impact of lobbying. Voters set the broad trends of public policy which all the other influences on policy must follow. It is for this reason that so many forces battle to manipulate public opinion. Public opinion is a factor which sets the boundaries for the policy struggle. On certain questions the boundaries are closely restricted, and the policy decisions of officials must closely follow public demands. On other questions, the boundaries may be broader, leaving wider discretion to decision-makers and more possibility for lobbyists to influence their decisions. Questions of large public attention and import are chiefly determined by considerations of political success and winning the next election. The chief executive, through his political leadership, his ability to mold public opinion, and his command of the resources and imagination of the executive bureaucracy, has the greatest single impact on the shape of public policy. Questions of small technical nature, which attract little public attention, are more subject to lobbying influence. The growth of one lobby group or coalition generally stimulates the development of an opposing group. Most careful observers of governmental decision-making have concluded that the over-all impact of lobbying is relatively minor. . . .

If the conclusion that lobbying has a relatively weak impact on policy is added to the conclusions that system controls and legal controls are adequate, that public decisions cannot be bought or stolen, and that the lobbying process is relatively clean, the result is clear: lobbying as we see it today in Washington presents little or no danger to the system. This does not mean that a dangerous situation could not arise or that lobbyists would not engage in unethical or unfair tactics if they believed these would be to their special advantage. The best insurance against danger and corruption in the process is an alert citizenry which elects responsible officials to public office. A wide-open communications system and viable and responsible public media are important preconditions to maintaining public alertness.

THE CONTRIBUTIONS OF LOBBYING

Eckstein raises the most fundamental question about lobbying and pressures groups: "What contributions do pressure groups make to the political system as a whole, and do these contributions tend to make the system more or less viable (stable and effective)? Are their consequences 'dysfunctional' or 'eufunctional' for the larger systems in which they operate?"[1] . . .

In this context it is relevant to point out . . . that lobbying is inevitable and is likely to grow in scope. One lobbyist says it is analogous to automobile drivers: there are a few bad drivers, but people continue to drive, and more cars are added to the road each year. Lobbying is protected by the First Amendment to the Constitution, and government officials are not disposed to hamper its growth or activities.

Granted the inevitability of lobbying, what are its positive contributions to the political process? Lobbyists provide information and other services which are welcomed by governmental decision-makers. These services are costly and

From "The Impact of Lobbying on Governmental Decisions," in *The Washington Lobbyists* (Chicago: Rand McNally & Company, 1963), pp. 354-358.
[1]Harry Eckstein, *Pressure Group Politics* (Stanford: Stanford University Press, 1960), p. 152.

somewhat wasteful; the public or the consumer pays for them ultimately; congressional officials even claim they could function quite adequately without them. In another sense, however, they are indispensable. If information from lobbyists and lobby groups was, for some reason, unavailable to government officials, they would be largely dependent on their own staff for information and ideas. Since the Congress is reluctant to staff itself adequately, it would have to turn primarily to the Executive for information. This would create an even further imbalance between Congress and the Executive in policy-making. More important, cutting off lobbying communications would eliminate a valuable, even indispensable, source of creativity. There is no assurance that government institutions can turn up all the possible alternative solutions to policy problems. A decision-maker who has his mind made up may well have to have new points of view forcefully thrust upon him before he can perceive and accept them. The clash of viewpoints between contesting groups is not only informative; it also is creative. Formerly unperceived alternatives may arise from the challenge to previously accepted possibilities.

Eckstein suggests that lobby groups perform two other indispensable functions in the political system: integration and disjunction.[2] Officials must know very specifically what the effects of a given policy will be and how citizens will react to that policy. Lobby groups and lobbyists define opinion for government with a sense of reality and specificity which political parties,

the mass media, opinion polls, and staff assistants seldom, if ever, can achieve. Aggregating and defining specialized opinions have both integrative and disjunctive aspects. The function is integrative in that persons with special interests or problems need group action to aggregate their views and communicate the positions to officials. The aggregation process requires some compromise on the part of group members and therefore is integrative. Group opinion is a more manageable consideration for officials than scattered individual opinions.

Specialized opinion is disjunctive as well, in that it encourages multiple group demands. Political parties (especially in a two-party system) strive for a very broad integration in order to win elections. That kind of integration can be achieved only by reaching a very low and vague denominator which may not be very functional for making policy. If special interests were confined to vague representation through political parties, they might begin to feel alienated from a political system which persistently distorts their goals. Affording disparate interests special representation through their own lobby group probably contributes to the stability of the system. There is reason to suppose, then, that the policy-making system produces wiser or more intelligent decisions and functions with more stability than might be the case if lobby groups and lobbyists were not present. If we had no lobby groups and lobbyists we would probably have to invent them to improve the functioning of the system.

WHOSE GAME DO WE PLAY?

E. E. Schattschneider

The final selection in this chaper on interest groups serves as a bridge to the next chapter, which focuses on political parties in the American political system. Schattschneider considers the relative contributions of interest groups and political parties to the process of government. From his vantage point there is no question about the greater importance of parties. His implicit advice to the person contemplating political participation is not to channel energy into pressure group activity.

Because his examination of two organizational alternatives for political involvement is carried out exclusively in the context of elections, Schattschneider's disparagement of interest groups does not adequately

take into account their impact *between* elections on ongoing legislative, administrative, and judicial behavior. The student who wishes to formulate valid conclusions about the alleged roles and functions of interest groups should juxtapose this selection with the earlier excerpts from Truman and Froman.

One of the more important aspects of this excerpt is its clarification of the notion of "balance of power." All too often, journalists and other impressionistic

[2]*Ibid.*, p. 162.
"Whose Game Do We Play?" Chapter 3 in *The Semisovereign People* by E. E. Schattschneider, pp. 47-60, copyright © 1960 by E. E. Schattschneider. Reprinted by permission of the author and publisher, Holt, Rinehart and Winston, Inc. All rights reserved.

political observers attribute a candidate's margin of victory to some specific group that "held the balance of power." For example, if a man wins by 10,000 votes an election in which 110,000 votes were cast, the temptation is to assign his plurality to the group to which he particularly addressed himself. However, a more reasonable explanation would attribute the margin of victory to any 10,000 voters of the total 60,000 who voted for him. A more sophisticated analysis would propose that the election hinged on the votes of those specific 10,000 individuals who were least likely to vote for the eventual winner but who finally did. Even if it were possible (by questionnaire) to identify these people, it would be most unlikely that all or even a majority of them would be members of a single interest group. True balance-of-power politics requires that an interest group have a membership which is in fact politically independent and that it be able and willing to switch parties or candidates *en masse* on instructions from group leader strategists. Such memberships are extremely rare. Furthermore, the balance-of-power strategy can be employed only in relatively close election situations, unless the interest group itself has a very large membership (which most do not).

This, then, is the logic of balance-of-power politics. However, the real world of politics responds not to logic but to people's perceptions. It is one thing to argue that interest groups cannot carry out their threats to swing a balance-of-power; it is quite another to claim that interest groups or politicians or parties believe this fact. Many politicians do not believe it at all, or only half believe it, or — in an attempt to follow the most conservative vote-getting route — decide not to risk even the very small chance of being wrong in calculating that a group cannot carry out its threat. It is safer to overestimate a group's strength than to underestimate it, they are likely to conclude.

The influence of interest groups on candidates and parties varies considerably with the political arena in question. When Schattschneider claims that the parties control interest groups, not vice versa, one assumes that he has national parties in mind. On a national scale, parties overwhelm individual interest groups by their size and diversity. But empirical studies have documented interest group ability to play a major role in party and governmental life at the state and local levels.

The scope and bias of the pressure system suggests some of the limitations of pressure politics as a form of political organization. The limitations of pressure politics become more evident when an attempt is made to use a pressure group in some dimensions of politics other than the relatively narrow range usually reserved for it.

Some of these limitations may be seen in our examination of a number of pressure groups interested in general public causes. What happens when pressure tactics are used to promote widely diffused interests? A survey of a few of these might easily give rise to some skepticism about the effectiveness of pressure tactics in this area.

Are the public-spirited people who invest time, energy and money in these organizations playing the right game? Would it not be intelligent to consider the relation between the resources mobilized by these organizations and the proportions of the task undertaken by them? What scale of political organization is appropriate to the tasks assumed by these groups?

What kind of "pressure" can the 350 members of the Shore and Beach Preservation Association exert on Congress? Would it not be intelligent to recognize that this kind of group is wholly dependent on the socialization of conflict? This is a trigger organization which may start a chain reaction, but what happens thereafter? Ultimately general policies make demands on the political system as a whole. Sooner or later we come to questions concerning the grand strategy of American politics — for what shall it profit us if we are organized to win all the little battles and lose all the big ones? Is it enough to start a multitude of battles if we cannot follow through?

In politics as in everything else it makes a great difference whose game we play. The rules of the game determine the requirements for success. Resources sufficient for success in one game may be wholly inadequate in another. These considerations go to the heart of political strategy. The contrast between pressure politics and party politics becomes evident as soon as we try to transpose the players from one game to the other.

How small the pressure system is does not become clear until we attempt to convert pressure-group membership into party votes. A presidential election involves the greatest mobilization of political forces in the country; a good test of the significance of the pressure system in party politics is therefore to estimate the potential weight of special interests in a presidential election.

We can make a beginning by examining a number of public opinion polls taken during presidential campaigns to show the party preferences of some of the larger special-interest groups, groups of which organized labor is the largest. What is the impact of organized labor in these elections?

About 70 per cent of *organized* labor (more pro-Democratic than nonunion labor) voted Democratic in 1940 and 1944 according to polls taken at the time. (The CIO membership voted 79 and 78 per cent Democratic in these elections.) In a series of polls taken in 1936, 1943, 1944, 1945 and 1946, the Democratic party preference of organized labor was 72, 72, 64, 74, and 69 per cent.[1] For the purposes of this calculation these figures may be taken as typical in spite of the fact that small variations in more recent elections have shown that organized labor may now be less strongly Democratic. That is to say, the statistics used here probably exaggerate the impact of organized labor slightly, as will be observed.

Some allowance must be made for the fact that it is never possible to convert the whole membership of any group into votes. The way in which the law of the imperfect political mobilization of social groups affects the calculus of politics is shown in the following model of the probable influence of the AFL-CIO in a typical election. The percentages and ratios shown are merely illustrative.

This analysis probably exaggerates the political weight of organized labor because it is doubtful that as many as half of labor union members actually vote in presidential elections. The 3,200,000 net contribution of organized labor to the Democratic total is important, but it is only one-fifth as great as it would have been if unions were able to control the vote of their whole membership.

TABLE I ORGANIZED LABOR AND PRESIDENTIAL ELECTIONS

Total membership of AFL-CIO	16,000,000
Since only about half of the membership votes in presidential elections, subtract	8,000,000
Votes actually cast by AFL-CIO members	8,000,000
Democratic share of the labor vote (70% of 8,000,000)	5,600,000
Republican share (30% of 8,000,000)	2,400,000
Subtract Republican share of the labor vote from the Democratic share to get net Democratic gain	3,200,000

The discussion has often been utterly confused by the tendency to attribute unanimity to special-interest groups. The law of the imperfect political mobilization of social groups forces us to revise the calculus of politics when we try to translate pressure-group power into party power.

The effect of *organization* is substantially less than the foregoing calculation suggests, however. For example, *a substantial percentage of workers would have voted Democratic even if they had not belonged to unions.* A fairly typical set of polls shows the vote intentions of union members and nonunion workers in three presidential elections.

TABLE II UNION AND NONUNION VOTES IN PRESIDENTIAL ELECTIONS*

	Per Cent Democratic	
Year	Union Members	Nonunion Members
1944	72	56
1940	72	64
1936	80	72
Average	74.7	64

*Gallup Political Almanac (1946), p. 205.

Apparently "organization" increases the Democratic bias of workers about 10 per cent. Now, if we apply this datum to the 3,200,000 net Democratic gain, shown by the calculation on page 71, we get a new set of figures [see Table III].

No mention is made here of the votes cast by the *wives* of union members because nonunion workers and Republican workers also have wives.

This calculation does not dispose of the matter because there are some "iffy" elements in it, but it does raise a question about the voting power of organized labor. If AFL-CIO, the largest special-interest group in the country can swing only about one million votes, what is the impact of ordinary pressure groups likely to be? Pressure politics and party politics are two different things, and the impact of the one on the other is not what it seems to be in a superficial analysis.

[1] Hadley Cantril, *Public Opinion, 1935-1946*, Princeton, 1951. 591, (2), 624 (9), 628 (18), 645 (7). See also Campbell and Kahn, *The People Elect a President*, pp. 24 and 25, for data on the split of workers and farmers in the 1948 election.

TABLE III   RECALCULATION OF LABOR VOTE IN A TYPICAL PRESIDENTIAL ELECTION

Members AFL-CIO	16,000,000
Do not vote	8,000,000
Do vote	8,000,000
64% who would probably have voted Democratic even if not organized by labor unions, subtract	5,120,000
36% who would probably have voted Republican if labor had not been organized, subtract	2,880,000
Net Democratic advantage (if workers had not been organized)	2,240,000
Net gain for Democrats as shown in previous calculation concerning the vote of organized labor	3,200,000
Net gain for Democrats if labor had not been organized, subtract	2,240,000
Net gain for Democratic party attributable to unionization	960,000

From the standpoint of party politics the margins within which pressure groups operate are limited. *If a group divides equally in an election, its impact is zero.* On the other hand, it is unusual for much more than 70 per cent of any large social group to support either of the parties. Thus for all practical purposes the "range" of discretion within which these groups operate is approximately 20 per cent. Twenty per cent of the membership is much less than the usual estimate of the impact of special-interest groups on party politics.

If we were to apply the calculation made in the case of organized labor to the American Bankers' Association (17,000 members), the end product would be insignificant, even if we make allowance for the probability that bankers are more highly mobilized than union members. As a matter of fact, nearly all business organizations are so small that the political mobilization of their members for voting purposes is pointless.

The impact of special-interest groups on party politics is further affected by the fact that they may actually have a *negative* effect in elections. Thus, in one poll, a cross section of American voters was asked how they would be influenced by the information that a candidate for Congress was endorsed by organized labor; the ratio of unfavorable to favorable responses was five to one.[2] If we follow the line of reasoning suggested by this poll, the calculus becomes something of a shambles.

The "reverse effect" of many special-interest organizations on party politics seems to be very strong. A 1944 poll indicated that the endorsement of candidates by the National Association of Manufacturers would have had marked adverse influence.[3]

A study made by the Washington Public Opinion Laboratory in 1950 showed that endorsements by each of thirteen well-known organizations was likely to have *some* adverse effect on the popularity of candidates.[4] All calculations of the influence of pressure groups in elections must take account of the *unpopularity of nearly all special-interest groups.* Pressure groups are not only small; they are widely disliked.

When allowance is made for all of the kinds of shrinkage (non-voting, imperfect mobilization, tendency of divided votes to cancel out and the reverse effect of special-interest groups), it becomes evident that *it is nearly impossible to translate pressure politics into party politics.* This discussion boils down to the proposition that pressure groups may have an impact on public opinion in general, but this is the point at which pressure politics ceases to be pressure politics. . . .

. . . The notion that parties are aggregates of special-interest groups held together by an endless process of negotiation and concession is unrealistic.

1. It underestimates the consequences of the fact that we have a two-party system. *The parties compete with each other;* they do not compete with pressure groups. The amount of bargaining that they have to do with special-interest groups is limited by the fact that each party must cope primarily with its *party* opposition. Neither party can afford to make excessive concessions to any pressure group.

2. A much better explanation of the process of majority formation is that majorities result automatically from the fact that we have a two-party system. In a two-party election one or the other of the parties is almost certain to get a majority. To win elections it is good strategy to

[2]American Institute of Public Opinion, September 7, 1938.
[3]*Ibid.*, May 23, 1944.
[4]See H. E. Freeman and Morris Showel, "Differential Political Influence of Voluntary Associations," *Public Opinion Quarterly* XV (1951), pp. 702 ff. The results of this study are less conclusive than they might have been if the authors had distinguished between organizations which are mutually exclusive and organizations which have no such directly antagonistic relations with rival organizations.

appeal to the general public broadly on matters of general interest and above all to *keep an eye on the opposition party.*

3. The scope and bias of the pressure system do not fit easily into the calculus of party politics. First, *the pressure system is much too small to play the role sometimes assigned to it.* Secondly, the supposed party neutrality of the pressure groups is largely a myth.

Since it is not easy to move special-interest groups from one party camp into the other, is it not better party strategy to try *to capitalize on the public hostility toward many of these groups than it is to woo them?* The shrinkage resulting from any attempt to convert pressure politics into party politics is so great that we might well conclude that it is never practical to attempt to translate one kind of political force into another.

It follows from the foregoing analysis that any description of political parties as aggregates of special-interest groups is not very convincing. Moreover, the notion that majorities can be formed by accumulating the support of a multitude of special-interest groups does not look like good political analysis because it substitutes a complex explanation for a simple one. If there are only two exits in a concert hall it is extremely likely that more people will use one exit than the other. The two-party system produces majorities as simply as that!

Finally something ought to be said about the logical fallacy of the straw that broke the camel's back. The fable is that the camel was able to bear up under the weight of 999,999 straws but that his back was broken by the millionth straw. This venerable fallacy ignores the obvious truth that each of the million straws contributed equally to the breaking of the camel's back. Unfortunately this kind of logic has been perpetuated in the literature of pressure politics. In a concrete instance the argument runs as follows: Iowa corn growers, incensed at the Republican party for its failure to provide adequate storage facilities, switched from the Republican party to the Democratic party in 1948 and elected Mr. Truman President of the United States. Let us examine the reasoning behind this story.

It is true that Mr. Truman carried Iowa by 28,000 votes and that Iowa corn growers might conceivably have provided that many votes in the election. However, Mr. Truman polled 522,000 votes in Iowa in the 1948 election, and obviously each of these 522,000 votes contrib-

uted equally to his victory. A vote for Mr. Truman counted exactly as much in the final result whether it was cast by a corn grower or a plumber or a school teacher, since all votes are mathematically equal. This would have been true even if Mr. Truman had carried the state by a single vote. In that event everyone who voted for Mr. Truman would have had an equal claim to the honor of having cast the decisive vote.

The power of pressure groups tends to evaporate when it is translated into other dimensions of politics because the calculus of party politics is entirely different from the calculus of pressure politics. Numbers are everything in one dimension and very little in the other. We are dealing with two different strategies of politics and two different concepts of political organization. Moreover, *the end product of party politics is inevitably different from that of pressure politics.* Inevitably some people prefer one game to the other.

Theoretically, pressure groups are nonpartisan (i.e., neutral in party conflict). The ancient assumption is that they reward their friends and punish their enemies regardless of party affiliation by throwing their weight either way as the circumstances warrant.

Actually the neutrality of pressure groups in party politics is largely a myth because political alignments are not as fluid as this concept implies. It is at least as likely that pressure groups are prisoners of the parties as it is the other way around, because pressure groups cannot easily negotiate with both sides in the party conflict. If business groups can do nothing but support the *Republican* candidates, *the Republican party dominates the pressure groups.* The Republican party enjoys a substantial latitude in its relations with business because its only competitor is the Democratic party and business has no party alternative.

The alignment in American politics does not array the parties on the one side against a great mobilization of pressure groups on the other side. Rather, each of the major parties attracts its own loose constellation of pressure groups. Thus the contest aligns the Democratic party and its ancillary groups against the Republican party and its affiliates. In this kind of alignment the relation of business and the Republican party is not that of master and servant (only the critics of the Republican party contend that it is the punching bag of business) because the party has what amounts to a political monopoly of the business interest. A party monopoly of any special interest implies that the *party* is the captor and the special-interest group is the captive.

The relation of business and the Republican party is much like that of organized labor and the Democratic party. Republican critics of the Democratic party like to portray the Democratic party as the slave of organized labor. Actually, labor usually has no place else to go. As long as it thinks that elections are important, it *must* support the Democratic party, generally. The facts of political life are that neither business nor labor is able to win elections by itself.

Once a two-party system is firmly established the major parties automatically have a monopoly of elections; they monopolize the greatest single channel to power in the whole regime. Control of elections gives the parties a very great position in the political system.

If there are twenty thousand pressure groups and two parties, who has the favorable bargaining position? In the face of this ratio it is unlikely that the pressure groups will be able to play off the parties against each other.

This analysis of the relations of pressure groups and political parties has been spelled out in some detail for a reason: *It has a bearing on the strategy of American politics.* It has been necessary to show, first, that the parties are not the prisoners of the pressure groups. The second proposition follows from the first: The *public* has a choice of strategies. The public has a choice of strategies and theories of political organization as well as a choice of issues. As a matter of fact, the choice of issues is apt to be meaningless unless it is backed up by the kind of organization that can execute the mandate.

It is an axiom of warfare that military commanders try to force the fighting on the terrain best suited for the deployment of their own forces, but less well adapted for the deployment of the enemy forces. Thus a small army tries to force the enemy to fight on a battlefield so narrowly restricted that he cannot take advantage of his greater numbers, as the Spartans did at Thermopylae. It follows that there is a strategy for large numbers and a strategy for small numbers.

Pressure groups are small organizations that do not have the political resources to play in the great arena for the highest stakes. The big game is the party game because in the last analysis *there is no political substitute for victory in an election.* This is the doctrine of the chosen battlefield. A wise political leader chooses the arena in which he makes his bid for power.

The problem of party organization is so different from that of smaller associations that it is often misunderstood. Parties are usually compared with smaller organizations, nearly always to the disadvantage of the parties, but parties cannot be judged by the standards used to measure other organizations. The most obvious criterion of the adequacy of either of the major parties is its ability to cope with its party opposition. In other words the parties establish their own standards of adequacy. Most of the organizational problems of the parties are unique. The party system is by a wide margin the largest mobilization of people in the country. The parties lack many of the qualities of smaller organizations, but they have one overwhelming asset of their own. *They are the only organizations that can win elections.*

The parties solve their greatest organizational problem very simply by maintaining the two-party system. This system makes it possible for the parties to get along with structures far more rudimentary than would be necessary otherwise, because each has only to be able to compete with another equally vast and loosely organized opposition. . . .

The parties organize the electorate by reducing their alternatives to the extreme limit of simplification. This is the great act of organization. Since there are only two parties and both of them are very old, the veterans of a century of conflict, it is not difficult for people to find their places in the system. The rivalry is so old, it has been renewed so often, that the problem of identification and organization is very different from that of the new, little, transitory groups which are sometimes regarded as models of efficiency. Most Americans are veterans of the party wars; they know where they belong in the system.

Actually, the parties are the most competitive large organizations in American society. They are far more competitive than the churches, labor unions or business.

In the end, theories of power and political organization get themselves related to what people want to accomplish. Automatism and theories of the disintegration of politics grow out of the assumption that the community is so well established and so stable that no one needs to think about its future. On the other hand, concern for the survival of the community in tumultuous times calls for ideas about conscious control of events by the community and places a high value on the public interest, majority rule and political parties.

Assuming that the general interest in survival is strong enough to be organized we must assume also that this interest will seek its characteristic forms of political organization, organizations capable of exploiting the potentials of the political system. . . .

CHAPTER **4**

THE ROLE OF THE PARTIES

The enthusiasm with which a growing number of political scientists view political parties is not widely reflected by the American public at large, whose feeling is better characterized as ambiguous at best, with a substantial streak of distrust and hostility.

It should come as little surprise that ambiguity and uncertainty are common responses to parties. There is initially the question of what to respond *to*. Is a party an organization with identifiable officers and members, or is it the sum of all voters who express loyalty to it, for example. V. O. Key, Jr., addresses himself to the problem of defining what a party is and what functions it serves. Confusion also arises from attempts to evaluate the ways in which important party functions are performed. Two central party activities are raising money for campaigns and marshaling voters. Although there are other organizations (interest groups) in American society that may also perform these tasks, none is as encompassing as the parties, nor would most of us wish to have interest groups replace parties as prime fund-raisers and vote-getters. Nevertheless, public appreciation for these two party contributions to the viable operation of large-scale democracy has traditionally been dampened by perceptions of the ways in which these two activities are carried out. The articles by Alexander Heard, on fund-raising, and Edward C. Banfield and James Q. Wilson, on one agency of vote-getting (machines), provide some basis for judging the fairness of this public assessment.

American political parties were formed at the end of the eighteenth century in an atmosphere of distrust. They emerged against a philosophy that clearly abhorred the ability of a society to develop strong majoritarian aggregates. The Sedition Act (1798), designed to check the growth of Jefferson's anti-Federalist party—for that was what the somewhat informal alliance of Jefferson's supporters had become—was not so much an awkward act of Federalist self-preservation as an indication of a yet imperfect comprehension that governments and the parties that hold governmental office at any given time are not synonymous. The Federalists did not fully understand that organized opposition to governmental policies does not constitute a threat to government itself.

The rudimentary condition of organized political action at the time of adoption of the Constitution was, in effect, mirrored in that document's failure to mention parties. As a consequence of this silence, the parties' role in our governmental scheme has had to be defined formally by specific laws and court decisions over the span of our history. Because parties sought to determine candidates, the states, which Constitutionally play the major part in conducting elections, inevitably found it necessary to control party procedures. And the parties themselves often sought state legislative assistance in such matters as enforcing criteria for party membership (e.g., for being able to vote in party primaries).

The deep and fundamental involvement of parties in the electoral process finally forced legalists to recognize parties as more than just another form of private interest group. In one of the most important series of Supreme Court decisions in our history, party primaries were established as part of the total formal election machinery, thus bestowing on parties much of the aura of formal governmental institutions. Most of the major Supreme Court cases dealt with exclusion of Negroes from "private" party primaries in the South. It is important to note that this increased recognition of parties as public organizations having a more-or-less "official" status has resulted not so much from a positive appreciation of their role as from a negative desire to regulate their activities.

Of course, popular reactions to political parties have never been, and are not today, homogeneous. Andrew Jackson tried to endow active participation in party organizations with greater respectability by pleading the justifiability of patronage. The Civil War spawned not only generations of hard-set party adherents but also substantial numbers of persons who proudly joined formal specific party organizations. And urban machines used nationality-oriented party clubs to attract the loyalty and participation of immigrants and their descendants.

The inability of contemporary Americans to reach consensus on the value of political parties in a democracy is demonstrated by the widespread tendency to defend the notion of "independence" in voting, or nonpartisanship in some kinds of elections, and at the same time to retain "the two-party system" as a central tenet in our political ideology. Formal nonpartisanship was a logical reform to follow turn-of-the-century revulsion with the performance of parties. But attachment to the two-party system is largely an historical accident; most Americans would find it hard to articulate a detailed rationale for this preference. Popular defense of the two-party system is rarely more than an indirect statement of generalized satisfaction with the governmental *status quo*.

When the two-party system is supported on more specific grounds, it is usually upheld in the face of one-party, not a multiparty, system as the meaningful alternative. The consequences of one-party systems are widely disapproved, yet few Americans realize how many thousands of essentially one-party electoral districts exist in this country. The Greenstein selection summarizes what we know about the interrelationships among categories of party competition and what happens in politics. The Downs excerpt is relevant in its consideration of the extent to which two-partyism does or does not provide electorates with clear choices of politics, programs, and ideologies.

Realization that parties have a crucial role to play, and a strong sense that they do not play it very well, have made the American party system a constant target of reform. Nonpartisanship, a major plank in the Progressive-inspired program for electoral change in cities in the early part of this century, should not be strictly classified as one of the reform possibilities, since it is a denial of party politics, not a proposed improvement. The direct primary is by far the most important reform effort—the one most widely adopted, the one with the most extensive consequences for the political system, and the one that recognizes the desirability (or inevitability) of parties in a free society. With more than a century of experience with primaries behind us, we are in a strong position to measure the actual consequences of the procedure against its intended consequences. This is done by V. O. Key, Jr., in an imaginative historical analysis of state election statistics. A less widespread but potentially important mode of party reform, the "amateur club," is described by James Q. Wilson.

And what of the *status quo*? We have spoken of the enthusiasm of many contemporary political scientists for parties. This enthusiasm is by no means necessarily contingent upon the administration of any particular set of reforms: Edward C. Banfield enters a strong defense of the party system as it is.

NATURE AND FUNCTION OF PARTY

V. O. Key, Jr.

Perhaps the most difficult task in dealing with the behavior and profile of American political parties is finding a broadly acceptable definition of parties. A voter who considers himself a party member will hardly agree that the main purpose of parties is to gain office rather than to obtain passage of policy—but a precinct worker might say so. The point is that the term "party" is used in a number of ways to describe quite different, although related, organizational and identificational phenomena. If confusion is the result, the substitution of a series of terms might help, but the advantage of common usage would then be lost.

Key approaches the problem of defining "party" not with any particular hope of synthesizing some new consensus of usage but rather with the intention of dispelling the semantic fog by systematically analyzing different usages of the term. In so doing, he initiates an exposition of what parties do in a democratic society.

Government derives its strength from the support, active or passive, of a combination of powerful elements in society. That support or acquiescence may be based on interest, fear, tradition, or a combination of these and other factors. The basis of governmental power differs with the traditions and nature of societies. In one instance a comparatively small group with control of instruments of violence may constitute the machinery of government and cow the populace into submission at least for a time. In other instances authority may rest to a far greater degree upon free consent of the governed. In some states those in the seats of power may claim the right to retain their places without challenge; in others, provision may be made for periodic changes in the personnel of government by orderly processes.

In times past, the right to rule was assumed —or grasped— by small groups who based their claim to authority on the rights of religion, birth, family, class, force, wealth. In modern times such narrowly based power has been challenged, if not swept away, by the demands of an ever larger proportion of the people for consultation and participation in the process of governance. The party politician, rather than the prince, becomes the characteristic contestant for power. The political party becomes the instrument for the organization of support in societies founded on the doctrine of the consent of the governed. Furthermore, basic to democratic doctrine is the proposition that there shall be competition for control of the government by party associations or groups.

The form and structure of associations competing for control of government depend somewhat on the nature of the society. In a highly specialized and differentiated society it is difficult for one of many interests to gain control of government. It is, for example, not probable that the Chamber of Commerce of the United States could put forward with any hope of success candidates for the Presidency, the Vice-Presidency, and Congress. Nor is it probable that the American Federation of Labor could do so. A combination of interests is necessary to win elections and to govern. Political parties attempt to form such a combination. They put forward candidates for public office. They compete by electoral means for control of the government apparatus. (This means, of course, that the "parties" of one-party states that brook no opposition are not parties in the western democratic sense.) Pressure groups, on the other hand, are mainly concerned with influencing the policies followed by the party after it gets into office.

Both pressure groups and political parties play important roles in American politics. The distinction often made between their functions is that pressure groups are interested in policy; political parties, in governmental personnel. That succinct differentiation is too simple. Private associations constantly seek to influence appointments to public office. They are not indifferent to the selection of holders of elective office; but, unlike political parties, they do not take the responsibility of nominating and supporting candidates for such offices. Nor are political parties indifferent about public policy. Party leaders may have, and often do have, strong convictions on matters of public policy. But there is a fundamental difference in the motivation of the policy attitudes of parties and of pressure groups. By the nature of the interests of their memberships, the attitudes of pressure groups toward public policy are fixed. Parties, on the other hand, are governed by no

From "Nature and Function of Party," Chapter 8 in *Politics, Parties, and Pressure Groups* (New York: Thomas Y. Crowell Company, 1953), pp. 215-223.

such rigid determination of their attitudes. They are apt to adhere to a doctrine of relativity of righteousness, and their stands on public policy may shift with the changing fortunes and influence of the various groups to which they must appeal for electoral support.

THEORIES ABOUT THE NATURE OF PARTY

Both parties and pressure groups are associations, but it is much more difficult to grasp the real nature of political parties than it is to gain a comprehension of pressure groups. Pressure organizations have well-defined bodies of members (usually dues-paying), constitutions, duly constituted sets of officials, and other usual institutional apparatus. Political parties have the same characteristics — except that most of their "members" pay no dues and the fact of membership rests fairly lightly on their shoulders. These superficial similarities between the two types of association conceal more fundamental differences. The definition of the nature of political parties is attended by no little difficulty, and no pat definition contains a foundation for thorough comprehension of their nature.

Parties inherent in social groups

One approach toward an understanding of political parties is to consider the nature of the functioning of social groups of which the state is only one type. Within all sorts of associations or groups "political parties" exist, although they may not ordinarily be so designated. Affairs of a group—be it a nation, a church, a union, or a chamber of commerce—do not and cannot take care of themselves; small factions of men must advance proposals and must put themselves forward as willing to assume responsibility for handling the affairs of the group. Even in the smallest of societies a minority of "ringleaders" or several minorities of such persons are almost invariably found. They propose ways of dealing with group problems and vie for public place; they exercise leadership. Parties are, it might be said, inherent in human society; these groups of leaders, of course, may or may not operate in every society as they do in a democratic society. They may simply be the strongest and best-armed men in a group. In a large and populous society the party group may become amorphous and ill-defined. Yet the function of public leadership is inherent in social existence; a society inherently has its leaders and followers and its would-be leaders. In a democratic society the principal leaders in political affairs are to be found in political parties.

These remarks, in essence, consist of the assertion that political parties are more or less axiomatic; they are inherent in social life, although they are not always called "parties" and they operate in different ways in different cultures. Perhaps the validity of the foregoing interpretation of the nature of party may be suggested by a brief excursion into some phases of the development of parties in the United States. The early theory of democracy spoke of the "general will" and the "consent of the governed," but was not always explicit about how the "general will" was to be expressed or the "consent of the governed" granted. Speculators about democracy seemed to believe that by some mystic process the "will of the people" would be expressed and rulers would be selected. But a mass of people cannot act as a unit; a small inner circle has to narrow the choices for public office and to formulate questions of public policy. Or perhaps it would be more accurate to say that small groups of men by working together can control the mass. At any rate, early in our history small groups began to act in concert by agreeing on candidates and policies they would support before the electorate as a whole. An early example of this sort of activity was recorded in February, 1763, by John Adams in his diary:

"This day I learned that the caucus club meets at certain times in the garret of Tom Dawes, the adjutant of the Boston regiment. He has a large house, and he has a movable partition of his garret, which he takes down, and the whole club meets in one room. There they smoke tobacco till you cannot see from one end of the room to the other. There they drink flip, I suppose, and there they choose a moderator who puts questions to the vote regularly; and selectmen, accessors, collectors, firewards, and representatives are regularly chosen before they are chosen in the town."[1]

If planning and agreement by a caucus to work in concert was a natural development in the town of Boston of 1763, it can readily be seen that the work of some such extragovern-

[1]C. F. Adams, ed., The Works of John Adams (Boston: Charles C. Little and James Brown, 1850), Vol. II, p. 144.

mental group is much more necessary to make representative government function over the entire United States. Yet the framers of the Constitution did not provide any machinery analogous to the caucus or party to carry on these duties in the formal mechanism of the national government; nor did they, apparently, foresee the rise of political parties in their present form. For the selection of the President, the framers devised the electoral college to be appointed in each state "in such manner as the legislatures thereof" might direct. The electors were to "meet in their respective states" and vote by ballot, and the ballots were to be forwarded "to the seat of Government," where they would be opened and counted. If there was a tie or if no person received a majority, the House of Representatives was to choose the President.

As soon as the new government got well under way, it became necessary to develop cabals and cliques outside the government to perform for the nation as a whole what the caucus club that met in Tom Dawes' garret did for Boston. That the electors in the several states would act independently and without concert was unlikely; in fact, prior to the first election under the Constitution, Hamilton himself "sent word in several States, advising that unanimous vote be given to Washington."[2] It was probably expected that the electors in the several states would represent the same interests and work together in the same manner as did the framers of the Constitution. At any rate, it was necessary to have some sort of machinery through which candidates could be agreed upon in advance. It was not likely that the workings of the electors would be left to chance, and later with the broadening of the suffrage it became even more essential that there be means for consolidating forces on candidates and for making their merits and beliefs known.

Parties an element of governmental apparatus

Political parties are ordinarily thought of as institutions separate and apart from the formal apparatus of government, but the foregoing discussion suggests that parties can be considered virtually as a part of the government, performing the vital function of leadership in the selection of governmental personnel and in the proposal of public policies. The conception of party as essentially an element in the governmental system is given further color by the fact that political parties have come to be closely regulated by law and thereby recognized as performing public functions. The caucus club in Tom Dawes' garret in eighteenth-century Boston operated without legal restriction or regulation. Presumably it could admit to its circle whom it wished and proceed as it desired, but the present-day party is hedged about by legal restrictions that grew out of abuses by the party when it was a purely voluntary association of individuals. As the party system developed, entrance to public office came to be almost exclusively through party nomination. The cliques in control of parties named the candidates from whom public elective officers were selected. The nominating system in general use at the time regulation of parties began was particularly susceptible to fraudulent manipulation. It was the convention system based on the selection of delegates at "primary" meetings of voters in each precinct—much on the order of the Boston caucus club. The controlling clique might call the primary without adequate notice, manage the meeting in an autocratic manner, intimidate the dissenting members, and falsify the ballot count, all without penalty of law, for the party was a voluntary and private association.

The assimilation of American parties into the state apparatus was gradual. The first laws governing parties were optional in character; that is, if a party, under the pressure of public opinion, elected to operate under them, a number of regulations governed the conduct of its primaries. Presently, mandatory laws were substituted for the optional and detailed regulation of party activity was built up. Parties have generally lost the unlimited right to establish qualifications for memberships; tests of membership are usually prescribed by law. Procedure to be followed in selecting candidates of the party is prescribed by law; generally the selection of party candidates is through a direct primary conducted by public officials under public regulation at public cost.

The development of public regulation of party activities was resisted by those groups controlling the parties; they anticipated that the power they derived from control of the party would be weakened by public regulation. The regulation of parties was urged as a means of

[2] Edward Stanwood, *A History of the Presidency* (Boston: Houghton Mifflin, 1926), Vol. I, p. 26.

wiping out abuses that had grown up around the party and of making the party less irresponsible and less independent of the wishes of the rank and file of the party membership. The culmination of the movement for regulation may be interpreted as an amalgamation of the machinery of private associations with the machinery of government itself; the party was found to perform an essential function in the governing process, and it was appropriated by the state. In practice, the regulation of parties is handled by the state legislatures; but the national conventions are not beyond state control in that delegates are often elected under procedures fixed by state law; and the national party organization is little more than a loose alliance of state organizations, each operating under the provisions of state law.

Contestants for power

Theories of the nature of political parties are sometimes phrased in terms of political power. The customary definitions of party, although usually in other terms, agree essentially with the conception of parties as groups exercising leadership within the state; that is, they seek power in the community for the sake of varying objectives. Yet whether the party is seen as inherent in social groupings, as a necessary extension of the apparatus of government, or as a contestant for power within the community, the essence is the same. These are only different ways of viewing the same phenomenon.

Commentators on parties as contestants for power sometimes confuse the discussion by disputes about the "true" objective of party and by failure to indicate sharply the limits of the subgroup within society that is said to be seeking power. What persons, thus, are to be included within the "party" contesting for power? Burke's often-quoted definition of party is: "Party is a body of men united, for promoting by their joint endeavors the national interest, upon some particular principle in which they are all agreed." This definition hardly fits all the facts in so far as American parties are concerned. American parties are not bodies of men "agreed" upon particular principles concerning the "national interest." Perhaps . . . parties never promote the national interest; they seek to advance something less than the national interest. Yet they also seek to promote something more nearly the national interest than do pressure groups. Burke's definition, however,

in its implicit recognition of the party's function of leadership in promotion of principle and of the party's striving to gain power to advance particular objectives touches on the reality of party.

The application of the criteria "united" and "agreed" in Burke's definition to the party groups within the American Congress leads to a rejection of his definition, at least in part, and suggests the importance of delimiting the group included within the term party. Neither the Republicans nor the Democrats within Congress maintain unity on many issues. Each party group finds many questions of principle that render party leaders impotent and split the ranks of the party group. On the other hand, the party machinery outside the government has less difficulty in maintaining unity during campaigns. The parties, in a sense, are bodies of men united to get into office. Thus, in May, 1946, at a time when the Democratic "parliamentary" party was beset by internal dissension, Robert E. Hannegan, the Democratic national chairman, stated: "After the primaries are over, we will support all the Democratic candidates vigorously. That has been our policy and it will continue to be our policy."[3] Party unity in Congress might be weak, but the party outside Congress had to unite to support for election each candidate bearing its label whether he subscribed to the darkest conservatism or the pinkest liberalism. . . .

But what of the nature of the "group" that seeks to control the personnel and policies of the government? A useful working distinction to keep in mind is that between the inner core of party workers and leaders and the mass of partisans whose principal contribution to party activity is a vote on election day. Professor E. E. Robinson asserts that to comprehend the nature of a political party we must concentrate attention on the inner core or organization of the party which comes

"into being for the purpose of fighting and governing. It is not concerned with matters of fact, or doctrine, or even of principle, except as they bear upon the great cause for existence: success at the polls. Such organizations not only contain men of divergent views; they must also appeal to voters of differing opinions, prejudices, and loyalties. It is folly to talk of finding

[3]*Washington Post*, May 23, 1946.

an actual basis [for political parties] in any set of principles relating to public welfare."[4]

. . . Emphasis on the importance of the inner group of leaders and workers in party activity serves to center attention on the main sources of party action, but the inner circle would amount to nothing without its following of faithful partisans. This is not to say that a more meaningful definition of party comes from defining party as a group consisting of those persons voting or registered as Democrats or Republicans, for party membership may carry with it no strong sense of group attachment. In many states membership in either of the major parties is gained simply by a person's indicating the party with which he wishes to affiliate when he registers as a voter; affiliation is even less formal in other states. The process of gaining membership in the party is a different matter from affiliation with more tightly organized groups. The party member does not go through an elaborate ritual of induction into the group; in most instances he neither is acquainted with nor knows the name of the ward or county chairman of his party; he probably never supports his party in any way financially; the privileges and responsibilities of party membership rest lightly on his shoulders.

Despite the informality of acquisition of legal membership in a party, the psychological attachment of the great mass of partisans to their party possesses remarkable durability. Even if the party member is an unfaithful attendant at party functions and an infrequent contributor to its finances, he is likely to have a strong attachment to the heroes of the party, to its principles as he interprets them, and to its candidates on election day. The mass of the membership thus conditions the attitudes of party leaders, who must act in a manner to retain its loyalty, and by its support gives strength to the leadership. Definition of party solely in terms of the inner core, the organization, directs attention to an extremely important part of the party group, but party is considerably more than the inner ring of leaders and workers.

THE MACHINE

Edward C. Banfield and James Q. Wilson

If the central function of a political party is to gain office by winning votes, the development in a free political system of efficient "machines" to accomplish this task should come as no surprise. The response of at least articulate Americans to "machine politics" has been overwhelmingly negative. One factor in this response has been the existence of romantic notions about the desirability and feasibility of an atomistic, amateur style of political operation, the same factor that has underlain such measures as nonpartisanship, token salaries, and heavy restrictions on campaign spending. Another factor has been the reaction to gross abuses in vote-getting procedures practiced in earlier decades by some of the more flamboyant party machines. It is these organizations, with their blatant vote-buying, multiple voting, and graveyard balloting, that most often come to mind when the term "machine" is used. Yet the same term is used (primarily by members of the opposition party) to characterize the legitimate get-out-the-vote activities of well-organized parties and their auxiliaries (such as the political action arms of some unions).

Party machines generally rely on the functioning of a tight network of personal relationships. The geographical proximity of potential voters is an important element in such a network, as is the organizations' access to large numbers of voters. Consequently, the history of political machines has been made primarily in cities. Banfield and Wilson describe the city political machine, past and present.

Emphasis in these comments has been on the vote-getting aspects of political machines, because their vote-getting activity has had the most bearing on the operation of party politics in the United States. But, as Banfield and Wilson point out, machines at one time or another have also become engaged in other aspects of the political process, particularly that of serving as broker between city agencies and firms who sell goods or services to the city. The future of machines is closely circumscribed both by increasing

[4]E. E. Robinson, "The Place of Party in the Political History of the United States," *Annual Reports of the American Historical Association for the Years 1927 and 1928* (1929), p. 202.

limitations on the vote-getting function—the decline of immigration, institutionalization and nationalization of welfare, greater voter sophistication, and closer scrutiny of election procedures—and by more strict regulation of governmental expenditures.

A political "machine" is a party organization that depends crucially upon inducements that are both *specific* and *material.* . . . A specific (as opposed to general) inducement is one that can be offered to one person while being withheld from others. A *material* inducement is money or some other physical "thing" to which value attaches. *Nonmaterial* inducements include especially the satisfactions of having power or prestige, doing good, the "fun of the game," the sense of enlarged participation in events and a pleasant environment. A machine, like any formal organization, offers a mixture of these various kinds of inducements in order to get people to do what it requires. But it is distinguished from other types of organization by the very heavy emphasis it places upon specific, material inducements and the consequent completeness and reliability of its control over behavior, which, of course, account for the name "machine."

Business organizations are machines in that they rely largely upon specific, material incentives (such as salaries) to secure dependable, close control over their employees. A political machine is a business organization in a particular field of business—getting votes and winning elections. As a Chicago machine boss once said of the machine in that city, it is "just like any sales organization trying to sell its product." Or as Lord Bryce put it in his famous work, "The source of power and the cohesive force is the desire for office and office as a *means of gain.*"[1]

The machine, therefore, is apolitical: it is interested only in making and distributing income—mainly money—to those who run it and work for it. Political principle is foreign to it, and represents a danger and a threat to it. As D. W. Brogan has remarked, "The true character of the machine is its political indifferentism. . . . It exists for itself."[2]

In the next section of this chapter we shall describe the machine in what might be called its classical form. Actually no big city today has a city-wide machine that is like the model (Chicago, Philadelphia, Pittsburgh, Albany, and Gary are some of the nearest approximations, but even they do not resemble it closely in all respects), and the party organization of most cities today is far from machine-like. One reason why we devote a chapter to the machine is its historical importance: between the Civil War and the New Deal, every big city had a machine at one time or another, and one cannot understand the present without knowing something about what went before. Another reason is its analytical importance: every kind of party organization employs inducements, and an extreme case of one kind—namely, almost exclusive reliance on specific, material ones—illumines the logic of the other kinds.

The model is by no means without present-day application, however. In many cities, large and small, there are elements of party organization that are surviving fragments of old machines or that are at any rate machine-like. In parts at least of every old city of the northeast, politics is organized on a machine basis. Tammany has been weakened and perhaps destroyed in Manhattan, but Democratic machines are still powerful in the Bronx and in Brooklyn. A revitalized machine plays an important part in Philadelphia. The Trenton Democratic Club flourishes in many parts of Baltimore. The Crump organization no longer exists in Memphis and James Curley has no successor in Boston, but some sections—particularly the Negro ones—of both cities have small-scale, ward-size "bosses" who behave very much like the famous bosses of old.

THE STRUCTURE OF THE MACHINE

The existence of the machine depends upon its ability to control votes. This control becomes possible when people place little or no value on their votes, or, more precisely, when they place a lower value on their votes than they do on the things which the machine can offer them in exchange for them. The voter who is indifferent to issues, principles, or candidates puts little or no value on his vote and can be induced relatively easily (or cheaply) to put it at the machine's disposal.

The votes most crucial to the machine are those cast in *primary* elections, for it is in primaries that party officials like precinct cap-

[1]James Bryce, *The American Commonwealth* (London and New York, 1889), II, III (italics added).
[2]D. W. Brogan, *An Introduction to American Politics* (London: Hamish Hamilton, 1954), p. 123.

tains and district leaders are chosen. Fortunately for the machine, primaries are the easiest elections to control. Most voters place less value on their primary vote than on their general election vote; there seems to be less at stake in the primary. Moreover, in the primary the machine does not ask them to forsake their normal party allegiances, which are often deep-rooted. The turnout of voters is also much lower in primaries, and the votes which must be controlled are therefore fewer. For example, although the 1953 New York mayoralty primary was bitterly contested, only about one fourth of the registered Democrats cast ballots.

Sometimes a machine gets the votes of people who are intensely interested in elections. It does this by asking them for their votes only on such offices — the minor ones at the bottom of the ticket — as are *not* of interest to them. The minor offices are the ones essential to control of the party machinery, and this, of course, is half the battle in the short run and the whole of it in the long run.

Even though the precinct captain asks for something that is almost worthless to the voter, he must offer something in return. What he offers is usually a personal, nonmaterial incentive, "friendship." A Chicago captain explained, "I never take leaflets or mention issues or conduct rallies in my precinct. After all, this is a question of personal friendship between me and my neighbors."[3]

Much has been made of the "favors" — turkeys at Thanksgiving, hods of coal at Christmas, and so on — with which the machine in effect buys votes. Such material inducements are indeed given in some instances. The voter, however, is the one contributor to the machine's system of activity who is usually given nonmaterial inducements, especially "friendship." The reason for this is, of course, that people will exchange their votes for "friendship" more readily than for cash or other material benefits; and the machine cannot afford to pay cash for many of the votes it needs.

Many voters, indeed, seem to have valued the turkeys and hods of coal mainly as tokens of friendship, and, accordingly, of the humanity and goodness of the "organization" and its "boss." Jane Addams, the settlement house worker, explained this long ago: "On the whole, the gifts and favors are taken quite simply as an evidence of genuine loving kindness. The alderman is really elected because he is a good friend and neighbor. He is corrupt, of course, but he is not elected because he is corrupt, but rather in spite of it. His standard suits his constituents. He exemplifies and exaggerates the popular type of a good man. He has attained what his constituents secretly long for."[4]

Working-class people, especially immigrants unfamiliar with American ways and institutions, have always been the mainstay of the machine. To use the terminology of the politician, the "delivery" wards are also the "river" wards, and they are a long way in both social and geographic distance from the "newspaper" wards. A delivery ward, of course, is one whose vote can be "delivered" by the machine, and a newspaper ward is one in which voters take the newspapers' recommendations seriously. The delivery wards are river wards because the oldest, and hence poorest and most run-down, parts of the city are those that lie along the river near the warehouses and the railroad yards. Almost without exception, the lower the average income and the fewer the average years of schooling in a ward, the more dependable the ward's allegiance to the machine. As one moves out from the river and the railroad yards first into lower-middle-class districts, then into middle-class ones, and finally (usually in the suburbs beyond the city proper) into upper-middle-class territory, fewer and fewer precincts are manned and the ties to the machine become fewer and weaker until they cease to exist.

The job of a precinct captain is to get out the vote for his party's slate and to keep at home the vote for the other party's. He usually has about 400 to 600 voters to keep track of; this keeps him busy one or two evenings a week ordinarily and full-time for a few days before elections. His superiors rate his performance according to how reliable — i.e., predictable — party voting is in his precinct.

The precinct captain is chosen by and works under the direction of a ward leader, usually an alderman or elected party official. The leader has under him thirty to forty precinct captains (the size of wards is extremely variable and some precincts are not manned). It is up to him to recruit and manage this force and to keep it

[3] Martin Meyerson and Edward C. Banfield, *Politics, Planning, and the Public Interest* (Glencoe, Ill.: The Free Press, 1955), p. 72.
[4] Jane Addams, *Democracy and Social Ethics* (New York, 1902), p. 254.

happy—he is the district sales manager. He also dispenses the larger items of patronage, favors, and protection to those who have earned them. One or two evenings a week he is available to all comers in his office. People come to him to inquire about welfare payments, to get their relatives into public institutions, to get something done about neighborhood nuisances (the garbage has not been collected from an alley or a policeman is needed at a school crossing), and to make complaints about the police or other city departments. Some, but not all, ward leaders sell illicit privileges such as protection for gambling, prostitution, and after-hours liquor sales. The ward leader is one of his party's high command in the city; he is consulted, more or less, in the choice of candidates and on matters of city policy that affect his ward.

A *good* precinct captain or ward leader has very little time for home life; he spends his evenings visiting his neighbors, doing chores at ward headquarters, traveling to and from city hall on errands, and talking politics. To get the services of men with the ability and energy that the job requires, the machine must offer precinct captains and ward leaders substantial inducements. Captains are often "payrollers," that is, they have appointive public jobs that they could not get or keep if it were not for the party. Some have "no show" jobs: they are carried on the public payroll without being required to show up for work. A larger number have "show" jobs and work like other employees —some more conscientiously than most—but their absence on election day and on other special occasions when the party needs them are overlooked. Some precinct captains look forward to running for office or to rising in the party hierarchy. The hope that the party will in due course run them for alderman keeps these captains at work.

Although ward leaders are sometimes payrollers, they more often have elective offices, such as that of alderman, which give them salaries without taking their time from politics. In addition, they almost always have some sideline which enables them to use their political connections to supplement their incomes. The alderman may be an insurance broker, for example, with an "inside track" at City Hall (insurance is all the same price, so why not give the business to one of the boys?). Or he may be a lawyer whose firm gets lucrative cases because clients think it is "good to be on the safe side." "Honest graft" of this kind shades imperceptibly into outright bribery, of course, and the ward leader, if he wants to, can always find some way to take money for misusing his office.

As a rule, however, there is not enough "gravy" to go around, especially among precinct captains. One consequence of this is that able people who can earn a living in less strenuous ways will not work for the machine. Or, to put the same thing another way, the machine is more likely to attract as workers those who, like Negroes, first-generation immigrants, and women, are at some disadvantage in the labor market. Many Irish, once the mainstay of the precinct, have, so to speak, been priced out of the market by the increase of their opportunities in other lines.

Another consequence of a shortage of "gravy" is that the ward and precinct workers are selected from among those people who will respond to nonmaterial inducements. Having a place where one can go to play cards and talk to "the boys" is the main inducement holding some ward organizations together. There is little doubt, however, that the substitution of nonmaterial for material inducements is not only an effect of the weakening of the machine but a cause of it as well: the fewer the material rewards, the less able and energetic the precinct and ward leaders, and the fewer the votes delivered on election day.

These conditions are dynamic elements in the internal life of the machine. Its relative attractiveness to young and aspiring representatives of the most recently arrived, lower-status ethnic groups means that the "old line" leaders who control it are continually challenged by men who are abler, more energetic, and more strenuously "on the make." Many of the "old line" leaders are receiving nonmaterial rather than material benefits for the most part and are therefore not easily disciplined. If they spend their time in the clubhouse when they should be canvassing the voters, there is not much the boss can do about it, for the comforts of the clubhouse are about all that the organization can offer them. To replace these clubhouse types with energetic, ambitious youngsters would be easy if—but only if—the boss were willing to accept the threat to his own position that their entry into the organization could represent.

The machine is run by a coalition of a few of the more powerful ward or district leaders or by a boss (himself a ward or district leader) who, through his control of patronage or by means of other material inducements, is able to exercise control over the others. In a survey of twenty bosses published thirty years ago, Professor Harold Zink found that only two had ever been mayors. In recent years, the situation has changed. Chicago's recent bosses (Cermak, Kelly, and Daley) were mayors, and so was Pittsburgh's (Lawrence). The reason for the change is perhaps to be found in the greatly increased authority of the mayor's office. Today's mayor has authority—especially over the police, the budget, and contracts and purchasing—which enables him to check, and ultimately to displace, any competing party leader. In general, having the authority of the mayor's office is today a necessary (but not a sufficient) condition of being the party leader in the city. That is, if the mayor is not the party leader there often *is* no party leader. This, of course, greatly affects the machine's internal life: it means that the boss must be a person who is reputable enough, and otherwise qualified, to face the electorate. The modern boss cannot run the city anonymously from a smoke-filled room, and this in itself has pervasive effects on the character of the machine.

EXTERNAL FORCES MAKING FOR CHANGE

The main reason for the decline and near disappearance of the city-wide machine was—and is—the growing unwillingness of voters to accept the inducements that it offered. The petty favors and "friendship" of the precinct captains declined in value as immigrants were assimilated, public welfare programs were vastly extended, and *per capita* incomes rose steadily and sharply in war and postwar prosperity. To the voter who in case of need could turn to a professional social worker and receive as a matter of course unemployment compensation, aid to dependent children, old-age assistance, and all the rest, the precinct captain's hod of coal was a joke.

Only those who are least competent to cope with the conditions of modern life, those who are culturally or personally incapacitated in one way or another, still value and seek the "favors" of the machine. They are, of course, the poorest of the poor, especially Negro slum dwellers, rooming-house drifters, criminals, and near criminals. Nowadays there is little that the machine can do for such people except

to give them information about where to go and whom to see in the city bureaucracy and (what is probably more important, despite its illusory character) to give them the feeling that they have a friend and protector. The ward leader cannot arrange to have welfare payments made to someone not entitled to them; he can, however, tell a needy person who *is* entitled to payments how to apply for them. In doing so, he may, of course, manage to leave the impression that if he had not made a telephone call and used his "influence" as "friend" the payments would never have been made. Even his opportunities to serve the voter by giving information (and thus to lay the basis for a later claim upon him) diminish, however, as the giving of information and other functions which are the politicians' special stock in trade are transferred to the executive departments. As Mayor Clark of Philadelphia remarked, "When the word gets around that you can't get things done by favor anymore, there tends to be a sort of channeling of complaints and desires to get things done away from the legislative branch and into the executive branch."[5]

"Friendship" is also harder to give. One reason is television. The precinct captain who visits in the evening interrupts a television program and must either stay and watch in silence or else excuse himself quickly and move on. Another reason is the changing ethnic character of the inner city. When, for example, a white neighborhood is "invaded" by Negroes, the white precinct captain cannot, or will not, form friendships among them as easily as he does among whites. He may even be afraid to enter a tenement of Negroes after dark. In time he will be replaced by a Negro captain, but meanwhile the organization suffers.

While the value to the voter of what the machine offers has declined, the value to him of what he has to give—his vote—has increased. This has happened because of the changing class character of the electorate. Except in the inner parts of the larger central cities, the proportion of middle-class people is greater than it was. Machine-style politics has rarely worked in predominantly middle-class districts. People who have, or pretend to have, opinions on political questions will not give away their

[5]Chicago Home Rule Commission, *Modernizing a City Government* (Chicago: University of Chicago Press, 1954), p. 47.

votes or exchange them for petty favors. Middle-class people do not want the precinct captain's "friendship" or the ward leader's help. It is easy for them to be virtuous in these matters: they don't have to worry about getting into the county hospital or out of the county jail. And they generally resent his efforts at persuasion. They think of themselves as well informed, able to make up their own minds, independent. Being qualified to pass upon public questions follows from their education status, they think, and therefore exhibiting the qualifications is a matter of pride. Whether justified or not, these claims to political competence make it hard for the precinct captain to exercise influence. Recently a Chicago captain told of calling on a voter one Sunday afternoon and finding him with three newspapers spread out on the floor and the TV set on. "What can you tell me that I don't already know?" the voter asked.

The assimilation of lower-class people into the middle class has, of course, entailed their assimilation to the political ethos of the Anglo-Saxon-Protestant elite, the central idea of which is that politics should be based on public rather than on private motives and, accordingly, should stress the virtues of honesty, impartiality, and efficiency.

Wherever the middle class is dominant, this ethos prevails and fixes the character of the political system. If, as seems likely, the middle class will in the very long run assimilate the lower class entirely, the final extinction of the machine is probably guaranteed.

Meanwhile, there remain enclaves that are heavily lower-class in all of the central cities and many of the older suburbs. In these, machine-style politics is as popular as ever. It does not flourish as of old, however, because of restraints and impediments imposed by the middle class, which constitutes the majority in the metropolitan area if not in the city proper, controls the legislatures, and has a virtual monopoly on federal office, both elective and appointive.

Some machines, however, are managing to adjust to the changing circumstances and to substitute, little by little as necessary, one kind of inducement for another so that they gradually become less machine-like. The Chicago machine is one which has survived by "reforming" itself piecemeal.

Other big-city machines have not adapted as successfully. The Pendergast machine in Kansas City was destroyed. Carmine DeSapio's efforts to refurbish the "image" of Tammany Hall in Manhattan not only failed but actually seemed to incite reformers to attack more energetically. Why is it that most machines did not adapt and survive as the Chicago machine has?

One reason is that the bosses have been too greedy for money. Tom Pendergast, for example, gambled heavily at the race tracks and thereby placed himself in a position where, even if he wanted to, he could not afford to cut the "take." Daley, by contrast, has not enriched himself. The satisfactions he gets from politics are apparently of an entirely different sort, and this has enabled him to use greedy lieutenants without exciting their envy and to gain personally in prestige, power, and whatever other such values he seeks by making reforms.

Some machines failed to adapt because their leaders waited too long before making reforms. The leader who makes a reform only under duress is not likely to be able to salvage the situation by making it on his own terms. This is what happened in New York. Carmine DeSapio tried in the early 1950's to remodel Tammany Hall but the power of the machine had by then withered away to such an extent that he could not make the kinds of changes in the situation that would have saved the organization.

In a word, the machines failed because bosses lacked statesmanship. . . .

SOME EVALUATIVE CONSIDERATIONS

It goes without saying that a system of government based upon specific, material inducements is wholly at odds with that conception of democracy which says that decisions ought to be made on the basis of reasonable discussion about what the common good requires. Machine government is, essentially, a system of organized bribery.

The destruction of machines would therefore be good if it did no more than to permit government on the basis of appropriate motives, that is, public-regarding ones. In fact, it has other highly desirable consequences — especially greater honesty, impartiality, and (in routine matters) efficiency. . . .

Great as the advantages of reform are, they are at least partly offset by certain disadvantages. Because these disadvantages are less obvious than the advantages, we will focus our attention upon them. In doing so we do not, of course, imply any derogation of the values sought by reformers.

The machine served certain latent social functions, functions which no one intended but which presumably would have had to be served by another means if not by that one. This has been remarked by Robert Merton, David Riesman, and other sociologists. According to Merton, it humanized and personalized assistance to the needy; afforded businesses, including illicit ones, privileges that they needed in order to survive; provided a route of social mobility for persons to whom other routes were closed; and was an antidote to the constitutional dispersal of authority.[6]

The last item on this list is of particular interest here. . . . The decentralization of authority in the city must be overcome in one way or another if public undertakings are to be carried forward. A system of specific, material inducements (i.e., a machine) is not . . . the only way of bringing about a centralization of influence; in principle, measures to weaken the machine may be accompanied by other measures to centralize influence. In fact, however, this never seems to happen; if any substitute at all is provided for the power of the boss, it is a partial one. La Guardia's reforms in New York, Clark and Dilworth's in Philadelphia, and Daley's in Chicago, although strengthening administrative authority, nevertheless weakened the influence of the city government as a whole. Because of this weakening of the city government, the reform of the machine, although increasing efficiency in routine matters, may at the same time have decreased it in those more important matters which call for the exercise of political power. . . .

The machine provided the politician with a base of influence deriving from its control of lower-income voters. As this base shrinks, he becomes more dependent on other sources of influence—especially newspapers, civic associa-tions, labor unions, business groups, and churches. "Nonpolitical" (really nonparty) lines of access to the city administration are substituted for "political" ones. Campaign funds come not from salary kickbacks and the sale of favors, but from rich men and from companies doing business with the city. Department heads and other administrators who are able to command the support of professional associations and civic groups become indispensable to the mayor and are therefore harder for him to control. Whereas the spoils of office formerly went to "the boys" in the delivery wards in the form of jobs and favors, they now go in the form of urban renewal projects, street cleaning, and better police protection to newspaper wards. Better police protection in white neighborhoods means greater police harassment in Negro ones. Appointment of white experts means non-appointment of Negro politicians.

Even though in the abstract one may prefer a government that gets its influence from reasonable discussion about the common good rather than from giving jobs, favors, and "friendship," even though in the abstract he may prefer government by middle-class to government by lower-class standards, and even though in the abstract he may prefer the rule of professional administrators to that of politicians, he may nevertheless favor the machine in some particular concrete situation. The choice is never between the machine and some ideal alternative. If there is any choice at all—and in some instances there may not be—it is between it and some real—and therefore imperfect—alternative. It is at least conceivable that in some of the large central cities the political indifferentism of the machine may be preferable to any likely alternative.

[6]Robert K. Merton, *Social Theory and Social Structure* (Glencoe, Ill.: The Free Press, 1957), pp. 71-81.

THE SOLICITORS — MIDDLEMEN IN INFLUENCE

Alexander Heard

Money may not make all things possible, but in the world of American politics it certainly helps. The relationships between money and political affairs have always fascinated political amateurs and professionals. Misuse of money has provided the grist for many a melodramatic tale of intrigue and manipulation of the political system, and imbalance in the amount of money available to each party or to competing candidates in election campaigns is always a source of concern.

The relationships between money and election results should also be of high interest to analytically oriented political researchers. Data on both the input — money — and the supposed and intended output — votes — are readily available in quantified form. But the many stages and variable relationships that intervene between input and output are so complicated and ephemeral that a truly *systemic* analysis of the role of money in American politics has yet to be developed.

Despite these difficulties, however, it is still surprising that only a handful of contemporary political scientists have devoted major research to the processes of party finance. For many years Professor Louise Overacker performed a notable task by assembling and analyzing party finance at the national level. Currently the only name prominently associated with large-scale analysis of political finance is the author of the following selection, Alexander Heard. The Citizens Research Foundation (a research operation rather than a foundation in the usual sense) is active in encouraging research in this area; its director, Herbert Alexander, is perhaps the person writing most often on the subject at the present time.

Heard's classic, *The Costs of Democracy*, is an exhaustive study of election finance based, for the most part, on the elections of 1952 and 1956. His insights into the methods of raising and dispensing funds are as relevant now as they were a decade ago. Because party activity is so heavily dependent on funds, the character of party politics and of our particular brand of democracy is significantly affected by who raises funds and by how he does it. The excerpt reprinted here develops a profile of this important link between the citizenry and the parties: the fund-raiser. Because he often is the channel through which interest groups gain access to the party organization, it is worth noting the extent to which this "middleman," the fund-raiser, views his prime loyalty as belonging to the party or to the contributors.

Much of the $100,000,000 or more that on the average is spent annually for campaign purposes requires intricate processes of solicitation to attract it into the political stream. True, some money snakes up from sinister sources, threatening the virtue of public men tempted to accept it. But in most campaigns, the truly burdensome chore is raising money. Those who do it occupy positions of singular importance in the political entourage. There are functional as well as legal reasons why candidates and party managers may depend more directly on solicitors than on contributors. This becomes especially so the more distant a candidate stands from his constituents — that is, the larger his constituency and the more complex his campaign operations.

Solicitors serve as middlemen between contributors and the candidates or the party they benefit. Just as a solicitor understands and explains the politician's need for money, he is aware of the political interests of those who provide it. . . . In the course of recruiting funds, solicitors create a type of informal organization among contributors who share common interests. Moreover, the network of solicitors that grows up around candidates, especially for high office, in some circumstances rivals in influence the more visible party organization. And in the pre-nomination processes of candidate selection that take place outside the public view and before formal procedures begin to operate, key fund-raisers often have a decisive voice.

The process of soliciting political money, with the liaison functions that often accompany it, is customarily focused around loyalty to either (1) a candidate, (2) a party, (3) a policy, or (4) a contributor. Some solicitors are attached to a particular candidate, as observable in direct primaries in states where the party organization takes little part. Others work from a formal or informal position within a party such as the finance chairmen of the national committees. Certain solicitors do not attach themselves primarily to candidates or parties but work with any party or candidate who will advance the policies they deem important. Some fund-raisers

From Alexander Heard, "The Solicitors — Middlemen in Influence," Chapter 10 in *The Costs of Democracy* (Chapel Hill: University of North Carolina Press, 1960), pp. 259-281.

operate chiefly as trusted advisers to contributors.

These concerns and relationships may be thought of as four postures from which solicitors work. Individual solicitors may move from one of these postures to another, at times may occupy more than one. A few solicitors fall neatly and consistently into one category, but most do not. The sort of objectives solicitors have in mind is not the basis for the classification. All, for example, are likely to be vitally interested in public policies, and one can hardly seek victory for a party and not its candidates. Neither are personal qualities the basis. Solicitors of all types must know, or come to know, the people to whom to appeal for money and how to win their confidence. The significant feature is the proximity of the solicitor to political power. Solicitors attached to successful candidates are closest to the processes of governmental decision-making. Those operating from party posts are next. Those attached to contributors are most remote. The political leverage a solicitor can exert depends on which one or more of these postures he operates from and how well he does it.

PARTY SOLICITORS AND THE CHARACTER OF AN ADMINISTRATION

A person with extensive White House experience concludes that the character of a president's administration is set by the persons who raise large blocks of money for the party. When matters that interest them are up for decision, around they come. A chance to state their case is guaranteed, which is all many of them need. The chief rustler of funds for the other party in an important state described with conviction how his fund-raising had brought him influence in party nominations from mayor to president. Moreover, he selected carefully which demands of his contributors were referred to Washington. No passive pipeline, he conveyed the messages he wanted received and let the others lie.

What kinds of people hold such power?

Republicans

The members of the Republican national finance committee are almost invariably successful businessmen, financiers, or their lawyers. So are the members of the state finance committees, though usually less prominent. At all levels, leading Republican fund-raisers characteristically possess impressive records of community service, including experience in nonpolitical fund-raising. The same type of individual customarily leads Republican volunteer committees.

Any New York committee headed in 1952 by the board chairman of the Chase National Bank constituted, by definition, a powerful engine for raising money. Winthrop W. Aldrich, Chase's chairman, was also chairman of the United Republican Finance Committee of New York. By his heritage (his father was Nelson P. Aldrich, Rhode Island's famed "dictator" of the United States Senate), by his family connections (among others, his brother-in-law is John D. Rockefeller, Jr.), by his schooling (Harvard College and Law School), by his directorships in America's leading corporations, and by his long and faithful support of religious, charitable, and educational enterprises (he held more than half a dozen honorary degrees), Mr. Aldrich was equipped by name alone to extract both energy and money from the financial and business world of metropolitan New York. In that same year the national Citizens for Eisenhower-Nixon operated nearby. Two of its principal leaders were Sidney Weinberg, widely experienced and widely known partner in Goldman, Sachs, & Company, investment bankers, and John Hay Whitney, financier, whose personal and financial connections were on the order of those of Mr. Aldrich. Mr. Whitney, in fact, succeeded to Mr. Aldrich's job as New York finance chairman in 1956. In Delaware, the Republican finance chairman has been Lammot du Pont Copeland. In Illinois, it was for a time Edward L. Ryerson, whose positions included the board chairmanship of Inland Steel as well as a host of business and civic directorships. Across most of the nation, to a greater or lesser extent, such has been the leadership of Republican fund-raising. In the context of subtle pressures that pervades any hierarchy of business relationships, men such as these can rally the assistance of countless others in a canvass for political donations. As one of them put it, any alert fellow will see an opportunity in the chore of soliciting to meet new people and to show his talents.

Democrats

A large proportion of Democratic fund-raisers are also successful businessmen, and typically they also have a record of civic activity including nonpolitical money-raising. Lacking a formal finance-committee system from which to operate, however, Democratic solicitors are more dependent than Republicans on their own knowledge of prospects and on personal skill in solicitation. With occasional exceptions, there are no ready-made lists to be handed Democratic solicitors to check the names they wish to approach. They have to provide their own lists. Moreover, the Democratic solicitor is usually on his own. He lacks formal organizational status that authenticates him as a party representative. Many a Democratic solicitor has been rebuffed by persons preferring to give via someone better known in party councils. A solicitor whose station in life gives him the knowledge and confidence of persons who will make healthy Democratic donations is a valuable party property.

A Republican solicitor speaks of raising $60,000 or $70,000 from his list of prospects; the chairman of a finance committee is given credit for a million and a quarter, meaning the receipts of his committee. Personal qualities always affect results, but on the Republican side it is the system that is essentially responsible for the results. To apportion a dollar-credit among individuals who took part at some level or other is impossible. Among Democratic solicitors, however, there is more exact identification between the sums raised and the persons responsible for them. In a way, Abraham Feinberg is the archetype of the Democratic fund-raiser. Mr. Feinberg's personal solicitations since the early 1940's have been measured in the hundreds of thousands of dollars. Like many political fund-raisers, he has remained relatively obscure, seldom mentioned in the press and rarely hailed outside close party circles for his vital role. Yet any discussion of Democratic fund-raising among those close to it during Mr. Feinberg's active period ultimately leads to mention of his importance. . . .

Not all important Democratic solicitors enjoy Mr. Feinberg's stable clientele with its stable interest in public policy. But each works a constituency of some kind, usually associated with his business or professional activities. The Democratic national committee does not publicize its key money-raisers, nor does any other unit of the party, but there seems to be agreement on the significant role played by a good many individuals at one time or another. Who is active in any given year depends on many variables including the leadership of the national committee, the presidential candidate if one is running, issues that are current, disappointments and rewards recently received, and factors affecting the personal availability of the individual — all, it may be noted, considerations that also produce changes in the corps of Republican solicitors from year to year. Whoever the solicitors may be, however, the process is the same. A large segment of the Democratic national committee's funds has traditionally come via persons who have solicited them from individuals who share economic or political interests: e.g., the fishing industry in the northwest, a section of the oil industry in the southwest, insurance in the midwest, assorted liberals in the east, the Cook County Democratic organization in Illinois, and the nation's clothing industry. Like the Republican party, the Democratic party could not survive under present conditions without blocks of funds like these. . . .

The rapport established between solicitors and persons in their own party who wield government power inevitably opens opportunities to influence public decisions. Individuals who have been on the receiving end of pressures, others who have themselves brought pressure to bear, and party people who have watched the exercise of influence at close range, all agree that solicitors in both parties often become channels of access to the decision-points of government. On jobs, clearance through regular party channels is customary and conflicts sometimes occur between finance people, desiring to reward generous donors, and others needing competent help to get a job done. On matters of party or government policy, fund-raisers may assert themselves independently. When a man who has raised $100,000 calls up, said one aide to a Democratic president, and asks that a friend be given a hearing, there is no way to say no, especially if the friend is a contributor, or may become one. A Republican with an overview of his party's affairs observed that the united finance committees constitute a source of power within the party separate from the hierarchy of regular political committees. State finance chairmen may go straight to Washington, straight to the White House. Since many state parties are deeply divided internally on policy questions, the views of individual fund-raisers may depart sharply from those of the party's political officers. One Republican state chairman remarked ruefully that at the national conclaves of his party the state finance chairmen were shown greater deference by national leaders than the heads of the regular state committees.

Edwin W. Pauley, independent California oilman and treasurer of the Democratic national committee from 1942 to 1945, is cited as his party's most successful money-raiser by many persons deeply experienced in Democratic finance. Mr. Pauley was systematic as well as hard working, which cannot be said of all who have held his job. A man of means himself, he was able to deal with other men of means. His reputation led his peers to trust their political contributions with him. He knew, and knew how to find out, who around the country could be productive solicitors, and he was willing to use them. No one charged with the Democratic party's national financing can succeed without this last quality. . . . But Mr. Pauley's real key to success was something additional. He looked about to find out who had benefited from the Democratic administration and then asked them for funds. In addition to being shrewd and diligent, Mr. Pauley is tough. Money was the result. The procedure assumes that for the *quid* there will be a *quo*. . . .

Party differences

Discussions with experienced financial operators in both parties led to the recognition of certain factors that help determine the amount of influence solicitors exercise in party councils. The importance of an individual solicitor, and therefore his potential influence, seems to vary with at least four factors: (1) how large the sums he collects are compared with the other income of the party; (2) how far short the party is of its essential requirements; (3) how personal the apparatus of solicitation is, as compared with an institutionalized set of fund-raising procedures and relationships; and (4) the ability of the solicitor to obtain funds with assurance and speed. When a party's candidate is desperately short of funds, lacking an adequate fund-raising organization, the man who can produce large sums of money fast becomes a crucial — though not necessarily visible — political figure. When he provides it from his own resources he stands in the same relationship to his beneficiaries as when he raises it from others. But the day when one or two giant contributors could finance an entire campaign is largely past; the role of the solicitor is steadily enhanced.

Republicans generally enjoy larger and readier financial resources than Democrats.

They have a widespread, well-formed hierarchy of continuing fund-raising committees to exploit these resources, a facility lacking throughout most of the Democratic party. Democratic lore brims with tales of financial crisis. Dwight R. G. Palmer, as treasurer in Mr. Stevenson's first presidential race, like others before and since, found it necessary to give personal guarantees before arrangements for certain broadcasts could be completed. Republican financial troubles are neither so frequent nor so acute, and as a consequence Republican dependence on individuals with special, quick access to funds is less than the Democrats. This is not to say that the viewpoints of their financial supporters in general are less well reflected in Republican actions and policies. But ironically, because theirs is the party of fewer funds, Democrats are often more dependent on particular sources of funds and therefore are potentially more vulnerable to pressures from those who provide them. . . .

COMPETING POLITICAL STRUCTURES

Aside from its importance as a path to access or specific privileges, political fund-raising may find importance as a basis for political organization. When a solicitor circulates on behalf of a common cause among politically interested people, he may create a structure of loyalties to himself personally. When he represents a fund-raising organization, institutional loyalties may develop. Not all solicitors seize the opportunities open to them. Others have with telling effect; as they have moved about among contributors and party officials, receiving and giving courtesies, certain solicitors have knitted together cliques or factions that have played a potent part in intraparty struggles. Such elements of factional and party organization have been influential in nomination contests, in marshalling the support of voters and of those who lead them, in the organization and functioning of legislatures, in fact wherever the haul and pull of politics go on. It is not surprising that party politicians often shy away from fund-raising schemes that might create a political organization to rival their own. . . .

Financial structures

There are many types of supplemental political structures. . . . It is no surprise that in an activity as close to the heart of politics as fund-raising there exists similar high potential for organizing political power. The ability of fund-raisers to pinch off the flow of cash, or part of it, enhances this potential. Whether the potential is invariably exploited, or whether the resulting political structure invariably dominates, is not here the point. The point is that both sometimes occur. The ways money is raised create sets of political loyalties within each of the parties, and even across party lines, that weaken the regular organizational hierarchies in representing the diverse and competing interests that make up American society.

The activities of any type of solicitor may lay the basis for a structure of personal influence. In internal party affairs, party-oriented solicitors are most likely to develop significant factional leadership. It was obvious in Georgia following 1952, for example, that behind the financial activities of the state finance chairman, Robert Snodgrass, lay the assumption that the expansion and invigoration of the Republican party could best be achieved through the development of a faithful corps of contributors and lower-level finance chairmen. The latter were for the most part different individuals from the regular party officers. In California, steps toward Democratic unity for years foundered on fears of rival organizational developments, the latter frequently rooted in fund-raising aspirations, as witness the conflict between the Dime-a-Day-for-Democracy movement and the Democratic Clubs. In at least one state, proposals to employ a full-time party executive to organize local party units for fund-raising and program-planning were rejected. Party leaders feared he would build organizational strength around himself. Henry Wallace seems to feel that Edwin W. Pauley commanded considerable influence as treasurer of the Democratic national committee. Wallace quotes George Allen on Pauley: "For more than a year before the 1944 Convention he toured the country raising money for the party and, incidentally, mobilizing opposition to Wallace's nomination. As he went from city to city on party business he primed local leaders to mention to Roosevelt, when the opportunities presented themselves, that the Democratic ticket would suffer seriously from the presence of Wallace on it in the 1944 campaign."[1] A presidential candidate who had been a governor was queried about the part of solicitors in his experience. Do they warrant the importance suggested by episodes like these? "Oh my God, yes," he

exploded, therewith to dwell on the troubles they had caused him.

The significance of fund-raising practices to the organizational characteristics of political parties is manifest in various settings. Not many members of the United States Senate or House of Representatives can control the destiny of more money than needed for their own campaigning. Occasionally one of them can, however, like the late Senator Robert A. Taft. The Senior Senator from Ohio commanded great confidence in certain circles of wealth. Campaign money found its way easily to colleagues in the Senate, and perhaps candidates elsewhere, whom he blessed. Regardless of how explicit Senator Taft was or was not in discussions of funds, his factional ties within and outside the Senate were unquestionably strengthened by the financial benefits that flowed to politicians with whom he kept political company. Senator Joseph R. McCarthy's influence with wealthy contributors accounted for donations made by them to other candidates, like Senator John Marshall Butler of Maryland. James F. Byrnes, influential senator from South Carolina during the New Deal, was able to direct financial aid to colleagues, some of it the money of his friend Bernard Baruch, who liked to collect southern "old masters" by backing them in southern Senatorial primaries. There seems little doubt that the Democratic party's chief pipeline for funds out of Texas long has been Sam Rayburn. Mr. Sam may off and on be Speaker of the United States House of Representatives, but his role, and that of his Texas colleague at the other end of the Capitol, Senate Majority Leader Lyndon B. Johnson, is also that of collector and distributor of Texas money. Both men fortify their other formidable talents for legislative and factional leadership with the ability to summon aid for friends in distress, a convenient resource in the logrolling, back-scratching reciprocity of United States politics.

The Republican trend [is] toward segregating and identifying publicly the money-raising organization of the party. . . . Perhaps the process had its beginning when the great American shopkeeper, John Wanamaker, made his price for service to Harrison's cause in 1888 the "cre-

[1] Text of an address by Henry A. Wallace for delivery to the Harvard Law School Forum, in *U.S. News and World Report*, April 6, 1956. The Allen quotation is from *Presidents Who Have Known Me* (New York: Simon and Schuster, 1950), p. 123.

ation of an advisory board of businessmen alone, with its own treasurer and unrestricted power to raise money and decide upon its expenditure." The finance committees did not then and do not now monopolize Republican money-raising, but they are becoming increasingly well set as party institutions and as formal avenues to party service. They are largely manned by persons without other political experience. They constitute distinctive political structures, and at times rival other political structures when particular decisions are to be made. Within the Democratic party the relationships are more confused, but divisive tendencies are present. What do these add up to in the broad scheme of American government?

FUNCTIONAL REPRESENTATION

... The American government does not accord formal recognition in its legislatures to the "instruments of power" that undergird the nation's social, economic, and political life. Yet no popular government in history has yet survived that did not in some way permit such interests to exercise effective means of petition.

The American federal and state governments have set up many procedures to facilitate consultation with interests directly touched by public policy (legislative committee hearings and executive commissions being only two of them). Hosts of less formal modes of consultation inexorably emerge whenever affected interests feel the need.

Solicitors have a special role in giving organized expression to the interests represented in campaign contributions.... Definite expectations accompany some contributions; none at all accompany others. Contributors, even of sums as large as $500, are too numerous and diverse for their voices to be heard effectively if each spoke individually. Certain solicitors serve as contributors' agents—relaying, explaining, screening, mediating, anticipating, in many subtle and varied ways conveying their expectations. At the same time, they interpret to contributors the problems, limitations, and conflicting demands faced by public officials. In sum, they supply a two-way communications system between important financial constituencies and government.

THE VARIETIES OF AMERICAN PARTY SYSTEMS

Fred I. Greenstein

The difficulty of defining and characterizing political parties is compounded and intensified by the existence of state boundaries and consequently of state parties. The relationship between state Democratic and Republican parties and their national counterparts is for the most part one of loose confederation. Because of the leeway this kind of relationship allows, there is great variation from state to state in parties bearing the same name—variation in ideological tone, type of personnel, mode of operation, and other important factors.

Consider fifty states, each with Democratic and Republican parties exhibiting this variation; add to the picture the many different ways in which any two state parties can relate to one another; the composite picture becomes one of a bewildering array of possible and actual political systems set in the context of particular state governments. Faced with this array, political scientists have devised a number of classifications intended to create meaningful, broad groupings of state political systems. The most effective schemes to date have been those distinguishing state political systems according to the extent of competition between

the two major parties. Some analysts have been content to contrast "one-party" with "two-party" systems; others have felt that more, and more refined, categories are necessary.

Greenstein summarizes much of the published research on party behavior in different settings of party competition. By implication, his brief case studies of Connecticut and Michigan suggest that classification based only on extent of party competition remains too broad at present—or that an entirely new basis might prove more useful.

Regardless of methodological questions, an important variable to keep in mind is the degree to which popular control over the development of public policy is affected by the several types of state party systems.

If the methods of the physical sciences could be neatly transferred to the social sciences, we

From Fred I. Greenstein, "State Politics: The Varieties of American Party Systems," Chapter 5 in *The American Party System and the American People.* © 1963. Reprinted by permission of Prentice-Hall, Inc., Englewood Cliffs, N. J.

might conceive of a quite elementary experiment which would help establish what functions are served by political parties. We would assemble a large sample of political units and divide it in two so that both halves were common in all characteristics. Into the political systems of the first half of our sample we would introduce political parties; the second sub-sample, our control group, would elect its officials and run its government by the same procedures as the first, but without recourse to parties. After a period of careful observation, we would note the shape that politics takes in each sub-sample, attributing the ways the first differed from the second to the effects of parties.

We might even conceive of a more sophisticated experiment, dividing our sample into three comparable groups, one of them with a party system in which the parties were closely competitive; one with a party system in which one party tended to dominate elections; and the third a control group. We also could vary, among other things, the number of parties in the party system, or the contexts in which the parties operated — e.g., the amount of basic social consensus or the distribution of interest groups. .

TYPES OF PARTY SYSTEMS

Needless to say, complex political units cannot be manipulated experimentally like the white rats run through mazes by psychologists. Yet something crudely approximating our controlled experiment actually exists in the United States, because of the remarkable panorama of partisan practices in the 50 states and thousands of localities of the nation.

In a number of the states and many of the localities, two-party competition of the sort we think of when we hear the phrase "the American two-party system" is full-blown. Some states (for example, Connecticut, in the years between 1930 and 1956) have had even more closely contested elections and more frequent alternations in party control of the government than does the federal government. With the exception of a few sparsely settled western states, close party competition has been most common in the large industrial states, where urban blue-collar workers who tend to vote Democratic are balanced by the Republican pluralities rung up in suburbs, small cities, and rural areas.

The closely competitive states may be thought of as being at one end of a scale measuring party competition. Adjacent to them we find states

which lean slightly in the direction of favoring Republican or Democratic candidates. Further along are states in which one party almost always elects the public officials, but the minority party has sufficient support to be within a hop, skip, and jump of taking office if the dominant party fails to keep its fences mended. Finally, at the far end of the scale are the one-party states — the states which have not elected officials or supported presidential candidates of the other party since the mind of man runneth back.

The states in which parties are not competitive are largely states which lack the underlying social heterogeneity of the two-party states. Often, also, the tendency toward one-party domination in these states has been encouraged by traditions of sectional conflict which developed in the aftermath of the Civil War. Thus, in the 11 states of the Old Confederacy, the best known of the one-party states, Democratic ascendancy has been a device for preserving a solid regional front in national politics, with the goal of maintaining white dominance in the South.

General elections decide nothing in the one-party states. In the South, for example, Republicans often do not even bother to contest elections. But this does not mean one-party states are without political conflict. Election contests are "pushed back" to the nominating stage. Under such circumstances a candidate's party affiliation has little meaning — the party is neutral, serving as the arena within which individual politicians and factions vie for office. It seems partly to have been in response to the meaninglessness of general elections in the one-party states that in the late nineteenth century and early twentieth century the uniquely American institution of primary elections developed.

Since primaries are in effect no-party elections and they also are the only real elections in the one-party states, it is rewarding to compare politics in the one-party states with politics in the states which have active parties. We also can add to our understanding of the functions of parties by glancing briefly at actual *nonpartisan elections*. In all of the American states, political parties play at least a nominal role in elections, even though in some states one party is of no practical significance. But in a good many municipalities, legislation has been passed barring the use of party labels on the ballot. This species of nonpartisanship, originally an outgrowth of early twentieth-century reformers' desires to destroy urban political machines, is to be found in 61 per cent of the cities over 5,000 in population in the United States. Two of the states—Minnesota and Nebraska—elect their state legislatures without recourse to party labels.

Strictly speaking, the reader should realize that the observations which follow are *not* comparable to a controlled experiment. We have already shown that the one-party states differ from the two-party states in respects other than degree of party competition. They differ, often profoundly, in characteristics such as the heterogeneity of their populations, per-capita income, economic resources, and so forth. Therefore the comparisons we make must be cautious; and we must occasionally resort to tentative inferences in an attempt to see whether differences relate to the presence or absence of competitive parties, or whether they relate to other factors, some of which are themselves responsible for the pattern of party competition in a state. In what follows we shall move from what might be called "the state of nature"—the politics of nonpartisanship and the politics of one-party states—to contexts in which parties are important.

NONPARTISAN POLITICS

The movement to bar the use of political party labels on the ballot was one of the many "direct democracy," "anti-machine" procedures which were advocated during the waves of reform and progressivism early in the century. Since the 1920's there has been little active agitation for nonpartisanship, but oddly the proportion of localities using nonpartisan elections has consistently increased, largely because nonpartisanship is part of the "package" of governmental arrangements associated with council-manager local government. The council-manager form has gained popularity and as more and more communities adopt it, nonpartisan elections have, as it were, slipped in the back door.

Political scientists had ignored the interesting possibility of comparing politics of nonpartisan and partisan localities until the early 1950's, when Professor Charles R. Adrian of Michigan State University pointed to the merits of such a research strategy and reported evidence supporting a number of interesting hypotheses about some of the unanticipated effects of eliminating parties from politics.[1] . . .

In some political settings nonpartisanship is essentially nominal. Removing party labels from the ballot seems to have made little political difference, since local Republicans and Democrats are sufficiently strong to take over the nonpartisan elections and to nominate and elect their own candidates. In other communities, nonpartisanship has led to what might be described in seemingly self-contradictory language as "nonpartisan parties." Citizens' groups—often business groups, such as a local chamber of commerce—nominate and endorse nonpartisan slates. In some cases several such slates may compete, each of them in effect a party, but without formal connection with the "real" parties in the state—the Republicans and Democrats. Finally, and evidently most commonly, nonpartisan elections often turn out the way reformers expected them to—neither parties nor slates are important in campaigns and each candidate runs as an individual rather than as part of some larger group or organization. Under the latter circumstances a number of interesting political consequences have been discovered.

1. *"Trivial" personal attributes of the candidates become more important.* [There are three major] criteria used by voters to make their electoral choices—party identification, issue orientation, and candidate preference. When parties are ruled out, we might expect the remaining two criteria to assume greater importance. Actually, it seems mainly to be response to the candidates—and sometimes what would seem to most of us to be extremely trivial characteristics of the candidates—which takes the place of party identification as a criterion for choice.

. . . Only a small proportion of the electorate observes politics closely and has well-crystallized opinions on the issues of the day. In nonpartisan elections the candidates on the ballot are not labeled. A good many candidates may be listed on the ballot, since party nominating procedures have not narrowed down the contenders to two. Voters may therefore find themselves choosing from lists of unfamiliar names. They also may have little understanding of the requirements of the offices for which candidates are running. As a consequence, anything that

---

[1]Charles R. Adrian, "Some General Characteristics of Nonpartisan Elections," *American Political Science Review,* Vol. 46 (September 1952), 766-776, later revised to take account of more recent findings and published in Oliver P. Williams and Charles Press, *Democracy in Urban America* (Chicago: Rand McNally, 1961), pp. 251-263. Unless otherwise indicated, the remarks on nonpartisanship are based on Adrian's revised discussion.

makes a candidate stand out on the ballot is to his advantage.

"Celebrities" are likely to have a political advantage in nonpartisan politics. Adrian refers to a successful candidate for Detroit's non-partisan city council who "stood largely on the implicit platform that he had been an able short-stop for the Detroit Tigers baseball club."[2] Political chameleons may be surprisingly suc-cessful. In primary elections (which are es-sentially nonpartisan elections), candidates whose chief distinction is the resemblance between their name and that of some distin-guished citizen sometimes are victorious, especially if they run for minor office. Thus, in the 1954 Massachusetts primary, a gentleman whose prior qualifications consisted of 18 years of employment by a safety razor company, culminating as head of the firm's stock room, won his party's nomination (and later the elec-tion) for state treasurer. His name was John F. (for Francis) Kennedy. There even is evidence that in nonpartisan elections candidates get significantly more votes if their names happen to be located at the top of the ballot.[3]

A more important consequence of nonpartisan voting is its effect on the electoral fates of certain types of public officials. Incumbent city council-men win re-election more often than do their counterparts in partisan areas. In the two states which elect their legislatures on a nonpartisan basis, there seems to be a similar bias in favor of officeholders. The chances are that these dif-ferences do not result from the greater ability of nonpartisan lawmakers to satisfy their constitu-ents. Voter awareness of the complex activities of legislatures is minimal, but names of incum-bent legislators do receive a degree of publicity. On election day the voter casts his ballot for the familiar name of the incumbent, even though his awareness of the incumbent's record might be slight.

2. *Influence shifts to non-party groups.* When parties do not nominate and back candidates, the illusion is created that no one is influencing elections. In fact other groups fill the vacuum. Because of the importance of the familiar name in nonpartisan politics, the power of those who control the press and the other channels for con-veying information to the public is increased. Candidates who are opposed by a nonpartisan city's newspapers may stand little chance of success; candidates who are *ignored* by the press may be even worse off. Without party resources

for financing campaigns, and without the grass-roots support of ward and precinct organizations, there is a greater likelihood that candidates will feel obliged to seek funds from other community groups. As a result, seeming independence may really signify hidden obligations to support the goals of various community interest groups.

3. *There is less campaigning.* Without party funds at their disposal, candidates are dis-couraged from bringing their case to the public. Massachusetts' "other John F. Kennedy" won his 1954 primary election on the basis of attendance at "three or four" rallies and a $10.50 purchase for automobile bumper stickers. In the campaign-ing which does take place, nonpartisan candi-dates may find it profitable to avoid discussing issues, especially controversial issues. The parti-san candidate, on the other hand, is not as able to ignore questions of public policy, since he is tied to a group that over the years has taken policy stands and acquired a public image.

4. *Protest voting may be frustrated.* Given the built-in bias in favor of incumbent officials, especially those who are protected by the ano-nymity and inconspicuousness of legislative service, government tends to be insulated from currents of public opinion. During periods of ferment and upheaval, when incumbent ad-ministrations classically are thrown out of office by American voters, nonpartisanship may make it impossible to distinguish and therefore punish the "ins" and replace them with "outs." In the depths of the depression ... control of partisan legislatures shifted dramat-ically, but the nonpartisan legislatures tended to be unaffected. ...

TWO KINDS OF ONE-PARTY POLITICS

Surprisingly enough, the study of state polit-ical parties did not begin by focusing on the states in which parties make an important con-tribution to politics. Rather, it began with the work during the mid-1940's of V. O. Key, Jr., and his associates, on the one-party Southern states.[4] In these states, as we have suggested, politics proceeds without benefit of parties. One-party state politics bears many resemblances to non-partisan city (and state legislative) politics. Because it is *state* politics, however, it is proba-

[2]"Some General Characteristics of Nonpartisan Elections," op. cit., p. 263n.
[3]Henry M. Bain and Donald S. Hecock, *Ballot Position and Voter's Choice* (Detroit: Wayne State University Press, 1957).
[4]V. O. Key, Jr., *Southern Politics* (New York: Alfred A. Knopf, Inc., 1949).

bly of greater interest to the student of parties, given the magnitude of the political responsibilities of the states and the similarity of many of the issues with which they wrestle to the great national issues of the day.

The naive northern observer of one-party southern politics is likely to assume that the South is all of a piece — draped with Spanish moss and peopled with characters from the novels of William Faulkner, Erskine Caldwell, and Truman Capote. Key's work effectively punctures this image. Politically and socially each of the southern states is distinct in numerous ways.

One political characteristic in which southern states vary is the pattern of their primary election and governmental politics. In most southern states, Key found that politics was fluid and "multi-factional." A typical gubernatorial or senatorial primary in such a state might see a half-dozen or more candidates in the field, each of them supported by his own temporary campaign organization and none of them very closely connected with any previous factional coalition. Under such circumstances voting becomes so splintered that if (as is the case in most American elections) the candidate with a plurality of the vote were to take office, many government officials would represent no more than a quarter of the electorate. Therefore, most of the southern states have adopted a special election procedure, the run-off primary, to preserve majority rule in the face of fragmented politics.

Some southern states — at the time of Key's writing these included North Carolina, Tennessee, and Louisiana — are not multi-factional. Factional politics in these states forms a rather rough approximation of a two-party system. Various factors contribute to what Key calls "bifactionalism." In the neighboring states of North Carolina and Tennessee, for example, the effect of a strip of traditional southern "Mountain Republicans" who dominate the politics of the hill areas between the two states has contributed to holding Democratic party factional politics down to a dual pattern. In each of these states one of the stronger Democratic factions (in North Carolina the "Shelby County Dynasty," and in Tennessee Boss Crump's Memphis machine) became allied for patronage reasons with office-hungry Democrats from the state's Republican-dominated areas. The combined strength of two such blocs usually was sufficient to lead other groups in the state to pool their strength in a second opposition faction, since

only by unifying could they hope to win. In Louisiana a traditionally powerful and unified New Orleans machine had a similar effect on factionalism, but even more important — after the early 1920's — was the tendency of prosperous citizens to band together in opposition to the flamboyant appeal to redneck farmers and other economically and politically distressed folk by Huey Long and his kin.

Quite commonly, when southern politics does assume a bifactional form (as is the case intermittently in a number of the normally multi-factional states), conflict has followed similar lines of cleavage to those in Louisiana — wealthy plantation owners and their urban industrial allies are represented by one faction; Bible-quoting, up-country, low-income farmers by the other. In Louisiana correlations can be found between support for the Long faction and support for the Populists in the 1890's. Anti-Long voting has parallels which go as far back as the Whig opposition to Jacksonian Democrats in the distant pre-Civil War past when party competition existed in the southern states.

The two patterns of southern politics are of interest to the political scientist because they enable him to compare politics *sans* parties with a sort of quasi-party politics. Since both dual- and multi-factional systems exist in the same region, we can compare the varieties of southern politics with somewhat more confidence than we can compare southern state politics with the politics of the industrial two-party states of the North. We will, however, also have to make the latter comparison since factions — even when there are only two of them and they are quite stable — differ (as we shall see) in at least one important respect from political parties.

Multi-factional politics

One of the defining characteristics of multi-factionalism is the number of contenders for office in the first primary. At Key's writing, Florida — partly because of its oddly dispersed population centers, but probably more basically because of its remarkable influx of new citizens — was the limiting case in multi-factional fluidity. It may be Florida that Key has in mind at one point in his over-all assessment of factionalism, when he almost sputters an array of modifiers — "multifacted, discontinuous, kaleidoscopic, fluid, transient. . . ."[5]

[5]*Ibid.*, p. 302.

No Florida candidates, Key found, had state-wide political organizations; virtually anyone who could afford the filing fee might be found running for office. In the especially chaotic gubernatorial primary of 1936, fourteen men competed in Florida's first primary, the front-running candidate polling about 16 per cent of the state's vote. Key and another student of Florida politics, Hugh D. Price, found evidence of a trend toward stability and dual factionalism in the state during the 1940's and 1950's,[6] but ... the pattern of state voting in the 1960 Democratic primary [suggests that] reports of the demise of fragmented politics are premature. There were ten candidates, of whom five received more than 12 per cent of the first primary vote. The man who ran third was squeezed out of the run-off primary by a mere 2.2 per cent. Elections of this sort, Key wryly comments, might better be considered lotteries.

When only two factions compete seriously in the politics of a southern state, the candidates' election appeals and the geographic distribution of votes often indicate that politics has made contact with underlying interest and issue cleavages, such as the conflicts ... between owners of large plantations and small up-country farmers. On occasion, voters will be presented with a rather clear-cut liberal-conservative choice. Multi-factionalism, on the other hand, is far less likely to tap such "gut" issues. Distinctions in the ideologies, or group appeals, of some of the various candidates may be evident to politically sophisticated observers of the multiple candidate elections, but there is little evidence that any of these distinctions have reached the mass of the electorate.

Friends-and-neighbors politics—voting for the home-town boy—is especially common in the multi-factional states. This pattern (which is paralleled by wheeling and dealing in which countless bargains are struck between county leaders and factional candidates) is revealed when each of several candidates wins 60, 70, or 80 per cent of the vote in counties near his home, but receives no more than a fourth of the state-wide vote. Under these circumstances special advantages may accrue to the candidate who spent his youth in one locality, his adult years in another, thus having *two* sets of friends and neighbors. In a politics of personalities, especially when much of the population is uneducated, it also often seems to be an advantage to be the politician with the loudest hillbilly

band, the most salty jokes, and the most aggressive white-supremacy argument. . . .

One consequence of this is that public officials of wondrously divergent types and ideological convictions may be elected simultaneously. Thus in one Florida primary the voters gave comfortable margins to a candidate who had acquired national repute for his liberalism and sympathy to the goals of organized labor and to another who was a vehement opponent of unions. Each of the candidates for state-wide office and the state legislative candidates (as well as candidates for local and federal office) run independently of the others in multi-factional states. Each raises his own campaign funds (Key estimated in the 1940's that $100,000 was a conservative estimate of the necessary resources for a successful southern gubernatorial campaign) and acquires his own obligations to his supporters. As might be suspected, such an election arrangement is hardly conducive to close cooperative relations between elected officials. Therefore, one pattern noted by Key, closely resembling the experience of Minnesota in the 1930's ... is the stymying of "reform" governors by their state legislatures. A gubernatorial candidate may campaign and win office by attacking the existing state of affairs and proposing alternative policies. Once in office, however, he finds himself faced with legislators who have no special reason to feel committed to his version of the public interest. In fact, given the low visibility of legislators' activities and the unlikelihood of effective voter retaliation, the reform governor's legislature may consist of a majority of the same "rascals" who were originally responsible for the castigated "existing state of affairs."

Bifactionalism

The best available account of southern bifactionalism is in the extensive work of Professor Allan Sindler on Louisiana politics.[7] Like the other southern states, Louisiana confines its intrastate politics to the Democratic primaries, but there are a number of clear-cut political differences between the Pelican State and its multi-factional neighbors.

[6]H. D. Price, *The Negro and Southern Politics* (New York: New York University Press, 1957), pp. 93-103.
[7]Allan P. Sindler, "Bifactional Rivalry as an Alternative to Two-Party Competition in Louisiana," *American Political Science Review*, 49 (September 1955), 641-662, and *Huey Long's Louisiana* (Baltimore: Johns Hopkins Press, 1956).

As already noted, each of the state's factions — Long and anti-Long — has distinct bases. Unlike some of the South's other flamboyant political products, Huey Long based both his appeal and his policies on clear-cut social and economic goals, as well as employing the ruthless manipulative skill and the spell-binding stump performances for which he is better remembered. In a state which ranked at the bottom of the national heap in the amenities of life available to its inhabitants, Long welded together a coalition of poor agriculturalists, and to a lesser degree industrial workers and Negroes. Well after an assassin's bullet had ended the Kingfish's life, the state's politics continued to be polarized in a bifactional mold around issues of taxation, education, and welfare policy.

During the years studied by Sindler, Louisiana had some of the appearance of the multi-factional southern states. Several candidates contended in its first primaries, for example. But by the second primary the field was regularly narrowed down to representatives of the Long and anti-Long factions. Judging from the consistency with which the prosperous and poorer groups supported the "appropriate" factions, and from the lack of friends-and-neighbors voting in the state, the bifactional alternatives must have been quite meaningful to Louisiana voters.

One indication of the strength of Louisiana factionalism is the use of a device seen nowhere else in the South — the ticket system. In most southern states, as we have seen, each candidate is on his own. The Louisiana tradition, begun by the old-time New Orleans machine and further developed during Long's years, is quite different. Candidates bound together on "tickets," much like the party slates offered to voters in northern states, run as common teams for the several state-wide offices, for the legislature, and sometimes also for local offices. Technically, the ballot lists only names of individuals, but in fact many voters take to the polling place with them a list of the names on "the Earl Long ticket" or "the Jimmie Davis ticket."

Tickets are a considerable asset to candidates, providing them with, in Sindler's words, "the benefit of a fully-organized campaign at cut-rate prices."[8] Since the candidates for such lower state offices as auditor, treasurer, and registrar of the state land office (and to a lesser degree legislators) campaign on the basis of their sup-

port for a gubernatorial candidate, the governor benefits by having a ready-made set of allies behind his program once he is elected. The voters also benefit, since — if they have a mind to do so — they can either elect a team or reject one.

Factionalism, with the ticket system, has led to a kind of politics of governmental activism, factional alternation in office, and attempts by each faction to woo the voter by providing him with services. Huey Long's ascendancy produced higher taxes, but also improvements in roads, education, hospitals, and other public services. When Longism went beyond this, producing egregious abuses of political power and corruption on a grand scale, the voters turned out the Long faction, replacing it with the conservative "reform faction." But the latter, in order to attain office, felt it necessary "to pledge liberal measures, which, in toto, made Huey's performance . . . appear conservative."[9]

This would seem to support one of Key's more interesting hypotheses about the effects of political parties or party-like organizations on the outcomes of politics. In a fluid, disorganized politics, Key believes that it is the "have-not" members of the population — the poor farmers, the sharecroppers, the textile-mill workers — who suffer, and the groups likely to profit from the status quo who gain. The former have few political skills and resouces for advancing their interests. They are uneducated and without the kinds of experiences which would prepare them to follow government closely, keeping track of such erudite matters as the record of a state legislator in office. But they do have one vital asset, if they are able to use it effectively — their numbers.

Parties and stable factions like those in Louisiana simplify the problem of perceiving and evaluating government for such citizens, enabling them to reward their friends and punish their enemies. Probably more important, the competition between fairly coherently organized groups of factional politicians, each of them desirous of winning office, encourages competitive efforts to *anticipate* the needs of such blocs of voters. Each group tries to outdo the other in its promises and in its accomplishments in office. Organized politics also is potentially helpful to have-not groups because it increases the likelihood of organized government — that is, of

[8] "Bifactional Rivalry as an Alternative to Two-Party Competition in Louisiana," op. cit., p. 654.
[9] Ibid., p. 644.

cooperation between state officials and between governor and legislature. When government is stalemated, only groups satisfied by the status quo will be helped; when positive governmental action is possible, groups desiring new schools, larger welfare programs, and other active policies may be able to achieve their goals.

Bifactional politics do not, however, approximate two-party politics in a number of important respects, Sindler believes. First, even a rather cohesive intra-party faction is likely to be muddier and less organized in its recruitment patterns than one might expect a party to be. In Louisiana there were no clear-cut standards for deciding who in the Long or anti-Long group might be next to serve as the faction's standard-bearer. As a result, it has been typical for governors and lieutenant governors to begin feuding toward the end of a governor's term in office. Disagreements over who is to run for office are resolved in the first primaries, but sometimes the period intervening before the second primary is not long enough for groups with common interests to forget campaign oratory and begin pulling together to win the election. Secondly, and related to this, Louisiana's factional politicians are less consistent in their allegiances than are the state's voters. There is a good bit of shifting of factional sides, accompanied by opportunistic bargaining and horse-trading. Instability seems to be especially great in alliances between local politicians and the state factions. Since the connection between local and state levels is tenuous, political organization in bifactional states resembles politics in states where most local elections are non-partisan — the state-wide political groupings have little solid grass-roots support, and the channels of mobility from local political experience to higher office are unclear.

Sindler also finds that although factional-ticket allegiances tie together the state-wide officials — at least during the early portions of a governor's term — they are somewhat less binding on state legislators. The latter traditionally support gubernatorial policy, but as much because of patronage arrangements as because of factional loyalty. Thus bifactional politics, if more orderly than multi-factionalism, is still rather confused.

The confusion, Sindler's analysis suggests, may partly be a consequence of a seemingly minor, but perhaps vital difference between factions and parties. Parties have labels. Shake-speare asked "What's in a name?" and perhaps the political scientist may answer that the name of a party, if it becomes rooted in historical traditions, voter identifications, and politicians' professional experiences can contribute remarkably to tying together the disparate units in a political system.

TWO KINDS OF TWO-PARTY POLITICS

The work of Key and Sindler suggests that within the one-party states, dual factional systems have certain advantages over multi-factional systems in terms of their contribution to popular control of government and effective policy-making. But even the dual factional systems, it is argued, fall short of two-*party* politics.

For a decade after the appearance of Key's *Southern Politics* the second of these hypotheses remained totally in the realm of speculation. There were no available studies of two-party states that considered the same questions raised by Key and Sindler about southern politics. This gap was filled by the work of Duane Lockard on New England politics.[10] Three of the six New England states — Massachusetts, Connecticut, and Rhode Island — seem, on Lockard's showing, to be competitive two-party states. Of these we shall consider Connecticut, a state in which the parties have had an especially substantial (and, Lockard believes, valuable) effect on politics. Then we shall glance briefly at another northern two-party state, Michigan, where the consequences of party competition have been less satisfactory.

Connecticut — party competition and effective policy-making

Up through the 1920's Connecticut was a safe Republican state. Following the shifts in political loyalties of the Depression and New Deal years, the Democratic party sprang to life in Connecticut, as it did in many other northern industrial states. During recent years the Connecticut parties have been remarkably competitive.

"In the 12 gubernatorial elections between 1930 and 1956 the Democrats have won seven times to the Republicans' five. The average Democrat percentage of the two-party vote

[10]Duane Lockard, *New England State Politics* (Princeton, N. J.: Princeton University Press, 1959).

in these elections has been a scant 49.9 per cent. ... In ten of the 12 elections the margin of victory was less than 25,000 votes and in three the margin was less than 3,000."[11]

At the same time, each of the parties is internally cohesive and disciplined to a degree which is unusual in the United States.

The closeness of Connecticut's party competition is not a consequence of the desire of party politicians to hew to some ideal model of politics. Both Democratic and Republican leaders would be delighted with a less competitive state of affairs, assuming, of course, that it was the other party which was less competitive. The state's even political division results from its even social division. Democratic support comes from urban groups — industrial workers, labor unions, ethnic minorities. ... The base of Republican power is small-town New England Yankees, suburbanites, and businessmen.

Neither party is monolithic. Labor-oriented Democrats do not invariably agree on policy with Democrats of the city machines, or with such ethnic organizations as the Polish Pulaski Clubs. Suburban Republicans and rural Yankee Republicans sometimes find themselves at odds. Furthermore, each party has at least some supporters in the other party's areas of strength, so there are both urban, ethnic Republicans and rural, Yankee Democrats. Nevertheless, the population groups and interests aggregated by each of the Connecticut parties are considerably more consistent in outlook and background than those represented by Republican and Democratic politicians nationally. This helps to explain why it is possible for the Connecticut parties to have rather clear-cut lines of authority and generally recognized leaders, giving them in some ways more the appearance of the well-disciplined political parties of Great Britain than of the disorderly formations in America.

A number of other factors are relevant to party unity in Connecticut. These include the closeness of state party competition, a considerable stimulus for politicians of each party to pull together in order to defeat the common foe; the failure of the state to adopt such party-weakening measures as nonpartisan local elections and state-wide primaries; and accidents of history which at various times have brought to the fore in each party skillful leaders who held office for many years and helped ingrain traditions of disciplined politics in the thinking of the state's politically active citizens.

The behavior of Connecticut politicians once in office is profoundly affected by both the internal cohesion of the parties and the competitiveness of the party system. Connecticut legislators hammer out party policies in caucus, often in consultation with the state chairman and with the governor, if he is of the same party. Each party's legislators vote together and oppose the legislators of the other party with much greater frequency than is the case in Congress, or in most other states.

The unity of Connecticut's parties and the state's slender electoral balance, Lockard believes, create a situation in which the parties contribute in a major way to effective policy-making. Unified parties, as we have seen, can contribute to policy-making by enabling a single group to control both the legislative and executive branches. Party government in Connecticut does not function this simply, however. Malapportionment in the legislature has prevented the Democrats from winning control of the lower house more than once in over 80 years, and the upper chamber is somewhat gerrymandered against the Republicans. Furthermore, because of the closeness of elections, even though it is common in Connecticut for many voters to support an entire party slate, governors have sometimes had to share control of the executive branch with lieutenant governors, treasurers, or comptrollers of the other party.

One would expect party cohesion and split party control of government to produce political stalemate, rather than effective policy-making. Yet this has not been the result. Much of the necessary legislation to keep the state operating is passed because Republican and Democratic leaders succeed in compromising their differences by agreeing to support one another's bills. More important, Lockard feels, although the parties have the power to obstruct policy-making, they do not do so. Party leaders must set their sights on making a record which will be appealing not only to their own supporters but also to members of the other party's coalition. Only this will bring victory in a state where the electoral balance is so close. The considerable influence of the state leaders of each party makes it possible for them to persuade legislators to take a broader outlook than might be

[11] *Ibid.*, p. 231.

expected from their ideological and constituency orientations.

Connecticut's small-town Republican legislators, for example, are in no danger of being voted out of office, given the heavily Republican composition of their districts. Nevertheless, they have often been persuaded that if they want the election of a Republican administration in the state, they must support policies which will appeal to the urban areas. Thus, Lockard points out, the state has "been among the vanguard in accepting new and relatively radical programs (as, for example, labor and anti-discrimination laws)."

"But none of those laws ever got on the books without the affirmative vote of most of the rural small-town Republican legislators whose general outlook is hardly daring. They are mostly true conservatives; they will wait awhile, thank you, and would rather not spend the money anyhow. But they voted yes on a good many innovations . . . [many of which] came when the Republicans had complete control over both Houses and the governorship. Many a law for which Democrats pleaded in vain when they shared power was rejected only to be passed the next session when the Democrats were out of power entirely. 'Let's act now, when there can be no doubt of who gets the credit,' is the plea of the Republican leadership. Among others the following acts got passed in just this manner: the first fair employment practices law in the state, minimum-wage increases, and the repeal of prohibitory taxes on oleomargarine."[12]

Connecticut's politicians, Lockard suggests,

". . . do not behave responsibly solely out of the goodness of their hearts any more than General Motors tries to build better cars out of sheer altruism. One seeks a payoff in the market, the other at the polls. The important thing is to facilitate the means by which the votes can influence the politicians."[13]

This is where Connecticut's party system seems to make its contribution.

Michigan—party competition and political deadlock

The Connecticut experience seems to offer a simple recipe for popular control of government and effective policy-making—electoral competition between cohesive political parties. Unfortunately, the case of Michigan suggests that matters are not quite so simple.

We are somewhat limited in our ability to compare Michigan with the other states we have discussed, since none of the several studies of Michigan politics fully parallels the work of Key, Sindler, and Lockard. This much, however, is clear. The Michigan party system has many of the same ingredients as the Connecticut party system. The Michigan constitutional arrangements also are similar to those of Connecticut, in that malapportionment makes it virtually impossible for the Democratic party to control the legislature. But the response of the parties to this constitutional situation has been radically different in the two states.

Although both of Michigan's parties have had their share of internal disagreements, party cohesion in the state legislature has been high. "The party caucus," Professor Norman C. Thomas of the University of Michigan reports, "dominates roll call votes in the State Senate to a degree that is almost unparalleled in American politics. The situation in the House of Representatives is almost as rigid."[14] As in Connecticut, Michigan's politics became competitive in the 1930's with the rise of the Democratic party. Alternation in office has not been quite as frequent in Michigan. In 1962, partly as a consequence of the vote-getting ability of G. Mennen Williams, the Democrats had controlled the governorship for 14 years. There was no question, however, that the Republican potential was sufficiently great sooner or later to break this string of victories. The Republicans demonstrated this in November 1962, when their candidate, George Romney, was elected governor.

Much of Governor Williams' career in office was marked by feuding with the Republican legislature. Conflict between the parties finally reached a head in a financial crisis that received nation-wide attention. This chain of events is best described by Professor Thomas:

"The recession of 1958 caused the state's sales tax revenues to fall far short of the estimated amount. Additional revenues were

[12] Ibid., p. 334.
[13] Ibid., p. 304.
[14] Norman C. Thomas, "Politics in Michigan: The Curse of Party Responsibility," Papers of the Michigan Academy of Science, Arts, and Letters, 47 (1962), 316.

urgently needed if the state was to meet its obligations and if the current level of state services was to be maintained. The Democrats . . . proposed the adoption of a personal income tax. Republican leaders countered by advocating an increase in the sales tax from 3 to 4 per cent. Neither side would yield. . . . [Each side persisted in blocking the other's proposals.] State employees suffered a 'payless payday,' the Administrative Board held biweekly sessions at which the General Fund was drained, and the fight raged on.

"After months of struggle, a temporary compromise was effected in December, 1959. Assorted 'nuisance' taxes amounting to approximately $65 million, an amount far short of the state's financial needs, were adopted. A referendum proposal to increase the sales tax was placed on the November ballot. But the state had acquired a monumental deficit, essential services had been neglected, and Michigan's national reputation had suffered grievous damage that will take years to repair."[15]

Perhaps if in the previous years the state's electoral margins had been as thin as Connecticut's, Michigan politicians would have been willing to compromise their differences in order to maintain voter support. Because of the long string of Democratic victories, the Republicans may have felt that they no longer were in the running for the governorship. The Democrats may have felt confident of continued state-wide victory, and embittered at their inability to surmount the state's "constitutional gerry-

mander." A more fundamental explanation of Michigan's difficulties, however, seems to lie in the ideological and interest bases of the two parties.

Much the same kinds of population blocs are aggregated by Michigan parties as by Connecticut parties. Democrats base their support on urban, ethnic, and labor voters. Republicans draw on rural, old-stock citizens and on businessmen. But the groups seem to be qualitatively different in their goals in Michigan and they are combined in different proportions. Party competition to a considerable extent pits the heavily Democratic Wayne County (Detroit) against the "outstate" areas. Much of Detroit's working population is organized by unions which operate in the militant CIO tradition of aggressively liberal political action. Pragmatic, oldtime politicians of the Boss Plunkitt variety . . . have largely disappeared in Detroit. Precinct work is carried on by union political committees. On the Republican side, executives in the state's big businesses, especially the automobile industry, allied with outstate interests, set much of the party's tone. Party competition therefore was to a considerable extent a simple projection into the political arena of the conflict between major economic interests. Under these circumstances, unified, policy-oriented parties led to the kind of politics described by the French as *immobilisme*, rather than to popular control, political stability, and effective policymaking.

THE ILLUSION OF POPULAR RULE

V. O. Key, Jr.

Ideally, political parties are devices for converting public policy demands into legislation. They should do this by presenting the electorate with candidates who represent differing policy stances. Elections convert some of these candidates into office-holders, and as office-holders they produce the desired legislation.

In reality, the process of converting public demands into legislation by relying on parties is not nearly so smooth as this simple model suggests, of course. Too often, some critics argue, the parties have failed to present the public with candidates whose policy positions are clearly defined and differentiated. And too often office-holders fail to respond to apparent

policy mandates, voting on legislation in ways that seem to distort the intent of the public as expressed through elections.

Without commenting on the validity of these criticisms, it is enough to say that from time to time a sufficient number of people have believed them to take major steps to try to alter matters. The introduction of the party primary has been one such step.

[15]*Ibid.*, p. 318.
Reprinted with omissions by permission of Alfred A. Knopf, Inc., from "Participation in Primaries: The Illusion of Popular Rule," Chapter 5 in *American State Politics* by V. O. Key, Jr., pp. 133-168. Copyright © 1956 by V. O. Key, Jr.

If it is true that the parties have done a poor job in nominating candidates, then, the reasoning goes, a suitable adjustment is to give that job to the electorate itself, leaving to party professionals the task of running campaigns.

Giving the responsibility of nomination to the electorate raises a host of questions about the nature of party membership. Most politicians in states employing primaries have clearly recognized that it is illogical to let the whole electorate choose either or both parties' nominees, so they have instituted an array of devices meant to separate Democrats from Republicans at primary time. The devices have not always been satisfactory, however. Under favorable circumstances, the adherents of one party can register in the other party, for the purpose of affecting its primary outcome, in numbers sufficient to alter the kind of choice among candidates offered the voters in the following general election.

But such technical difficulties are only part of an adequate assessment of the contribution of primaries to the democratization of political parties. One major "plus" for primaries has been their introduction of an element more closely approximating competition of ideas and programs in one-party states or districts (although Greenstein, in the preceding selection, showed that it has been only an approximation of "two-party" politics). Two fundamental "minuses" of primaries as they have actually operated are the focus of this selection by Key. First, the large-scale apathy and nonparticipation of the electorate in primary elections leaves the outcome of these elections to persons constituting something considerably different from a population cross section. Second, primaries deprive party professionals of a great deal of latitude in establishing and following campaign strategy, thereby jeopardizing what both party professionals and adherents want — control of government.

The American political tradition caps decisions made by popular vote with a resplendent halo of legitimacy. Therein lies a source of the strength of the direct primary as an institution. In its form and spirit the primary appears to be a means for mass decision. In practice, not many people go to the trouble of using this great mechanism for the registration of the popular will. While it is well enough known that few voters turn up at the polls on primary day, relatively little effort has been devoted to the determination of precisely how many do so. Random thoughts about the significance, if any, of wholesale boycotting of the primaries by the voters have run to the effect that a small turnout assures a victory for the party organization's slate or that the whole problem has no importance one way or another. Yet reflection on the actual facts of primary participation suggests important questions about the nature of the politics of the states. Here some preliminary explorations of the numbers and sorts of people who vote in direct primaries may at least get some of the facts out on the table and indicate tentative conclusions about the consequences of variations in levels of participation.

LEVELS OF PARTICIPATION IN GUBERNATORIAL PRIMARIES

A few simple facts about the numbers of persons who vote in the direct primaries will aid in the estimation of the extent to which the primary is an instrument of popular government. To lend significance to such figures, it need not be assumed that the larger the number of voters the more "democratic" the process or the better the results. If 90 per cent of the potential electorate shares in the nomination of candidates, obviously a different sort of political order exists than if only 10 per cent of the maximum possible number of participants feels sufficiently concerned to go to the polls on primary day.

How many people do vote in primaries to nominate candidates for governor? The answer to so simple a question becomes a bit involved. It all depends on the time, place, and circumstances. The level of participation must be described in terms of distributions, frequencies, ranges, and averages rather than by a set figure.

In a sample of 15 nonsouthern states over the period 1926-1952, in three out of four primaries not more than 35 per cent of the potential electorate voted in the primaries of one or the other of the major parties. That is, the total Democratic primary vote plus the total Republican primary vote did not exceed 35 per cent of the number of citizens 21 years of age or over. In about one of six primaries the voters in Democratic and Republican gubernatorial primaries did not exceed 20 per cent of the number of citizens 21 and over. At the extreme of high participation in only one out of twelve primaries did more than 50 per cent of the potential vote turn up at the polls. Most often between 25 and 35 per cent of the potential electorate voted in the primaries. About four out of ten of the primaries in the sample states fell within this range of participation. . . .

The levels of interest . . . in gubernatorial primaries are far exceeded, of course, by the participation in gubernatorial general elections. Characteristically, well over one-half the potential electorate votes in the general elections while the great bulk of primaries draw less than one-third of the voters. . . .

What factors account for the variations in the rates of participation in gubernatorial primaries? Perhaps some meaning may be squeezed from the figures on participation rates by a search for the explanation of why one primary day sees 10 per cent of the voters at the polls and another 50 per cent. One broad category of explanations for these differences consists of factors peculiar either to a particular state or even to a particular primary. In any state when neither primary is contested the turnout is apt to be low. In Illinois, for example, when the state organization happens to be split and a factional fight occurs in the primary the turnout tends to the high side. When the party organization unites on a candidate for the nomination the vote is small. An especially warmly fought primary may pull the turnout for a particular primary far above the usual level for a state. Thus the 1938 Pennsylvania Democratic primary, in which the Mine Workers and the regular Democrats fought out their differences, brought the turnout much above the usual level for the state.

In a few states the entire primary voting record is considerably higher. . . . The mean rate for the North Dakota primaries . . . is 53 per cent; for West Virginia, 49; for Wyoming, 40. These deviant rates are undoubtedly clues to peculiar characteristics of the political systems of these states. In all three of these states a habit of high political participation prevails; they rank, for example, quite high among the states in the percentage turnout at general elections. Perhaps that habit spills over into the primaries and brings a high primary turnout. The high rate for North Dakota doubtless flows also in part from the lively duels within the Republican party between the Non-Partisan League and the Republican Organizing Committee.

Some of the variation in primary turnout undoubtedly comes from factors common to all states. Studies of public concern about presidential politics have shown that great waves

TABLE I

Mean Proportions of Potential Electorate Voting in Major-Party Gubernatorial Primaries in Sure Republican States and in More Competitive States, by Years, 1926-1952

Year	Sure Republican States[a]	More Competitive States[b]
1926	30.8	25.9
1928	24.4	33.1
1930	34.1	26.4
1932	41.3	41.1
1934	34.9	36.3
1936	34.7	39.3
1938	35.8	35.7
1940	31.9	37.9
1942	20.0	20.0
1944	20.0	20.6
1946	23.6	16.9
1948	29.1	28.0
1950	29.1	24.0
1952	35.2	31.8

[a] Vermont, North Dakota, Maine, Wisconsin, Michigan, New Hampshire, Pennsylvania, Kansas.
[b] Massachusetts, Illinois, Wyoming, Ohio, Colorado, West Virginia, Missouri.

of interest and disinterest affect the voters of most of the states in much the same manner. At times the gravity of public issues brings a larger proportion of the potential electorate into the circle of the politically involved. At other stages tranquillity prevails, or perhaps hope dies, and the circle of the involved shrinks. It is evident that to some extent these variations in the public's political temperature affect interest in direct primaries as well as participation in presidential elections. These variations in primary turnout from time to time appear in Table I, . . . a pair of time series showing the average rates of primary turnout by years for a group of sure Republican states and for a group of more competitive states. In both sets of states the primary turnout responded to the great waves of political concern or unconcern that swept the country during the period 1926-1952. In 1932, the numbers of primary voters jumped quite sharply over that of 1928, and a high level of interest was maintained in 1934, 1936, and 1938 in keeping with the intensity of the political debates of the time. In 1942, 1944, and 1946, primary turnout dropped sharply as did interest in other types of elections, while in 1952 there was a marked upturn in primary voting as well as in turnout at the presidential election.

An interesting, and perhaps significant, feature of the data of Table I, is that total primary turnout in the group of sure Republican states runs at about the same level from year to year as in the group of states called more competitive. That is, no matter how those persons sufficiently concerned to vote in primaries divided between the parties, roughly similar proportions voted in one or the other major party primaries. To show in more detail what underlies the figures of Table I, the data of the table are broken down by the primaries of the major parties in the graphs in Figure l. The curves in that figure show the average percentages of the potential vote participating in the primary of each party over the period 1926-1952. In the sure Republican states, shown in the upper panel of the drawing, the mean participation rate in the Republican primaries consistently

exceeded by a wide margin that in the Democratic primaries over the entire period. In the more competitive states the participation rates ran more closely together over the period, although, insofar as primary participation measures competitiveness, the Democrats occupied a weak position in these states in the early period covered by the graphs.

About the only indisputable conclusion to be drawn from this analysis of the levels of participation in gubernatorial primaries is that not many people take a hand in this sort of political business. Yet the tendency toward similar levels of turnout under similar conditions suggests a speculative inference about the workings of state political systems. Perhaps there exists a sector of the population, of more or less the same relative size from state to state, with an especially strong concern about state affairs. This concern expresses itself through voting in the primaries of one or the other of the major parties. Who these people are and whether they have the same characteristics from state

FIGURE 1 MEAN PROPORTIONS OF POTENTIAL ELECTORATE VOTING IN REPUBLICAN AND DEMOCRATIC GUBERNATORIAL PRIMARIES IN SURE REPUBLICAN STATES AND IN MORE COMPETITIVE STATES, 1926-1952

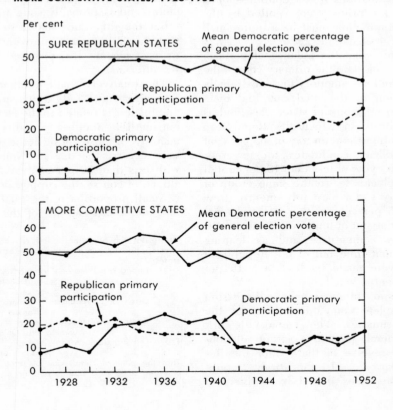

to state it is impossible to say. Nevertheless, few though they are, it is their votes that control the gateways to the governorship. In fact, in the strong one-party states, this more highly concerned sector of the electorate makes, in effect, the final choices. As states approach dual competition the final decision tends to be taken from the hands of the narrow group of primary participators and transferred to the much larger sector of the population that votes in general elections.

SIZE OF CONTROLLING MINORITIES

The fact that voters stay away from the direct primaries in droves profoundly affects the strategy of gubernatorial politics in the American states. So few votes determine the party nomination that aspirants for office need only command the loyalties of a relatively small following to win a place on the party ticket. Once on the ticket, the candidate's fortunes may be governed by the traditional voting pattern of the state, the great accidents of general election politics, or even by the sound preferences of a majority of those who vote in the general election.

From earlier analyses it has doubtless been deduced that the primary vote polled by the winner of a nomination must be a quite small proportion of the electorate. . . .

. . . No matter what the balance of partisan power may be in a state the primary vote of the Republican nominee amounts to an extremely small proportion of the total potential electorate. Even in [a] group of states classified as strong Republican, in which the Republican nominee was almost certain to win, 63 per cent of the Republican candidates for governor polled a primary vote of less than 15 per cent of the potential electorate. In the same group of states a primary victor most infrequently drew as much as 25 per cent of the potential electorate — about one out of ten times. In the states categorized as competitive and as leaning Democratic about nine out of ten Republican nominations were made by less than 15 per cent of the potential vote.[1]

It is unnecessary to encumber the discussion with the complete companion table for the Democratic primaries. The Democratic primaries, in general, present a set of relationships just the reverse of that . . . for the Republican primaries. . . . In the strong Republican states, the votes polled by winners of

Democratic gubernatorial primaries are minute proportions of the potential electorate. Of the Democratic nominations in these states, 64 per cent were made by less than 5 per cent of the electorate. On the other hand, in states with relatively stronger Democratic parties the winners of Democratic nominations attract a higher proportion of the potential electorate. The proportions of Democratic nominations made by less than 10 per cent of the potential electorate for the various groups of states were as follows:

Strong Republican	96%
Less-strong Republican	93
Competitive	77
Leaning Democratic	55

Generally, Democratic nominations are made by smaller proportions of the total electorate — at least in the states analyzed[1] — than are Republican nominations. And turnout at Democratic primaries tends to be smaller in relation to the party's general election vote than at the Republican primaries. In part this difference reflects the fact that in most of the states examined the Republican nomination is worth more — and is probably sought more diligently — but the difference may also reflect the fact that the Democratic following consists in the main of persons less disposed to vote than are Republicans.

The relatively small numbers of voters that an aspirant must rally to his support to win the nomination is related to the fact that commonly outside the South a plurality, rather than a majority, of those voting at the primary is necessary to carry the day. . . . Nominees who win with less than 50 per cent of the primary vote attract, of course, the support of an exceptionally small proportion of the total electorate. Nor in general did capture of the nomination by

[1]Using data covering the period, roughly, of 1910-1952, Key develops the following classification scheme and illustrative states:
    Strong Republican — Vermont, North Dakota, Maine, South Dakota, Wisconsin, Michigan, Iowa, and New Hampshire
    Less-strong Republican — Minnesota, Pennsylvania, and Kansas
    Competitive — Massachusetts, Illinois, New Jersey, Wyoming, and Ohio
    Leaning Democratic — Colorado, West Virginia, Idaho, Missouri, and Nevada
That the political complexion of some of these states has changed since 1952 has no bearing on Key's analysis here. — Ed.

less than half the primary vote reduce the chances for ultimate victory.

Whether men who squeeze through the primaries with the support of a small proportion of the electorate are any better or worse than those with slightly larger followings it is impossible to know. More or less horrible examples may be found to be sure. In Ohio in 1934 Martin L. Davey won the nomination with votes equal to 5.3 per cent of the potential electorate and carried the state in that year of great Democratic strength over the nation as a whole. In 1920 Len Small received a primary vote of 10.9 per cent of the potential Illinois electorate and rode into office on the great Republican landslide of that year. On the other hand, many governors with eminently respectable records have gained office in the same manner. The records suggest something of the fortuitous and capricious nature of elective process. A man who chances in the primary to win the votes of 5 to 10 per cent of the potential voters, with the aid of luck and landslides, can be elevated to the governorship of an American commonwealth. The seemingly rational processes of democratic politics contain an element of the lottery.

Yet the small size of the blocs of voters necessary to win nominations has a most significant consequence for the nature of the party within the states. The direct communion of potential candidates with small groups of voters places enormous difficulties in the way of those party leaders disposed to look beyond the primaries to the general election and to put forward the most appealing slate. Individual politicians with a grasp on a small bloc of voters which can be turned into a primary victory are difficult to discipline or to bargain with. The support of even a weak personal organization, the loyalties and admiration of an ethnic group, a wide acquaintance within a religious group, simple notoriety achieved in a variety of ways, an alliance with an influential newspaper—these and a variety of other elements may create power within the narrow circle of people who share control in the politics of the direct primary.

BIASES IN PRIMARY CONSTITUENCIES

The smallness of the primary vote would not affect the results if those who voted constituted a representative sample of the adherents of a party. A minute group of voters—as small even as one of Mr. Gallup's samples—would make about the same nominations as would a turnout of 100 per cent, if the principal elements of the party were proportionately represented in the group. The fact seems to be, however, that those who vote in the primaries do not make up miniatures of the party membership. Perhaps in those one-party states with extremely high primary participation and in which the primary is indubitably the election the primary voters approximate a more or less representative sample of those who would vote in the general election if the general election were of any importance. Yet in states with a modicum of interparty competition primary participants are often by no means representative of the party.

Although a sample survey could be used to determine with some exactness the characteristics of those few persons who bestir themselves to express preferences for party nominations, an exercise in the arithmetic of election returns can reveal some gross dimensions of the active primary constituency. A plausible hypothesis with which to begin an inquiry is the supposition that in statewide direct primaries—to make nominations for governor, United States Senator, and other offices filled by elections at large—a disproportionate part of the vote would be cast by residents of areas strongly attached to a party. Virtual one-party Republican counties, for example, would be agitated over Republican nominations for local office and the Republican primary turnout would be exceptionally heavy in such counties. Their contribution to the total vote in statewide nominations would incidentally also be large. In the same counties Democrats, faced by hopeless prospects in local races, would vote in small numbers in the primaries and incidentally contribute a relatively small proportion of the state vote in the gubernatorial primaries. In counties controlled locally by Democrats the reverse of this pattern of participation would be expected to prevail.

The hunch is, then, that strong Democratic localities would vote especially heavily in statewide primaries, while strong Republican areas would contribute a similarly large part of the total vote in statewide Republican primaries. Whether this state of affairs actually prevails can be determined quite easily. An illustrative calculation on a New Hampshire gubernatorial primary will explain a technique to be applied to a few other situations. In the 1950 gubernatorial primaries in New Hampshire the Democrats nominated Robert P. Bingham, while the Republican nomination was won by Sherman Adams, a man later to gain some notoriety on the national political scene. In Hillsborough County, the strongest Democratic county in the state, the total Democratic primary vote was 89.6 per cent of the total Republican vote. This ratio, which we may call the index of primary balance, [is] . . . a convenient measure of the relative strength of partisan groups within the electorate. In Hillsborough County the Democratic primary vote was 43.2 per cent of the Democratic general election vote and the Republican primary turnout was 64.8 per cent of the Republican general election vote. At the opposite extreme from Hillsborough County was Carroll County, an area of dedicated Republicanism in which the Democratic primary turnout amounted to only 3.8 per cent of the total Republican primary vote. In Carroll County the Democratic primary vote was only 13.2 per cent of the Democratic general election vote and the corresponding Republican figure was 81.4 per cent. . . .

. . . The same type of analysis applied to the 1950 Colorado primaries for the nomination of candidates for lieutenant-governor yields another confirmation of the supposition that primary participation is warped by variations in the balance of power between the parties. Special heed ought to be given to . . . the average numbers of Democratic county officers for the counties. . . . The counties ranked high in numbers of Democratic county officers also ranked high in Democratic primary participation and low in Republican primary participation (in relation to general election vote). If our general suppositions are correct, the primary contests for Democratic county nominations in strong Democratic counties attract voters to the primaries and help swell the vote in these counties on Democratic statewide nominations. Meanwhile, local Republicans, unmoved by the prospects for local victory and relatively untouched by the urgings of local candidates for their vote, stay away from the primaries. A reverse set of relationships apparently prevails in the strong Republican counties.

An extensive analysis would be necessary to ascertain whether these broad differentials in primary participation prevail in all states and at all primaries. Doubtless in some sets of circumstances the relationships do not exist, yet the tendency for areas strongly attached to a party to gain a disproportionate weight in statewide primary nominations is doubtless sufficiently widespread to be of importance. . . .

CONSEQUENCES OF UNREPRESENTATIVE PRIMARY TURNOUT

Our analyses make it clear enough that the effective primary constituency may often be a caricature of the entire party following. The question immediately arises, what of it? The answer must be to a considerable degree conjectural. A suggestive line of speculation may be to consider the problem as a special case of the more general question of the interaction between public officials and their constituencies. A time-worn axiom of American politics proclaims the proposition that politicians keep their ears to the ground. Different politicians keep their ears to different sorts of soil, a fact that makes it possible to ascertain whether they pay any heed to what they hear. It is quite plain, from several systematic analyses, that not only does the character of the constituency affect the type of person elected but that after representatives are elected their voting records have, on the average at least, a demonstrable relationship with the characteristics of the people of their constituency. The same general idea has served to explain some of the differences in the behavior of a variety of public functionaries. Thus, it is often said that United States Senators, with their large constituencies including many interests and types of people, are apt to take a different viewpoint than Representatives who often speak for relatively homogeneous — farmer, worker, suburban — districts. Or that the President must concern himself with all the people and, hence, may be moved to take a position diverging from that of a Senator or a Representative who responds to the tugs of a narrower constituency.

This broad tendency for the elective official to reflect the characteristics of his constituency may have a special significance if it also applies to the highly unrepresentative "constituencies" of actual participators in statewide direct primaries. Over the long run, the effect may be to mold the party leadership, or at least the bulk of the party candidates, more and more toward the image of that sector of the party stimulated by circumstances to participate in the primaries in high degree. By the same token, the composition and orientation of the party leadership would come less and less to take into account those elements of the party indisposed by circumstances to play a role in the primary.

The exact form of these consequences would, of course, be expected to be a product of the facts of the situation as they existed in a particular state at a particular time. Depending on the precise nature of those facts, the effective primary constituency of the state as a whole may come to consist predominantly of the people of certain sections of a state, of persons chiefly of specified national origin or religious affiliation, of people especially responsive to certain styles of political leadership or shades of ideology, or of other groups markedly unrepresentative in one way or another of the party following. The consequences would, thus, probably be most notable when the party following contained large and diverse groups of voters. Under some circumstances the minuscule and unrepresentative primary constituency may project its features upon the party leadership and handicap the party in polling the maximum party strength in the general election. On occasion, when extraneous influences such as presidential landslides control state elections, nominations dominated by warped primary constituencies may lead to general election victories mightily embarrassing to the responsible elements of the party as well as impairing the usefulness of the party in the larger cause of the government of the state.

The testing of these general notions and precise identification of the types of circumstances under which they would tend to prevail would require the most extensive investigations. An examination of the workings of the primary system in Massachusetts, however, will serve as an illustrative instance, although it should by no means be supposed that the effects of the primary system take exactly the same form in other states. As a first step in the examination of the transformation of Massachusetts parties under the direct primary system Tables II and III deserve careful inspection, for they identify some long-run tendencies that suggest lines of speculation in relation to our general proposition about the effects of the primary.

Since the introduction of the primary system of nomination for statewide office in 1912 the geographical distribution of Democratic nominees for statewide offices has been gradually but radically altered. In the first decade of the century only one out of four Democratic nom-

TABLE II

Trend in Residence of Democratic Nominees for Statewide Office in Massachusetts, 1900-1952

Period	Number of Nominees[a]	From Boston and Vicinity[b] #	%	Elected[c] #	%
1900-1911	72	18	25.0	3	4.2
1912-1920	56	26	46.4	11	19.6
1922-1930	34	15	44.1	6	17.6
1932-1940	32	21	65.6	17	53.1
1942-1952	41	34	82.9	22	53.7

[a] Includes nominees for all statewide elective offices and for the United States Senate since 1916.
[b] Includes Suffolk County, Cambridge, Medford, and Somerville.
[c] That is, percentage of all Democratic nominees elected, not of those from Boston and vicinity only.

inees for such posts resided in Boston and vicinity, as defined in Table II. By a slow but steady movement Boston Democrats after the introduction of the primary increased their proportion of the nominations to 82.9 per cent for the decade 1942-1952.

Over the same period the geographical distribution of the membership of Republican slates also underwent drastic changes, which are pictured in Table III. The shifts in the sources of Republican candidates differed from those for the Democrats although probably the same types of underlying influences brought them about. Under the convention system the strong Republican territory of western Massachusetts

TABLE III

Trend in Residence of Republican Nominees for Statewide Elective Office in Massachusetts, 1900-1952

Period	Total Nominees	From Boston #	%	From Eastern Counties[a] #	%	From Western Counties[b] #	%
1900-11	72	29	40.3	14	19.4	25	34.7
1912-20	56	17	30.3	22	39.3	14	25.0
1922-30	34	9	26.5	23	67.6	2	5.9
1932-40	32	9	28.1	20	62.5	3	9.4
1942-52	41	5	12.2	36	87.8	0	0.0

[a] Included in this category are nominees from Essex, Middlesex, Norfolk, Bristol, and Plymouth counties.
[b] This group of counties consists of Berkshire, Franklin, Hampshire, Hampden, and Worcester.

contributed about one out of three Republican candidates for statewide office. Under the direct primary the leaders of the loyal Republicans dispersed over the western counties gained smaller and smaller shares of the posts on the slate and eventually they came to win no places on the ticket. Fewer and fewer Republican nominees claimed Boston as their residence. In 1900-1911 about 40 per cent of the Republican statewide nominees were Bostonians; in 1942-52, only 12 per cent. It may be suspected that this shift parallels the movement of Yankees from Beacon Hill to the suburbs, but it also probably reflects a gain in capacity to win nominations by persons with a claim on considerable local concentrations of Republican voters.

The analysis of changes in geographical distribution of candidates rests on no assumption that geographically balanced tickets are a "good thing." Rather the changing pattern of the nominees suggests that under the direct primary a marked alteration in the location of the controlling power points in the nominating process has occurred. That alteration is mirrored in the changing geographical distribution of the party nominees.

In the Democratic party the changes in sources of statewide nominees apparently paralleled a gradual disintegration of the statewide Democratic organization. In the convention epoch that organization allocated nominations over the state. Even after the adoption of the primary the state organization continued to sponsor more or less balanced slates in the primaries. Its capacity to carry its slate in the primary became less and less with the passage of time as the organization became weaker and weaker. Ultimately in large measure the determination of nominations came to rest largely in the hands of those leaders with a hold on large concentrations of primary voters in strong Democratic territory. And these leaders tended to be individualists who got themselves nominated.

It might well be supposed that the primary system of nomination had nothing to do with these tendencies. Undoubtedly other factors were at work. One possibility, however, can be ruled out. Did the changing origins of candidates simply parallel a change in the location of the Democratic vote? In fact, the division of the Democratic vote between Boston and vicinity and the rest of the state remained fairly constant. The primary, in combination with the distortions in primary participation, gave the Boston Democratic vote a mighty leverage in nominations. Some averages for the periods 1913-1920 and 1942-1952 will make clear what happened:

	1913-20	1942-52
Average percentage of total Democratic primary vote on statewide nominations from Boston and vicinity	56.0	52.4
Average percentage of Democratic candidates' general election vote from Boston and vicinity	33.1	29.6
Average percentage of total general election vote from Boston and vicinity	26.0	23.9
Total Democratic primary vote in Boston and vicinity as percentage of nominee's statewide general election vote, mean	18.8	15.4

These figures give the characteristics of the situation which facilitated the pyramiding of a small following of voters into a nomination for statewide office. Boston and vicinity, as defined in Table II, accounted for about one-half the statewide Democratic primary votes against around one-third of the statewide general election vote for Democratic candidates. The total Democratic primary vote in Boston and vicinity averaged in the two periods 18.8 and 15.4 per cent of the Democratic nominees' statewide general election vote. Men with the capacity to win the support of voters in Boston equal to 10 per cent or so of the statewide Democratic general election vote obviously would have enormous advantage in capturing statewide nominations.

A factor that doubtless contributed to the disintegration of statewide Democratic organization, as reflected in the distribution of nominees, arose from the increasing prospects over the period for Democratic statewide victory. So long as Democratic candidates had little chance for victory the state organization could designate and nominate through the primary more or less balanced slates. In truth, when the nominations were worthless, it took precious little statewide organization to produce a balanced slate. As the probability of victory grew, however, the latent cleavages within the party became manifest through sharp competition for primary nomination. In other words, when the Democratic nominations for state office became worth something, Boston Democratic politicians had a stronger incentive to exert the great leverage of their local followings in the statewide primaries. The right-hand column of Table II indicates the changes over a half century in the probability of victory for Democratic nominees.

For many years after the introduction of the direct primary the Democratic state organization, through the state committee, the state convention, or less formal means, prepared slates of organization candidates for the primary nomination. Gradually whatever cohesiveness the organization ever possessed became inadequate to curb the tempting opportunity to fight out differences in the primary. In fact, in due course even the factional elements of the party became so ineffectively linked with the voters that the outcome of the primary contests, at least for the lesser offices, became almost a matter of chance.

For well over thirty years important actors in the internal wars of the party were David Ignatius Walsh, of Fitchburg, and James Michael Curley, of Boston. Although they never met as opposing candidates, their allies and associates often sparred in the primaries. Walsh, with the benefit of the Republican rifts of the Progressive era, won the gubernatorial election of 1913 and as governor established a record as a progressive himself. In 1918, a year of Democratic disaster over the nation, he won a United States Senate seat and remained in the Senate most of the rest of his life. Over the years he built up and maintained a following adequate to keep him in the Senate yet not sufficient to control the Democratic party of the state. The first Catholic governor of the state, Walsh's style of politics was adapted to political longevity in his environment. Irish by origin and for his day liberal, he had an appeal to the Massachusetts Irish, an appeal re-enforced by his isolationism. Yet he proclaimed, "Let every man of Irish blood face his duty as an American citizen in passing judgment on national and international questions. Let us remember to be Americans first."[2] So mellow a view coupled with a moderate economic outlook earned for him independent and, on occasion, Yankee Republican support that contributed to his capacity to survive despite the misfortunes of his party.

Curley's style of politics, radically different from that of the upstater Walsh, served his purposes and needs also. Curley, his biographer Joseph F. Dinneen observes, was a "creation of a curious society known everywhere as 'The Boston Irish,' as distinguished from all other Irish."[3] Curley built a political career on his uncompromising championship of the Boston Irish. A man of exceptional histrionic skill, he had great capacity to play upon the sentiments of the more exuberant strains within the Boston Irish community.

Scarcely had the direct primary been put into operation when Curley, from his base as mayor of Boston, challenged a primary recommendation of the Democratic state committee. In 1913 the committee backed Walsh for the gubernatorial nomination and Richard H. Long, of Framingham, for the nomination for lieutenant-governor. Curley's man, one Edward P. Barry, of Boston, won the latter nomination. At intervals over the years Curley men and Walsh men crossed swords. In 1930 Joseph B. Ely, a western Massachusetts Democrat, a Protestant, and early in his career a protégé of Walsh, easily won the gubernatorial nomination over a stalking horse backed by Curley. The state convention of 1934 endorsed Walsh for the United States Senate and Charles H. Cole, an Ely-Walsh man, for governor. Curley carried the fight to the primaries and won the gubernatorial nomination for himself but his man Edward P. Barry made a poor showing in the primary against Senator Walsh. Curley won the senatorial nomination in 1936 but, in a year when any Democrat should have won, lost to young Henry Cabot Lodge. Again in 1938 he won the primary nomination for governor but lost to Leverett Saltonstall in the general election. Curley's strong hold on a substantial block of Boston voters made him a formidable candidate in statewide Democratic primaries. No matter how faithfully he mirrored his own immediate constituency, he made a poor candidate in the larger arena of the state. He managed to win only one statewide race, that for governor in 1934, a year when probably Democratic popular strength in the nation generally reached its peak.

The gradual increase in the proportions of Democratic nominations captured by Bostonians did not reflect by any means solely the fortunes and exertions of prominent factional leaders.

[2]Dorothy G. Wayman, *David I. Walsh, Citizen-Patriot* (Milwaukee: Bruce, 1952), p. 108.
[3]*The Purple Shamrock* (New York: W. W. Norton & Company, Inc., 1949), p. 9.

It came more and more to result from the unguided and unbossed actions of primary voters in supporting names familiar to them, usually those of local notables. Primary maneuvers to divide the vote, by a multiplicity of candidacies, became more common and increased the probability that this or that extremely small minority would control the nomination. . . .

These cases suggest that the direct primary in Massachusetts, along with its distorted effective constituency, had consequences for party leadership that are not so easily measured as are changes in residence of candidates. In any case the problem of geographical balance is generated by the practice of electing officials who might in the main better be chosen otherwise. Geographical balance may not be a matter of as great importance in party victory as is balance in the sense of selecting candidates whose style of politics and whose policy orientations strike somewhere near the common denominator of the party membership. In this sense a ticket with only one candidate may be "balanced" or "unbalanced." In the internal politics of American parties a recurring problem of party leadership is to keep in check the extremists in the party—ideological extremists, regional special pleaders, deviant groups of whatever sort—and to nominate candidates and advocate causes that hold the support not only of most elements of the party but reach out and attract the uncommitted voter and the milder adherents of the opposition. The accomplishment of that task is inevitably difficult, but under some circumstances the primary procedure creates especially formidable obstacles. . . .

The saga of the Hurleys in Massachusetts politics further illustrates [another difficulty]. In 1930 Francis X. Hurley won the Democratic nomination for auditor and Charles F. Hurley won the Democratic nomination for treasurer. Both went on to victory and in 1932 were re-nominated and re-elected. Four years of publicity for the Hurley name gave it a political potency. In 1934, as Charles F. Hurley, unsuccessful in his bid for convention endorsement for governor, had to be content with a re-nomination for treasurer, one Joseph L. Hurley turned up on the scene and won the nomination for lieutenant-governor. Elected as lieutenant-governor, he shared the stage with Treasurer Hurley for a couple of years and the name of Hurley became more and more of a household

word. The two Hurleys, Charles F. and Joseph L., vied in 1936 for the convention endorsement for governor. Charles F. won the nod and Joseph L. disappeared from the limelight. The magic of the name Hurley seeped over into the Republican ranks and, also in 1936, the Republicans endorsed and nominated a William E. Hurley for treasurer, the post held by the Democrat, Charles F. Hurley, now running for governor. Simultaneously, the Democratic convention proposed J. C. Scanlon for the treasury post, but one James M. Hurley won the primary nomination for the place that had been so adequately filled by Charles F. Hurley. Mr. Charles F. Hurley went on to win the governorship but his colleague Mr. James M. Hurley, of Marlborough, fell before the campaign of Mr. William E. Hurley, the Boston Republican.

Obviously when candidates of questionable capacity whose names are household words—or who have the same name as somebody whose name is a household word—can become formidable contestants in primaries, party organization no longer has much capacity to lead the voters, a condition that may be more ominous than that which prevails when the primary rubber-stamps the organization slate.

The impact of different groups within the highly restricted primary constituency upon party nominations differs from state to state with the structure of the groups within the party, with the sorts of people who make up the high participating element of the party, and doubtless with many other variables. Yet it is probably correct that the fact that primary constituency bias tends to determine the nature of party leadership may become of special significance for the minority party which is especially weak, i.e., not too weak to hope for victory but not strong enough to win except on infrequent occasions. Leaders of such a party who are ambitious for statewide victory confront a real difficulty in overcoming the preferences of a primary constituency for its own peculiar kind. Yet to win now and then such a minority must put forward nominees with an appeal to the independents and to the inconstant fringe of the majority party. In the states of the North the minority's problem in fielding an attractive ticket is principally a Democratic problem. Where the Republicans normally occupy the minority position, they have their difficulties.

In New Mexico, Jack E. Holmes has pointed out in an able analysis,[4] to win state elections the Republicans of the small number of Republican counties must desert their own and put up candidates from elsewhere in the state. Nevertheless, during the period 1940-1950 most of the voters in the Republican primaries and a majority of the Republican nominees came from five counties of the Rio Grande Valley. Republican personalities of these counties can readily obtain primary nominations for statewide office. Yet, Mr. Holmes observes, "individuals nominated from such a narrow base of old friends and neighbor's support will hardly appeal to the dissident Democrat from the East side who is looking for a respectable chance to vote his convictions on policy on those occasions when he might feel that his own party has not given him and his neighbors a fair shake."[5]

QUERIES ABOUT MASS CONTROL OF PARTY HIERARCHIES

A favorite argument of some of the more sophisticated advocates of direct primary used to be that the primary afforded a means for popular correction of the errors and misjudgments of the party organization in the nominating process. They recognized the uses of party organization and thought that the party leadership would and should propose slates of candidates to the judgment of the party membership in the primaries. The party voters could then approve or reject or selectively substitute in the primary the virtuous challengers of the wicked men proposed by the organization. The facts of experience about mass interest and participation in the direct primaries make it evident that the expectation that the primary would function as a mechanism for control of the party hierarchy requires revision. The data on participation over a long period and under widely varied conditions make it plain that only under the most exceptional circumstances will more than a handful of the voters turn out at the primary. The thinness of participation is perhaps not so significant a factor in the re-estimation of the possibilities of membership control of the party hierarchy as is the unrepresentative character of the segment of the party that does participate.

If any moral at all obtrudes from the various comparative analyses, it is that the practical realities of particular institutional arrangements vary with the nature of the situation into which they are introduced. So it is with the estimation of the significance of the biases in the effective primary constituency. The form of the bias is fixed by the peculiar situation in each state as are its consequences and significant elements of that situation may change from time to time within an individual state. It is therefore most perilous to attempt any general observations on the basis of the sample inquiries reported [here]; far more extensive study would be required to estimate the frequency of occurrence of particular types of actions associated with the primary system of nomination and to define the circumstances under which particular types of actions might be expected to take place. About all that can be said is that under some circumstances the unrepresentative block of participators in the primary, by nominating candidates in their own image, seriously handicap the party in carrying the battle to the opposition in the general election. The elevation of such minorities to power within the nominating process —through the smallness of total participation and its bias along with the accidents of plurality nomination— may affect more than the capacity of the party to wage political war. At times the swings of partisan sentiment are enough to throw into office the most improbable sorts of characters who have won nominations through the vagaries of the primary.

It may well be that these sorts of consequences of the bias in participation are most apt to occur in states fairly competitive between the major parties and in states in which one or the other of the parties contains within itself a congeries of groups of voters susceptible to management and manipulation by would-be candidates. Another range of consequences may develop as one moves into states that are dominated by a single party although the difference may be one of degree.

A focus of attention on these aspects of primary participation points to special difficulties in maintaining a cohesive party hierarchy extending over an entire state under the statewide direct primary. A party organization, representative of all segments of the party and with an eye on statewide victory, would almost

[4]Jack E. Holmes, *Problems Relating to Various Nominating Procedures in New Mexico* (Santa Fe: New Mexico Legislative Council Service, 1954).
[5]*Ibid.*, p. 34.

of necessity propose slates in one way or another unappealing to the unrepresentative sector of the party voting in the primary. Statewide party hierarchies seem to disintegrate under the impact of the influences given free play by the primary. They cannot thrive under repeatedly successful assaults upon their proposals by those who, on the basis of some special or parochial appeal, can manage to win nominations through the primary. Only under rather exceptional sets of circumstances — of party homogeneity, of monopolization of sources of campaign funds, of common desire for victory — can formal party leadership maintain much control over the nominating process. The more common tendency seems to be that competing centers of power — competing informal hierarchies based on localities, regions, groups, personal followings — develop their electoral support in the direct primary. These little hierarchies — under one-party conditions — approach, of course, the reality of political parties themselves.

The dilemma with which the analysis confronts us is essentially that the introduction of means for popular control of party hierarchies also plants the seeds for the fission, if not the destruction, of statewide party organization. The primary mode of nomination gives free play to forces that make it difficult for the party hierarchies to do much by way either of good or evil. The observation that such consequences tend to prevail should not be interpreted as an argument for the return of the old-style convention system, which had its erraticisms as well. The point is rather that under the processes of the primary we have a wide range of consequences, by no means all to the good, more or less totally unforeseen by the architects of this system of nomination.

THE AMATEUR DEMOCRAT

James Q. Wilson

The reform drive that produced the party primary in America, as well as such tools of popular political control as the referendum, has been motivated chiefly by a deep concern that party politics, as played by professionals, tends to be issueless. Ideology and program lose focus in the pragmatic scramble to gain office.

Popularly, primaries are viewed as one means of bringing the party closer to its membership and of reintroducing programmatic substance into party consciousness. Key has laid that expectation open to serious question. An alternative is to mount an effort to displace, or at least to rival, the existing core of party professionals in the performance of party tasks. Once in a while, reform groups or interest groups of other sorts do "capture" party organizations by successfully contesting ward elections and by other means. The United Automobile Workers' take-over of the Democratic Party in Detroit and Michigan in 1948 is one of the more dramatic instances. It is also one of the rare instances in which the new leadership has maintained its ascendancy. More often, program-oriented reform groups have been able to gain power only for short periods, rather quickly succumbing to their own lack of organizational skills and their members' decline in interest and enthusiasm.

Major American campaigns often give birth to *ad hoc* "citizens committees," whose job, as both they and the ongoing party organization usually define it, is to attract to the party's candidates money and votes that might otherwise be repelled. The motives of these committees are less suspect than those of the party organization, in the eyes of voters and campaign contributors who are program- or ideology-oriented and who often like to think of themselves as "independents." But the life span of such committees rarely exceeds the duration of a campaign, and therefore they constitute at most only a temporary annoyance to the professional party organization.

The amateur party clubs that Wilson describes in this selection are quite a different matter. They display attributes of skill and tenacity that party professionals must view as serious competition for control of the party's main operations and future directions. The clubs are a relatively new phenomenon, a more effective attempt to achieve some closer correspondence between the life of a party and the preferences of its adherents. Wilson takes a close look at the kinds of people who form the amateur clubs and at their impact on American politics.

Reprinted from *The Amateur Democrat* by James Q. Wilson, pp. 1-28, by permission of The University of Chicago Press. Copyright 1962 by the University of Chicago Press.

Since the Second World War a new kind of politician has appeared in large numbers in several of the biggest American cities. Although they are nowhere in complete control of their parties, these new politicians have played a crucial part in the defeat of the boss of Tammany Hall and have contributed to the election of several important officials: a governor in California, a mayor in New York City, and a state's attorney in Chicago. Their ambitions extend far beyond these offices, however, for they intend to alter fundamentally the character of the American party system, and accordingly of all governing institutions.

The new politicians are known by several names. In California, they are referred to, most generally, as the "club movement" and more specifically as the "CDC" – the California Democratic Council. In New York City, they are called the "reformers" or sometimes the "Lehman group," after one of their chief sponsors, former Senator Herbert H. Lehman. In Illinois, one group is known as the "IVI" – the Independent Voters of Illinois, a local affiliate of the Americans for Democratic Action – while another wing is called the "DFI" – the Democratic Federation of Illinois. Wherever they are found and whatever their name, however, they display certain common characteristics. . . .

Although the traits these new politicians have in common are easy to list, it is difficult to find a single word which will describe them adequately and distinguish them from the more conventional politicians found in large cities. That they are so distinguished can scarcely be doubted. In every community where they are found in large numbers, a keen antipathy inevitably develops between the new and the conventional politicians. The former accuse the latter of being at best "hacks" and "organization men" and at worst "bosses" and "machine leaders." The latter retort by describing the former as "dilettantes," "crackpots," "outsiders," and "hypocritical do-gooders." Most of the new politicians in the Democratic party are also liberals, but it is not their liberalism that is their chief distinguishing characteristic. They can be found in the Republican party as well, and there they are likely to be extremely conservative. What is necessary is a definition that distinguishes the new from other politicians but which is applicable equally to liberals and conservatives.

THE NATURE OF THE AMATEUR

It is not his liberalism or his age, education, or class that sets the new politician apart and makes him worth studying. Rather, it is his outlook on politics, and the style of politics he practices. This is sensed by the politicians themselves; the conventional and the new politicians, in almost every case, find it hard to "understand" one another or to "get along," even in those cases in which their interests or policies happen to coincide. Although in New York the new politicians are called "reformers," their counterparts in Wisconsin or California are not reformers at all, for in these states they are not preoccupied with matters of reform. Nor, as we shall see, are they all "intellectuals" or "eggheads," although some of the new politicians are fond of describing themselves and their colleagues in these terms. Although no single word is completely satisfactory, the word which I will use . . . is "amateur."

By amateur is not meant a dabbler, a dilettante or an inept practitioner of some special skill; many amateur Democrats have a highly sophisticated understanding of practical politics and have proved their skills in the only way that matters – by winning at the polls. Similarly, a good many undoubted professionals – by which word I mean all non-amateurs – are hopelessly incompetent and have proved themselves so in the only way that matters.

Nor does amateur here mean a person who is in politics for fun or as an avocation, rather than for money or as a career. To be sure, most amateurs do get their incomes from sources other than politics and regard it as other than a career. But there are also many professionals, as the word will be used here, who do not make money from politics and who think of it mainly as a game. In Chicago, of course, most professional politicians do as a rule have public jobs or get some income from politics, but this is not the case everywhere. In California few professionals other than those holding elective office are supported mainly by politics, and even in Manhattan there are as many or more workers in Tammany clubs who do not have political jobs as there are those who do.

An amateur is one who finds politics *intrinsically* interesting because it expresses a conception of the public interest. The amateur politician sees the political world more in terms of ideas and principles than in terms of persons. Politics is the determination of public policy, and public policy ought to be set deliberately rather than as the accidental by-product of a struggle for personal and party advantage. Issues ought to be settled on their merits; compromises by which one issue is settled other than on its merits are sometimes necessary, but they are never desirable. If the arena in which the amateur acts is the city and the question at hand a limited one, his tendency is to endow the issue with generality—either by making it a national issue or by finding in it wider implications. The amateur takes the outcome of politics—the determination of policies and the choice of officials—seriously, in the sense that he feels a direct concern for what he thinks are the ends these policies serve and the qualities these officials possess. He is not oblivious to considerations of partisan or personal advantage in assessing the outcome but (in the pure case) he dwells on the relation of outcome to his conception, be it vague or specific, of the public weal. Although politics may have attractions as a game of skill, it is never simply that.

The professional, on the other hand—even the "professional" who practices politics as a hobby rather than as a vocation—is preoccupied with the outcome of politics in terms of winning or losing. Politics, to him, consists of concrete questions and specific persons who must be dealt with in a manner that will "keep everybody happy" and thus minimize the possibility of defeat at the next election. The professional politician rarely broods about his function in society, the larger significance of the issues with which he deals, or the consistency of his procedures with some well-worked-out theory of democracy. Although he is not oblivious to the ends implied by political outcomes, he sees (or, since he is rarely given to theorizing, acts as if he sees) the good of society as the by-product of efforts that are aimed, not at producing the good society, but at gaining power and place for one's self and one's party.

The principal reward of politics to the amateur is the sense of having satisfied a felt obligation to "participate," and this satisfaction is greater the higher the value the amateur can attach to the ends which the outcomes of politics serve. The principal reward of the professional is to be found in the extrinsic satisfactions of participation—power, income, status, or the fun of the game. The ideal amateur

has a "natural" response to politics; he sees each battle as a "crisis," and each victory as a triumph and each loss as a defeat for a cause. The professional tends, by contrast, to develop a certain detachment toward politics and a certain immunity to its excitement and its outcomes.

The difficulty with this distinction is not only that it is somewhat overdrawn, but that its applicability tends to vary with the rank of the politician. Anyone with even a casual familiarity with amateur club politics in the Democratic party will object immediately that many so-called "amateurs," particularly those who seek elective office or who lead amateur clubs, are obviously and deeply ambitious, power-seeking, or eager for patronage in a way that is indistinguishable from the professional politician. This is true. Many, but not all, of the amateurs with long experience and personal stakes in politics acquire the habits and motives of the professional; indeed, it is entirely possible that an amateur club movement could not endure if there were not in it at least a few pseudo-amateurs who had made politics a career and who had a careerist's detachment about or even contempt for the "meaning" of politics.

This consideration raises the question of what, if anything, keeps all amateurs from either dropping out of politics or becoming professionals. If higher-ranking amateurs and professionals tend to become indistinguishable in motive, what keeps them distinguishable in style and rhetoric? In the long run, of course, it may well be that nothing keeps them apart; indeed, the brief course of most reform movements in American politics suggests that the amateur spirit cannot endure permanently. Eventually, the amateur either loses interest or becomes a professional and plays the game by professional rules. But in the short run at least—and perhaps . . . even in the long run— the sharp distinction between amateur and professional is maintained by the existence of amateur clubs.

The ultimate source of the amateur spirit is found in the expectations of the followers, not in the motives of the leaders. The amateur Democrats are not just a small caucus of notables but a large movement with, by any party's standards, a numerous and active rank and file. This rank-and-file is organized into neighborhood political clubs and it is these clubs which provide the principal resources of the amateur political leader. The need to maintain these clubs is the principal constraint that moves amateur leaders, whatever their private motives, to protect their "amateur standing" carefully. Whether or not the leaders are amateurs, they must act as if they are in order to take advantage of the resources which the clubs can offer. The militantly amateur political club, like the militant religious sect, does not tolerate a professional leadership and is quick to detect and criticize those who reveal some relativity of attitude, detachment of spirit, or selfishness of ambition. . . .

Even among the amateur leaders, however, there are men and women who are genuinely disinterested; not all, or perhaps even most, amateur leaders are ambitious men clever at manipulating the slogans of reform or liberalism. Among the group which came of age politically after the Second World War, there were both ambitious opportunists and dedicated idealists. A major point of this analysis, however, is that, in certain areas and for certain largely fortuitous reasons, ambition was harnessed to idealism and both the opportunist and the visionary were led to play the same game. In these areas, a new generation of leaders saw that a challenge to established party rulers could be made by mobilizing the chronic discontent among certain members of the educated, urban middle class and directing it into primary election contests. To organize this discontent, one had to demonstrate that he was more concerned with issues and candidates than with personal success or organizational maintenance. This placed constraints on ambition. And, added to the ambitious, there were articulate men in leading positions in the clubs who genuinely cared neither for personal political success nor for perpetuating a party organization, and these men, by demonstrating their disinterested, idealistic, and even ascetic approach to politics could set the tone for the movement as a whole by providing standards against which all others could be judged.

New political leadership in times of party crisis or organizational decay is frequently provided by young men who are politically "marginal"—who stand between two worlds, the old and the new, the ascendant and the dying, and who because of their unique position can create a new alliance which will perpetuate the political system. Typically they have a background which symbolizes different and even competing values in the community. For example, one might be an Irish Catholic with a Harvard education and an intellectual manner; another might be the liberal scion of a conservative, Main Line Philadelphia family; a third an able Jewish lawyer with a heavily Puerto Rican and Negro clientele; a fourth a respectable Italian businessman with close connections in the underworld. New groups can be brought into politics or new coalitions formed between formerly warring elements through the mediation of such marginal politicians. In some cases, however, circumstances are such that these men lead, not a new coalition which restores the political equilibrium under a modified version of the conventional rules, but instead a frontal assault on the very foundation of the old political system which requires a radical redistribution of power in the community. This can occur when the new leaders find themselves, usually for reasons beyond their control, in charge of an army of new entrants to politics—a group of idealistic amateurs who are a new force to be reckoned with. Being at the head of such an army places constraints on the leaders which often prevent them from negotiating a new alliance among professional politicians under the old rules; instead, the expectations of their amateur followers require them to challenge, not simply certain professionals, but the very concept of professionalism itself.

The source of these expectations which account for the behavior of the amateur seems to be found in a "political ethic" which has been characteristic of the Anglo-Saxon, Yankee Protestant middle class in the United States and which is profoundly different from the political ethic of the immigrant, the Eastern and Southern European workers, and perhaps from that of the lower classes generally. Richard Hofstadter has given an excellent description of these competing political ethics in his book, *The Age of Reform.* One ethic,

"founded upon the indigenous Yankee-Protestant political traditions, and upon middle-class life, assumed and demanded the constant, disinterested activity of the citizen in public affairs, argued that political life ought to be run, to a greater degree than it was, in accordance with general principles and abstract laws apart from and superior to personal needs, and expressed a common feeling that government should be in good part an effort to moralize the lives of individuals while economic life should be intimately related to the stimulation and development of individual character.

"[In contrast,] the other system, founded upon the European backgrounds of the immigrants, upon their unfamiliarity with independent political action, their familiarity with hierarchy and authority, and upon the urgent needs that so often grew out of their migration, took for granted that the political life of the individual would arise out of family needs, interpreted political and civic relations chiefly in terms of personal obligations, and placed strong personal loyalties above allegiance to abstract codes of laws and morals."[1]

The political ethic of the immigrant became, of course, the basis of the big-city political machine, while the ethic of the Yankee Protestant became the basis for civic reform and assaults on that machine. Today, powerful, city-wide machines of the old style are hard to find; Chicago may be the only important example remaining. But the ethic of the machine persists, in modified form, in the habits of professional politicians for whom the value of organization and leadership are indisputable, personal loyalties and commitments remain indispensable, and the lower-class basis of the big-city electorate is unchanging. Similarly, contemporary amateur politicians are critical of the naïveté of older reform efforts which sought to capture elective offices without first capturing the party organization. Nonetheless, the essence of the reform ethic persists: the desire to moralize public life, the effort to rationalize power with law, and the insistence that correct goals will be served only if goals are set and officials selected by correct procedures. . . .

In [professional] organizations, the extrinsic rewards of politics may be intangible, but they are by and large unrelated to issues, the ends of government, the abstract desirability of citizen participation, or the need for the "better element" to control the party. Rather, the intangible rewards of the professional arise from the prestige, sociability, and personal loyalties which politics can provide: being a "big man" to one's neighbors, placing voters under an obligation to one's self, expressing one's gratitude to a district leader from whom a favor was received, taking pride in the congratulations from the leader when one has "delivered" his district or precinct, or simply being able to meet regularly with one's neighbors and friends as one canvasses for votes or petition signatures and thus overcome loneliness or boredom. An amateur may derive some of these satisfactions also, but not in a club where there is not at least a verbal concern for issues and "reform"; the professional, on the other hand, gets more out of politics precisely in those clubs where no one upsets pleasant relations with issues and reforms. When an amateur club splits into factions, the issues at stake quickly become infused with ideology; when a professional club suffers from internal friction, it is in the nature of a family fight over ethnic claims, the division of patronage, or the conflict of personalities: in short, over the rupture of *personal* ties. For the amateur politician, personal ties are mediated through a nexus of general ideas; for the professional, they are direct. Thus, an essential aspect of an amateur's relation to politics is that he is what Robert K. Merton has called a "cosmopolitan"; the professional, on the other hand, is a "local."

A local, from whose ranks most professional politicians are drawn, is a person who is preoccupied with the local community to the exclusion of affairs outside his community.[2] He is "parochial," and has lived in his community for many years, knows many people and is anxious to know more, and defines power in terms of interpersonal influence based on a network of friendships. He joins organizations which are local in order to avail himself of contacts and in order to associate himself with the broadest, most widely accepted symbols of community integration. A cosmopolitan, on the other hand, is a person with minimal ties to the locality but a strong attachment to "the Great Society" of national and international problems, ideas, movements, fashions, and culture. He is often a recent arrival to the community and, if it is small, anxious to move on to large cities which are themselves "cosmopolitan." He is selective in his friendships, seeks out other cosmopolitans, joins organizations which have a professional and civic flavor, and endeavors to be influential through the display of his *expertise* and special skills. His attachment is to symbols

[1] *The Age of Reform* (New York: Vintage Books, 1960), p. 9.
[2] Robert K. Merton, "Patterns of Influence; Local and Cosmopolitan Influentials," in *Social Theory and Social Structure*, rev. ed. (Glencoe, Ill.: The Free Press, 1957), pp. 387-420.

which are not widely shared but esoteric and which are, thus, often divisive rather than integrating for the community as a whole.

Professional politicians, even those who do not earn their living in politics, are usually drawn from the ranks of the locals. The local is a man who can himself symbolize the shared sentiments of the community rather than any special set of ends or virtues. The most successful local politician is able, as George H. Mead said, "to enter into the attitudes of the group and mediate between them by making his own experience universal, so that others can enter into this form of communication through him."[3] These qualities are uniquely those which enable a man to grasp the motives of others by entering imaginatively into their feelings, and, by understanding them, turning these motives to his own benefit. A cosmopolitan often lacks these qualities, for to him, action is or ought to be governed by general principles. If he should enter politics, as the club leaders have, he must rely on the force of his ideas and the worth of his principles to provide him with standing and insure his success. This is a very difficult undertaking. . . .

Because the amateur is attracted to politics by principles, there is some overlap between those who are interested in a politics of principle and those who are, in a broad sense, intellectuals. But the overlap between the world of intellectuals and the world of club politics is not great, for although many amateur politicians, particularly in the Democratic party, are intellectual "consumers," few are intellectual "producers." As intellectual consumers, they may be engaged in disseminating cultural or intellectual products (as are teachers and journalists), in applying them (as are lawyers and physicians), or simply in enjoying them by having a style of life which is vaguely intellectual (as do people who collect books, recordings of serious music, and works of art). There is, however, a striking shortage of intellectual producers such as creative scholars, artists, and writers. Few university professors of stature are found active in club politics, and serious writers are usually active in politics, if at all, at a different level (for example, as contributors to liberal or conservative periodicals). Amateur, club-based politics can be found in certain parts of the Republican party as well as in the Democratic, and here the overlap between intellectuals and amateur politicians is, one suspects, even less.

The relative absence of professors is a complex phenomenon. In part it is because, as in New York, professors do not live in great numbers in the central city. But there is little academic participation in amateur politics even where, as in Chicago, almost the entire faculty of the university lives in the center city in the area of greatest amateur club activity. And there participation has been declining rather than growing. . . .

In California Democratic clubs around the University of California at Los Angeles and the California Institute of Technology, university teachers are from time to time active as club officers or candidates for assemblyman or congressman, but such men are almost always younger, relatively unknown academics who often are engaged in politics as a kind of substitute for scholarly research and publication. Prominent and ambitious university personnel are rarely in amateur politics or noted as spokesmen on behalf of amateur political causes; those who are involved are usually neither prominent nor productive.

The club movement has attracted many kinds of people to it, and no single description will suffice for all, but to a great extent the principal shared characteristics are precisely those which support the description of them as cosmopolitan, intellectually oriented amateurs. For the most part, they are young, well-educated professional people, including a large number of women. In style of life, they are distinctly middle- and upper-middle class; in mood and outlook, they are products of the generation which came of age after the Second World War and particularly after the Korean conflict; in political beliefs, they are almost entirely among the liberals of the left. They bring to politics a concern for ideas and ideals.

In Manhattan, between one-half and three-fourths of the members of three clubs studied were under forty years of age. Not only were they young, they were fairly recent arrivals to the city. Over three-fourths did not live in their present neighborhood before 1949, and between one-half and two-thirds did not live there before 1953. Many were raised in New York, but most had left home to attend a university and had only recently returned. Between two-thirds and three-fourths had not joined a political club before 1957.

[3]George Herbert Mead, *Mind, Self, and Society* (Chicago: University of Chicago Press, 1934), p. 257.

In two of the three clubs examined, over half of the members were of Jewish background; on the other hand, there were very few Catholics, never more than 10 per cent of the total. Only in one club did the proportion of married people exceed one-third; the rest were single, separated, or divorced. Often those who were married were childless; although about 30 per cent of the members were married, only 10 per cent had a family. Most club members, at least the most active ones, appeared to be sufficiently young and lacking in extensive family or professional obligations so that a considerable amount of time and energy could be devoted to politics. Often husband and wife were both club members; presumably this reduced the problems which might result if one or the other were perennially absent on political tasks. The wives of volunteer politicians were not, unlike their Tammany counterparts, the kind of women who were likely to remain at home and raise children while husbands pre-empted all the diversions and excitement of political activity. Many of the married but childless women in reform politics were anxious not to let marriage and the demands of a husband's career compel them to give up their interests, "lose their personalities," or become absorbed by household duties.

Lawyers represented between one-tenth and one-sixth of the membership but a much higher percentage (in one case, half) of the officers and activists. Nearly a quarter of the members of two clubs were in what are described as the "communications" business — public relations, advertising, journalism, editing, publishing, radio, and television. There were often as many members from medicine (physicians, psychiatrists, nurses) as from law, a rather striking fact given the general beliefs about the reluctance of such persons to become associated with political or controversial causes. Business, service, and clerical occupations accounted for one-fourth to one-third of the membership.

The backgrounds of the officers show even greater similarities. Officers were far more likely to be male, married, Jewish, and lawyers. In 1960, there were 36 men and women nominated for office in the Lexington Democratic Club, the oldest of the reform organizations. Of these, 26 were men and 10 women. Of the 34 who had graduated from college 19 had attended the desirable schools of the Ivy League. The majority (20) had completed law school and were practicing law in New York City (mostly with firms in and around Wall Street). Most of the rest were in public relations, advertising, the theater, college teaching, radio and television, and so on. Of the five who were in other businesses, most were associated with investment houses. In many cases, these young professionals were academically distinguished: there were 16 instances of school honors, including five Phi Beta Kappa members, two teaching fellows, and at least two law review editors. Although no precise determination of ethnic background is available, a rough estimate based on family name suggests that there were about 20 or 21 Jewish and 15 or 16 non-Jewish candidates for office.

When another reform club, the Riverside Democrats, was organized in 1957, all eight of its officers were college graduates and seven had done graduate work in prestigious eastern universities such as Harvard, Yale, Columbia, and Princeton. Despite the fact that the Seventh Assembly District, in which the Riverside Club was organized, includes Morningside Heights and Columbia University, there were few academic personnel associated with the club. No officer and only one member of the nineteen-man board of directors was a university teacher.[4]

The ranks of the amateur politicians seem constantly to be replenished by new, young recruits as age, professional preoccupations, or family responsibilities cause older members to fall away. Many stay active in the movement only while they are still on the lower rungs of their career ladders. As a result, there is a high turnover of activists.

Essentially the same kinds of people are found in club politics in California as in New York. The active members of eight clubs studied in Los Angeles County in early 1961 were similar to club members in Manhattan in most respects. Over half were under forty years of age, over 60 per cent had a college education or better, most were in professional occupations, and practically no one was Catholic while nearly half were Jewish in their religious background. (But not in their current beliefs. A large number of respondents from a Jewish background took the trouble to write on their questionnaires that they were no longer believers.) Contrary to the observations of some who have interpreted the California club movement as an organization providing social contact and a sense of belonging

[4]Robert Lekachman, "How We Beat the Machine," *Commentary*, April, 1958, 292.

for the rootless, newly arrived intelligentsia in this rapidly growing state, the overwhelming bulk of club members who responded were, by California standards, old-time residents. Over 80 per cent had lived in the state ten years or more, and nearly half had lived there twenty or more. But there were some differences between New York and California as well. Among California club members there was a higher proportion of older people (over one-third were fifty-five years of age or older), a somewhat larger number were married and had children, and more had belonged to the clubs for a considerable period of time (many California clubs are much older than the reform clubs in Manhattan).

THE FUNCTION OF PARTIES

Political parties perform, to some degree, at least three functions in a democratic government. They recruit candidates, mobilize voters, and assemble power within the formal government. . . . All three party functions will in some degree be performed differently by amateur as contrasted to professional politicians. . . .

The professional, for whom politics primarily has extrinsic rewards, is preoccupied with maintaining his position in party and elective offices. Winning is essential, although sometimes electoral victory must be subordinated to maintaining the party organization.[5] Candidates will be selected on the basis of their electoral appeal. A ticket will be constructed which maximizes this appeal by offering "representation" to candidates of important ethnic, religious, racial, and nationality groups and to important geographic regions and civil divisions. This is the "balanced" ticket. Since most voters support parties out of traditional allegiances, these traditional loyalties will be reinforced. Added to them will be appeals to "interests" — private advantage, sectional loyalties, and ethnic and nationality claims. Issues will be avoided except in the most general terms or if the party is confident that a majority supports its position. Should a contrary position on the same issue seem best suited for winning a majority at the next election, the party will try to change or at least mute its position. Votes will be mobilized not only by such appeals but also by personal contacts through precinct captains. These workers will appeal to the voter on the basis of party loyalty and personal friendship; sometimes material inducements (money, favors, jobs) will be offered. To the extent that the party

can enable its candidates to win by providing them with these resources (loyalty to a party name, a balanced ticket, appeals to interests, and the efforts of party workers), it places them under an obligation to it. Re-election without party support would be costly (in terms of money, time, effort, obtaining support from new groups in exchange for commitments to programs, and so forth). Since the party enables the candidate, in effect, to economize, his behavior in office can be controlled to some extent by threatening not to re-slate him for office if he acts independently. In this way, and through the distribution of patronage and money, the party is able to assemble power in the government.

The amateur politician, on the other hand, would in the ideal situation prefer to recruit candidates on the basis of their commitment to a set of policies. Voters would be mobilized by appeals to some set of principles or goals. The party would be held together and linked to the voter by a shared conception of the public interest. A politics of principle would necessarily attach little value to — and indeed would criticize — appeals to private, group, or sectional interest. Private interests, which for the professional are the motive force of politics, the amateur would consider irrelevant, irrational, or immoral. The task of assembling power in the formal government would be met, not by using sanctions to discipline elective officials, but by electing to those posts candidates who were committed to the policies of the party and who would therefore act in concert, not from coercion, but out of conviction. Amateur politicians thus seek to alter fundamentally the way in which the functions of parties are carried out. Instead of serving as neutral agents which mobilize majorities for whatever candidates and programs seem best suited to capturing public fancy, the parties would become the sources of program and the agents of social change. They would control the behavior of public officials by internalized convictions rather than external threats and for the purpose of realizing certain social policies rather than of enhancing the party's prospects for retaining power in the next election. . . .

. . . The amateur asserts that principles, rather than interest, ought to be both the end and motive of political action. Government should not only serve desirable goals, but the power

[5]James Q. Wilson, "The Economy of Patronage," *Journal of Political Economy*, LXIX (August 1961), 369-380.

to attain them ought to be assembled by appealing to those ends. Politicians ought to work for certain ends, not because such action is expedient or self-serving, but because they are convinced of the intrinsic worth of those ends.

This approach stands in sharp contrast to the actions of professional politicians who behave as if they believed that politics, like other forms of human activity, only occurs when individuals can realize their private aims and maximize their self-interest. Public policies are the by-product of political self-seeking just as the distribution of goods and services is the by-product of economic self-seeking. In both cases, the incentive for individual action is not the same as the ends served by the system as a whole. The social function of human action is not the reason that action is undertaken.

The amateur politicians maintain, in effect, that the ends of government and the incentives for political action ought to be identical. Many economists, as Anthony Downs has pointed out, have tacitly agreed with this theory by assuming that the government ought to act to maximize a "social welfare function" and that it in fact will act in this way because the end is intrinsically desirable.[6] There is thus a general intellectual tradition which supports the view that government officials do or should act in a disinterested manner, as contrasted to businessmen and party bosses who act out of "selfish" motives.

A fundamental question . . . is whether a democratic society is better served by a system in which the motives of politicians are identical with their social function or by a system in which motives and social function are unrelated. The amateur subscribes, by and large, to the sometimes unspoken assumption that desirable social policy can only or best result from action undertaken out of a desire to see that policy realized. But there is no reason why this should always be the case. In fact, when one considers economic activities, most people will quickly agree that the desirable consequences of that activity (the distribution of goods and services in some manner) are usually the result of activity undertaken for self-serving reasons (the attempt to maximize individual utilities). To be sure, a socialist will argue that the best distribution of goods and services is only achieved when production and distribution are undertaken out of community-regarding rather than private-regarding motives; thus the slogans, "production

for use, not profit," and distribution "to each according to his needs (or abilities)." But most amateur Democrats, though liberals, are not socialists; indeed, many of them are conspicuously successful in their economic occupations and will defend the consequences of action undertaken to maximize their wages or profits. But although they may not be economic socialists, they act as if they desired to "socialize" politics. Obviously, they are convinced that politics must be based on principle even though economics is based on interest.

This anomaly is seen most clearly, of course, when the amateur politician is a conservative Republican rather than a liberal Democrat. The amateur conservative typically is outspoken in favor of an economic system which depends on the pursuit of private interests to provide a common good through the intervention of the "invisible hand" of which Adam Smith wrote; at the same time, the conservative urges politicians to act on principle.

EVALUATING THE AMATEUR DEMOCRAT

Since people who read books about politics are likely to be instinctively sympathetic to the aims, if not the achievements, of amateur politicians, the contrast (necessarily oversimplified) between the amateur and the professional sketched [here] may make the choice appear an easy one. Politicians, one immediately feels, *ought* to be high-minded and committed to policies; they *ought* to "talk sense" to voters rather than rely on empty slogans, selfish appeals, and political payoffs; elective officials *ought* to vote and act on the basis of conscience rather than at the dictate of party "bosses." But the choice is not a simple one. An amateur politics of principle may make certain highly valued ends difficult or impossible to attain, whereas a politics of interest may, under certain circumstances, realize these ends much more easily. Institutions should be judged by the ends they serve, not by the motives of their members, and on this basis it is an open question whether the professional politician is not the person best equipped to operate a democratic government in a way that will produce desirable policies. A preoccupation with the propriety of methods, while a legitimate concern, can be carried too far. No one used the power of patronage more

[6]Anthony Downs, *An Economic Theory of Democracy* (New York: Harper & Brothers, 1957), pp. 280-286.

ruthlessly than Abraham Lincoln; no one appealed more cleverly or more successfully to "irrational" sentiments of nationalism and race pride than Fiorello H. La Guardia; no one relied more heavily on big-city machines than Franklin D. Roosevelt.

Adlai Stevenson, the man who, more than anyone, has served as the patron saint of the amateur politicians, voiced similar concerns when he raised but did not answer these questions:

"It does not belittle the movement to ask some questions, as a perceptive California friend of mine has done, about at least the West-Coast type of club development. What are the effects of an almost exclusively 'ideological' political motivation? Is some degree of instability the likely price of a lack of the restraint of economic interest and of part-time interest in politics? What are the implications of all-out election campaigning by highly vocal groups who assume little responsibility for legislative follow-up of either their nominees or their programs? What is necessary to prevent hit-and-run politics—even by one's highest minded political friends? These seem to be worthwhile questions."[7]

These questions can be placed in perspective by suggesting some historical parallels. America has had many experiences with political reform, and although the goals and strategies of the reformers have changed from decade to decade, the essential features of the reform mentality have not. The Yankee Protestant political ethic can be detected in the writings of the municipal reformers, the advocates of the direct primary, and the supporters of party reform.

Each successive political reform has proved many times to be either unattainable or defective, and hence the aims of the reformers have steadily shifted. The commission form of government advocated by reformers did not prevent Frank Hague from becoming the boss of Jersey City. The initiative and the referendum are devices often used, not for "direct democracy," but for overloading state constitutions with amendments protecting special-interest groups. The direct primary has, at least in some states, weakened party organization to the point that responsibility for government action is diffuse and hard to assign. The 1936 reforms in New York City resulted in a charter which was

workable for Fiorello La Guardia but apparently for no other mayor, since the changes praised by the reformers in 1936 were damned by them fifteen years later. Cross-filing, once hailed in California as a device for returning government to the people, became, to a later generation of reformers, an obstacle to good government which they labored mightily to eliminate. Nonpartisanship proved to be ineffective in Chicago because the machine continued to control "nonpartisan" aldermanic elections; in Detroit and Los Angeles, on the other hand, it proved to be so effective that liberal amateurs now regard it as a principal institutional block to the success of the Democratic party at the local level.

At the same time, there have been certain reforms which have attained some of the goals of their proponents. Civil service legislation, where it has been enacted and defended, has unquestionably reduced, if not eliminated, patronage. The city manager form of government has taken hold in 38 per cent of all American cities (although in only 6 per cent of those over 500,000 population)....

...Throughout this century, there has always been a "reform mentality" in American politics and in this broad sense the amateur Democrats have their forebearers in the Progressive and municipal reform efforts of fifty years ago. The non-business urban middle class has sought to implement the Yankee political ethic. That many, if not most, contemporary amateurs are Jews, while the earlier group was Anglo-Saxon Protestant, has not affected the premises of the reform mentality, for the Jewish tradition is similar in most important respects.

Today, the major thrust of the liberals active in local party politics has been, not to institute the direct primary, but to take advantage of it. The hopes of the early reformers had been dashed; the procedural reforms in strong-party states such as Illinois had not led to the emergence of "good" leaders, and in weak-party states such as California the procedural reforms had led to a situation in which virtually no leaders at all, good or bad, could emerge. And there were still some states, such as New York, where no procedural reforms had been adopted (in great part because they had always been two-party states). It was obvious that reforms were not enough; those concerned with improving the quality of

[7]Adlai Stevenson, "So You Want To Be in Politics?" Review of *Elm Street Politics*, by Stephen A. Mitchell, in *New York Times Book Review*, April 12, 1959, p. 1.

public life would have to enter it on a long-term basis in order to *become* the leaders which they had originally hoped the new mechanisms would generate spontaneously. . . .

IN DEFENSE OF THE AMERICAN PARTY SYSTEM
Edward C. Banfield

The party primary and the amateur club are two responses to a perceived flaw in American political parties: their issuelessness and their consequent lack of correspondence with the will of their adherents. This is by no means the only flaw that critics have found. In 1950 a highly respected group of political scientists wrote on behalf of the American Political Science Association a critical analysis of party operation in the United States.* The heart of the analysis and the series of recommendations flowing from it was that parties today fail to distinguish themselves sufficiently from one another; the result is that the electorate is given no distinct choices among candidates and issues through which they may "speak" in a clear voice. In a similar vein, other prominent political scientists have pressed for greater internal homogeneity in party ideology and for sharper differentiation of the parties along "liberal" and "conservative" lines.

The remaining two selections in this chapter deal in quite different ways with criticisms of contemporary American parties. Banfield strongly disagrees with those who find the *status quo* seriously at odds with democratic objectives. Downs indicates why a two-party system tends to generate more-or-less indistinguishable party ideologies, implying that reforms designed to separate two parties ideologically would be effective only for a short time.

The American party system has been criticized on four main grounds: (1) The parties do not offer the electorate a choice in terms of fundamental principles; their platforms are very similar and mean next to nothing; (2) they cannot discipline those whom they elect, and therefore they cannot carry their platforms into effect; (3) they are held together and motivated less by political principle than by desire for personal, often material, gain, and by sectional and ethnic loyalties; consequently party politics is personal and parochial; and (4) their structure is such that they cannot correctly represent the opinion of the electorate; in much of the country there is in effect only one party, and everywhere large contributors and special interests

exercise undue influence within the party. . . .

If [critics] were to evaluate the party system on the basis of results, they would have to conclude that on the whole it is a good one. It has played an important part . . . in the production of a society which, despite all its faults, is as near to being a good one as any and nearer by far than most; it has provided governments which, by the standards appropriate to apply to governments, have been humane and, in some crises, bold and enterprising; it has done relatively little to impede economic growth and in some ways has facilitated it; except for the Civil War, when it was, as Henry Jones Ford said, "the last bond of union to give way,"[1] it has tended to check violence, moderate conflict, and narrow the cleavages within the society; it has never produced, or very seriously threatened to produce, either mob rule or tyranny, and it has shown a marvelous ability to adapt to changing circumstances. . . .

. . . [The critics] are in error when they do not recognize that other values of equal or greater importance are often in conflict with democratic procedure, and that when they are, some sacrifice of it is essential in order to serve the other values adequately. If they faced up to the necessity of assigning priorities among all of the relevant ends, they would not, it is safe to say, put "democratic procedure" first. Probably they, and most Americans, would order the ends as follows:

1. The party system must above all else provide governments having the will and capacity to preserve the society and to protect its members. Any sacrifice in other ends ought to be accepted if it is indispensable to securing this end.

From "In Defense of the American Party System" in Robert A. Goldwin, ed., *Political Parties, U.S.A.* (Chicago: Rand McNally & Company, 1964), pp. 21-39.
*American Political Science Association, *Toward a More Responsible Two-Party System* (New York: Rinehart & Company, Inc., 1950).
[1]Henry Jones Ford, *The Rise and Growth of American Politics* (New York: The Macmillan Company, 1900), p. 303.

2. The party system must insure periodic opportunity to change the government by free elections. Any sacrifice of other ends (except the one above) ought to be accepted if it is indispensable to securing this one.

3. The party system should promote the welfare of the people. By "welfare" is meant some combination of two kinds of values: "principles," what is thought to be good for the society, described in rather general terms, and "interests," the ends individuals and groups seek to attain for their own good, as distinguished from that of the society. The party system should produce governments that assert the supremacy of principles over interests in some matters; in others it should allow interests to prevail and should facilitate the competitive exercise of influence.

4. The party system should moderate and restrain such conflict as would threaten the good health of the society. Other conflict it should not discourage.

5. The party system should promote and exemplify democracy, meaning reasonable discussion of matters affecting the common good in which every voice is heard.

These ends have been listed in what most Americans would probably consider a descending order of importance. In devising a party system, we ought not to try to serve fully each higher end before serving the one below it at all. The first two ends are exceptions to this rule, however: each of them must be attained even if the others are not served at all. With respect to the remaining three, the problem is to achieve a proper balance— one such that no reallocation from one end to another would add to the sum of value.

Finally, we must realize that we can rarely make important social changes by intention. The most we can do is to make such minor changes as may be consistent with, and more or less implied by, the fixed features of the situation in which we are placed. Even to make minor changes in an institution like a political party requires influence of a kind and amount that no group of reformers is likely to have or to be able to acquire. It is idle to propose reforms that are merely desirable. There must also be some possibility of showing, if only in a rough and conjectural way, that they might be carried into effect.

With respect to the American party system, it seems obvious that the crucial features of the situation are all fixed. The size of our country, the class and cultural heterogeneity of our people, the number and variety of their interests, the constitutionally-given fragmentation of formal authority, the wide distribution of power which follows from it, the inveterate taste of Americans for participation in the day-to-day conduct of government when their interests are directly at stake—these are all unalterable features of the situation. Taken together, they mean that the party system can be reformed only within very narrow limits.

A MODEL PARTY SYSTEM

Let us imagine a system free of the alleged defects of ours. In this model system, every citizen is motivated—highly so—by political principles, not subsidiary ones, but ones having to do with the very basis of the society.... The electoral system, moreover, is such as to give every side on every issue exactly the weight that its numbers in the population warrant; no group or interest is over- or under-represented....

Assuming that the society is divided by the usual number of cleavages...the following would result:

1. There would be a great many parties, for no citizen would support a party with which he did not agree fully.

2. The parties would tend to be single-issue ones. If logically unrelated issues (for instance, segregation and isolationism) were linked together in a party program, only those voters would support the party who chanced to be on the same side of all of the linked issues. The number of these voters would decrease as the number of issues so linked increased.

3. Parties would be short-lived. They would come into and pass out of existence with the single issues they were organized to fight.

4. In their election campaigns and propaganda, parties would emphasize their single defining principles. This would tend to widen the cleavages along which the parties were formed.

5. Ideological issues, not practical problems, would constitute the substance of politics.

6. The number of such issues pressing for settlement at any one time (but being incapable of settlement because of their ideological character) would always be more than the system could accommodate.

7. Coalitions of parties would seldom form, and such as did form would be highly unstable. Party leaders would find compromise almost impossible because it would lead to loss of highly principled supporters.

8. Coalitions of parties being unstable, governments would also be unstable and therefore lacking in power and decision.

9. Those selected for positions of political leadership would tend to be ideologues skilled in party dialectics and symbolizing the party and its positions. Practical men, especially those with a talent for compromise and those symbolizing qualities common to the whole society, would be excluded from politics.

10. Matters having no ideological significance (a category that includes most local issues) would either be endowed with a spurious one or else would be left outside the sphere of politics altogether.

These points should suffice to show that a system with a perfectly democratic structure would not produce results acceptable in terms of the criteria listed above.

Now let us introduce into the model system one of the alleged defects which the critics find most objectionable in the American party system. Let us suppose that at least half of the electorate is prevailed upon to exchange its vote in matters of fundamental principle for advantages that have nothing to do with principle, especially private profit, sectional gain, and nationality "recognition."

One effect of this would be to reduce greatly the intensity of ideological conflict and to make political life more stable and conservative. . . .

Another effect would be to encourage the formation of a few (probably two) stable parties. These might begin as alliances among the profit-minded, the sectional-minded, and the nationality-minded, but to attract support from principled voters the parties would have to seem to stand for something—indeed, for anything and everything. Since no faction of them could hope to win an election by itself, principled voters would attach themselves to those parties that they found least objectionable. The parties would develop corporate identities and mystiques; principled voters would then subordinate their differences out of "loyalty" to the party and in response to its demands for "regularity." Competition for middle-of-the-road support would cause the parties to offer very similar programs. This competition might lead to there

being only two parties, but this result would probably be insured by introducing another supposed defect into the system: a principle of representation (single-member districts and plurality voting) which, by letting the winner take all, would force small parties to join large ones in order to have some chance of winning.

In one way or another, the "defects" of the system would tend to produce these consequences—consequences which have in fact been produced in the United States:

1. A strong and stable government would be possible. The country would be governed by the party that won the election, or (given the particular complexities of the American system) by two closely similar parties engaged in give-and-take and, therefore, in a sense constituting one party under two names.

2. There would be a high degree of continuity between administrations elected from different parties. Elections would not shake the nation to its foundations because the competing parties would be fundamentally in agreement. Agreement would be so built in by countless compromises within the parties (each of which would be under the necessity of attracting middle-of-the-road support) that a change of party would seldom entail complete reversal of policy in an important matter.

3. There would exist many substructures of power that would be largely or wholly impervious to the influence of political principle or ideology. "Machines"—party organizations of the profit-minded, the sectional-minded, and the nationality-minded—would not be inclined to offer pie in the sky or to stir the emotions of the masses because they could count upon getting their votes in other ways. These essentially apolitical centers of power would therefore exert a stabilizing and conservative influence throughout the political system. By making businesslike deals with the leaders of the "machines," the President could sometimes buy freedom to do as he thought best in matters of principle.

4. The diversity of the principles and the multiplicity of the interests within the party would be another source of strength to the leader elected from it. He could afford to offend some elements of the party on any particular question because there would be enough other elements unaffected (or even gratified) to assure his position. The more fragmented his

party, the less attention he would have to pay to any one fragment of it.

5. The assertion of interests (as distinguished from principles) would be encouraged. The profit-minded, the sectional-minded, and the nationality-minded would in effect give up representation on matters of principle in order to get it on matters involving their interests. Thus two different systems of representation would work simultaneously. The party leader would act as a trustee, disregarding interests in favor of principles. ("Congress represents locality, the President represents the nation," Ford wrote in 1898.)[2] Meanwhile legislators dependent on machines and, in general, on profit-minded, sectional-minded, and nationality-minded voters would act as agents of interests. The trustee of principles (the President) and the agents of interests (Congressmen) would of necessity bargain with each other; by allowing the agents of interests some successes—but only in this way—the trustee of principles could win their support in the matters he considered most important. Thus, there would be achieved that balancing of interests and of interests against principles (the most important principles usually being vindicated) that a good party system should produce.

6. The formation of deep cleavages would nevertheless be discouraged. The competition of the parties for the middle-of-the-road vote; their tendency to select practical men of wide popular appeal, rather than ideologues, for positions of leadership; and the definition of the politicians' task as being that of finding the terms on which people who disagree will work together, rather than that of sharpening ideological points—these would all be unifying tendencies. . . .

MAKING PARTIES "RESPONSIBLE"

Some think that the American party system can be reformed without changing its nature essentially. Several years ago, a Committee on Parties of the American Political Science Association proposed making certain "readjustments" in the structure and operation of the party system to eliminate its "defects." These readjustments, the Committee said, would give the electorate "a proper range of choice between alternatives" in the form of programs to which the parties would be committed and which they would have sufficient internal cohesion to carry into effect. Thus,

the two-party system would be made more "responsible."[3]

What this means is not at all clear. "Responsibility" here seems to be a synonym for accountability, that is, the condition of being subject to being called to account and made to take corrective action in response to criticism. In the case of a party, this can mean nothing except going before an electorate, and in this sense all parties are by definition responsible. . . .

The hope that the two-party system might be made to offer a choice between distinct alternatives is illusory for at least two reasons. One is that a party which does not move to the middle of the road to compete for votes condemns itself to defeat and eventually, if it does not change its ways, to destruction. But even if this were not the case, the parties could not present the electorate with what reformers think of as "a valid choice." The reason is that the issues in our national life are such that there does not exist any one grand principle by which the electorate could be divided into two camps such that every voter in each camp would be on the "same" side of all issues. The idea of "left" and "right" is as close as we come to having such a grand principle, and it has little or no application to many issues. . . .

The hope that the parties might commit themselves to carry out their programs is also illusory. A party could do this only if its leaders were able to tell the President and the party members in Congress what to do, and could discipline them if they failed to do it. Therefore, unless, like the Russians, we were to have two sets of national leaders, one in governmental office and another much more important one in party office, it would be necessary for our elected leaders—in effect, the President, since only he and the Vice President are elected by the whole nation—to control the Congressmen and Senators of their party. This would be possible only if the President could deny reelection to members of Congress who did not support the party program. Thus, instead of merely bringing forward and electing candidates, as they do now, "responsible" parties would have to govern the country. We would

[2]Ibid., p. 187.
[3]Committee on Political Parties of the American Political Science Association, Toward a More Responsible Two-Party System (New York: Holt, Rinehart & Winston, Inc., 1950), pp. 1, 85.

have a parliamentary system with the President in a position somewhat like that of the British Prime Minister, except (a very important difference) that, not being a part of the legislature, he could not use it as a vehicle through which to exert his leadership. The legislature would in fact have no function at all.

This great shift of power to the President would remedy another "defect" in the party system: its receptivity to the demands of interest groups. With the President in full control of Congress, logrolling would cease or virtually cease. It would do so because no one could any longer make the President pay a price for assistance in getting legislation passed; the traders who now sell their bits and pieces of power to the highest bidders would have to lower their prices and would probably go out of business. With their opportunities for exercising influence vastly reduced, interest groups would be less enterprising both in their efforts to anticipate the effects of governmental action and in bringing their views to the attention of the policy makers.

The making of policy would thus pass largely into the hands of technical experts within the majority party, the White House, and the executive departments. These would be mindful of principles and impatient of interests. They would endeavor to make "coherent" policies, meaning, presumably, policies not based on compromise. In all important matters, however, "the public interest" would prove an insufficient guide; the experts, when confronted with the necessity of choosing between alternatives that were equally in the public interest— that is, when no authoritative, ultimate criterion of choice existed for them to apply— would by the very necessities of the case have to balance the competing values as best they could, which means that they would have to fall back upon their personal tastes or professional biases.[4] Thus they would do badly (but in the name of "impartial administration") what is now done reasonably well by the political process.

The destruction of political traders and of local centers of power would mean also that the President's power would derive from somewhat different sources than at present. Instead of relying upon logrolling and patronage to get the votes he would need in Congress, he would have to rely upon direct appeals to the electorate. To some extent he might manipulate

the electorate by charm and personality; TV and the arts of Madison Avenue would become more important in politics. But in order to get elected he would have to depend also, and to a greater extent, upon appeals to political principle or ideology. Whereas the political trader maintains his control by giving and withholding favors to individuals (a circumstance which makes his control both dependable in its operation and cheap), the President would have to maintain *his* by the uncertain and costly expedient of offering to whole classes of people— the farmer, the aged, the home owner, and so on—advantages that they would have only at each other's expense. If charm and the promise of "something for everybody" did not yield the amount of power he required to govern the country, the President might find it necessary to exploit whatever antagonisms within the society might be made to yield more power. Class and ethnic differences might in this event serve somewhat the same function as logrolling and patronage do now....

That a President might rely more upon appeals to political principle does not at all mean that better judgments or results would follow. For the discussion of principles would probably not be *serious;* it would be for the purpose of securing popular interest and consent, not of finding a wise or right course of action....

THE DANGER OF MEDDLING

A political system is an accident. It is an accumulation of habits, customs, prejudices, and principles that have survived a long process of trial and error and of ceaseless response to changing circumstance. If the system works well on the whole, it is a lucky accident—the luckiest, indeed, that can befall a society, for all of the institutions of the society, and thus its entire character and that of the human types formed within it, depend ultimately upon the government and the political order.

To meddle with the structure and operation of a successful political system is therefore the greatest foolishness that men are capable of. Because the system is intricate beyond comprehension, the chance of improving it in the ways intended is slight, whereas the danger of disturbing its working and of setting off a succession of unwanted effects that will extend throughout the whole society is great.

[4]This argument is developed in E. C. Banfield, *Political Influence* (Glencoe, Ill.: The Free Press, 1961), Ch. 12.

TWO PARTY COMPETITION AND SIMILARITY

Anthony Downs

Because the following excerpt is rather spare, some explanation may be of help. The analytical scale Downs uses assumes that equal numbers of voters hold the political beliefs indicated by the continuum markings 0, 25, 50, 75, and 100. For example, in a total electorate of one hundred thousand, 20,000 voters hold extreme left-wing views (zero on the scale), 20,000 voters hold extreme right-wing views (100 on the scale), and 20,000 maintain each of the other three ideological positions.

The two parties in a two-party system may initially develop ideologies that differentiate them sharply, Downs argues, but over a series of elections both parties will moderate their ideological stances — will "move toward each other" on the scale — in the following manner: When the two parties occupy the extreme positions (zero and 100), each attracts half, or 50,000, of the hypothetical 100,000 voters. The left party attracts those 40,000 voters whose ideologies place them at zero and 25 on the scale; the right party attracts those 40,000 voters whose ideologies place them at 100 and 75; and since the two parties are equidistant from the ideological center, the 20,000 voters at 50 split randomly — 10,000 for one party and 10,000 for the other. In order to garner more votes, the right party may decide to change its ideology and move to the 75 point on the scale. It then attracts 60,000 votes, because it is "closer" than the left party to the voters whose preferences are 100, 75, and 50. To counteract this gain by the right party, the left party is virtually forced to move to the 25 position, whereby it re-establishes the ideological balance between the two parties and regains an equal split of the total vote. Finally, each of the two parties in turn moves to the 50 position.

This is a very simple model with several obvious flaws that preclude its being entirely valid. In the excerpt, however, Downs introduces an important modification that would tend to keep the two parties from moving to exactly the same ideological position. In a portion of the article not reprinted here, he also adjusts the model to account for the fact that not all ideological positions are likely to attract equal numbers of adherents in the electorate. The model needs to be further adjusted to rectify its incorrect assumption that voters' ideologies are totally inflexible, that only parties can change points of view. Nevertheless, the basic dynamics of the model are sufficiently sound to retain relevance even when complications of the real world are brought into the picture.

Parties in a two-party system deliberately change their platforms so that they resemble one another. . . .

[To demonstrate this,] we borrow and elaborate upon an apparatus invented by Harold Hotelling. It first appeared in a famous article on spatial competition published in 1929, and was later refined by Arthur Smithies.[1] Our version of Hotelling's spatial market consists of a linear scale running from zero to 100 in the usual left-to-right fashion. To make this politically meaningful, we assume that political preferences can be ordered from left to right in a manner agreed upon by all voters. They need not agree on which point they personally prefer, only on the ordering of parties from one extreme to the other.

. . . If [for example] we assume that the left end of the scale represents full government control, and the right end means a completely free market, we can rank parties by their views on this issue in a way that might be nearly universally recognized as accurate. In order to coördinate this left-right orientation with our numerical scale, we will arbitrarily assume that the number denoting any party's position indicates the percentage of the economy it wants left in private hands (excluding those minimal state operations which even the most Hayekian economists favor). Thus the extreme left position is zero, and the extreme right is 100. Admittedly, this apparatus is unrealistic for the following two reasons: (1) actually each party is leftish on some issues and rightish on others, and (2) the parties designated as right wing extremists in the real world are for fascist control of the economy rather than free markets. However, we will ignore these limitations temporarily and see what conclusions of interest we can draw from this spatial analogy.

Both Hotelling and Smithies have already applied their versions of this model to politics.

From "The Statics and Dynamics of Party Ideologies," pp. 115-117 of *An Economic Theory of Democracy* by Anthony Downs. Copyright © 1957 by Harper & Brothers. Reprinted by permission of Harper & Row, Publishers.

[1]Harold Hotelling, "Stability in Competition," *The Economic Journal,* XXXIX (1929), 41-57, and Arthur Smithies, "Optimum Location in Spatial Competition," *The Journal of Political Economy,* XLIX (1941), 423-439.

Hotelling assumed that people were evenly spaced along the straight-line scale, and reasoned that competition in a two-party system would cause each party to move towards its opponent ideologically. Such convergence would occur because each party knows that extremists at its end of the scale prefer it to the opposition, since it is necessarily closer to them than the opposition party is. Therefore the best way for it to gain more support is to move toward the other extreme, so as to get more voters outside of it—i.e., to come between them and its opponent. As the two parties move closer together, they become more moderate and less extreme in policy in an effort to win the crucial middle-of-the-road voters, i.e., those whose views place them between the two parties. This center area becomes smaller and smaller as both parties strive to capture moderate votes; finally the two parties become nearly identical in platforms and actions. For example, if there is one voter at every point on the scale, and parties A and B start at points 25 and 75 respectively, they will move towards each other and meet at 50, assuming they move at the same speed (Fig. 1). Like the two grocery stores in Hotelling's famous example, they will converge on the same location until practically all voters are indifferent between them.

FIGURE 1

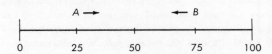

Note: Horizontal scale represents political orientation. Vertical scale represents number of citizens.

Smithies improved this model by introducing elastic demand at each point on the scale. Thus as the grocery stores moved away from the extremes, they lost customers there because of the increased cost of transportation; this checked them from coming together at the center. In our model, this is analogous to political extremists becoming disgusted at the identity of the parties, and refusing to vote for either if they become too much alike. At exactly what point this leakage checks the convergence of A and B depends upon how many extremists each loses by moving towards the center compared with how many moderates it gains thereby.

In another volume of this American Government Readings Series, Michael Reagan discusses political scientists' pretensions about being *scientists.*[1] He suggests that if political science is to have sufficient relevance to the real world, at least a few members of the profession will have to remain content to pursue their investigations and establish their policy recommendations on a basis of intellectual operations that are less than scientific. By "less than scientific" he means operations that do not approximate the natural scientist's controlled experiment. Alternatively, "scientific" can mean the use of statistical manipulation to determine with specific levels of certainty what contribution one or another independent variable makes to some observed political event (dependent variable).

Reagan is correct in seeing the necessity of, and defending the less-than-scientific political scientist. Interestingly, however, it is not this kind of political scientist whom lay people usually take to task. In spite of our culture's general awe for "science," we tend not to have much patience with those social scientists who, in the name of science, seem to produce articles, books, and other outputs that have little bearing on the immediate problems facing contemporary society.

Yet there is no *a priori* reason why political science must have direct relevance to present realities — no reason, that is, why it must address itself to the political questions that people engaged in government and politics want or need answered. Not all physicists or chemists — or, for that matter, mathematicians — are motivated in their work by a realization that what they discover will be of use to mankind in the solution of practical problems of health, shelter, survival, and so forth. As long as men treasure knowledge and discovery as intrinsically good, there will be room for the "irrelevancies," for the kinds of empirical investigation and theory-building that are sometimes characterized (rather grandly) as "pure science." Not all political scientists need be "engineers." In a similar vein, it is hoped that students do not always choose the books they read or the social science courses they take according to some calculation of immediate or eventual utility; hopefully, some of these choices are made be-cause of intrinsic interest, enjoyment, or excitement.

These comments are important to consider both in review of the readings that have been included in this volume and in looking ahead to developments in political science in the substantive areas of voting, interest groups, and parties. This group of readings was chosen not with the objective of creating a handbook for prospective candidates nor even for prospective voters. By presenting selections of description, quantitative empirical research, middle- and "grand"-level theory, I have tried to cast light on the subject of political involvement and activity from many angles and, in the process, to illustrate the many ways in which individual political scientists approach the study of a common subject.

These comments should not leave the impression, however, that scientific political analysts have nothing to contribute to immediate problem solving. On the contrary, they would insist that where statistical or experimental techniques can be used to solve immediate problems, these methods are much to be preferred in order to gain reliable knowledge. With this conviction, then, scientific political analysts devote a fair amount of attention to immediate problems. What they investigate strays from what laymen expect in that they draw somewhat different outside boundaries for their work: on the one hand, they conservatively tend to exclude the study of those immediate problems which cannot be handled scientifically (statistically or experimentally); and on the other hand, they extend their work boundaries to include theoretical problem solving that is of little interest to laymen and has little direct utility for politicians and others directly engaged in the political process.

RESEARCH PROSPECTS: VOTING AND PARTISANSHIP

Fortunately, many forms of research can be both intrinsically "good" and instrumentally helpful. This has tended to be the case with the study of voting, which has offered political science one of its most promising opportunities to develop, test, and refine tools of analysis.

[1]Michael D. Reagan, *Politics, Economics, and the General Welfare* (Chicago: Scott, Foresman and Company, 1965), pp. 141-142.

Exploration of what happens during elections has triggered remarkable advances in an understanding of how data collection methods affect later findings and interpretations; of how statistical procedures can help overcome lack of experimental control in an ongoing political system; and of how theory can integrate discrete bits of information and isolated relationships, escalating comprehension and revealing research gaps at the same time.

One of the reasons that such potential lies in the study of voting is, of course, the fact that the investigator is able to deal with numbers when he deals with votes. Many types of political phenomena seem incapable of scientific study not because of their complexity but because there is no way of translating the relevant components of the phenomena (the independent and dependent variables) into numbers. Information on voter behavior, however, comes with a central dependent variable—the votes cast—already quantified, and the tally is often available broken down into relatively small geographic units. A second advantage of studying voting is the fact that voting involves *large* numbers, which are required if a political analyst is to be able to offer more than the most superficial explanation of voting preferences. Finally, the fact that in a two-party system each person has only three possible options (to vote for one or the other party, or to abstain) makes voting research much more manageable than, for example, attitudinal research, in which there are a multitude of individual options.

The classic voting studies did not use actual election tallies as sources of data. Because they wanted to test, as independent variables, characteristics which in part cannot be obtained from public sources (age distributions can be obtained from the Census Bureau, but religion and authoritarianism data cannot), they had to utilize personal interviews and questionnaires. Some important avenues of voting analysis still can, and perhaps must, rely on public information. For example, a major study of Negro political behavior in the South, carried out by scholars at the University of North Carolina, explored (among many other things) the relationship between Negro registration and voting and basic characteristics of the political districts Negroes live in—without relying (in this particular segment of their project) on interviews or questionnaires.[2]

The major thrust of voting research in decades to come, however, *will* concentrate on interview data, primarily because the focus of this research is increasingly on psychological correlates of voting decisions, and psychological data can effectively be obtained only through direct contact between researcher and voter. Significantly, it is the Survey Research Center at the University of Michigan, with its strong orientation to psychology, which currently stands as the predominant academic investigator of national voter behavior.

There is undoubtedly a great wealth of information still awaiting discovery by those who continue to explore with greater and greater sophistication the psychological dynamics of voting. The process by which adults crystallize their political preferences during a campaign or between campaigns is still only a partially charted phenomenon. As a matter of chance or fashion, however, it is the process by which *children* acquire their political preferences and establish their total patterns of response to politics which currently has caught the imagination of some of the most able and imaginative political scientists. The two excerpts from Hyman and Greenstein on political socialization, in Chapter Two, are forerunners of what may be a modest flood of books on this subject in the next few years. At this writing, three substantial studies of political learning are in final stages of preparation. One of these, which will be published by Robert Lane, builds in part on the type of data reported by Greenstein. Another is a large undertaking by David Easton, Robert Hess, Jack Dennis, and others; it concentrates on the youngest children yet examined, dipping down to the third grade. At the other end of the preadult scale, M. Kent Jennings of the Survey Research Center has completed the data collection for a monumental study of 25,000 high school seniors in which he attempts to reconstruct the political education of the final three school years.

A projection of this trend of interest suggests a further probe deeper into the early years. This would bring researchers face to face with the problems of eliciting information from preliterate children. But there are compelling theoretical and empirical justifications for attempting such a probe.

[2]Donald R. Matthews and James W. Prothro, "Political Factors and Negro Voter Registration in the South," *American Political Science Review*, LVII (1963), 355-367.

A second important thrust for research during the next decade is likely to be in the area of Negro politics. The North Carolina study heralds what will be, or should be, a massive attempt by social scientists to understand contemporary American Negroes. Because researchers in political socialization have been so persuasive in emphasizing the importance of early learning on later behavior, one can anticipate that the early political socialization of Negroes will become a strong focus of analytical efforts. Ironically, a hindrance to research in this field is the attitude of major foundations: because the Negro problem in America is so immediately urgent, funds are granted far less often for research activities in this area than for substantial action programs based on only modest foundations of knowledge.

RESEARCH PROSPECTS: INTEREST GROUPS

After the spate of studies, many of them case studies, in the 1950's, a distinct decline of research into interest groups occurred and has not been reversed. A prize-winning exception is the 1963 publication *American Business and Public Policy;* a portion of which appears in Chapter Three, but even in this case much of the research itself was done during the mid-1950's. Even so, this project and Milbrath's *The Washington Lobbyists* are outstanding not only because of their innate quality but also because they stand virtually alone.

While specific attention to interest groups has waned, broader-gauged research into organizational behavior has been carried on much more frequently during the last fifteen years. The central personality in this area of group analysis is Herbert Simon, who, by insisting on the relative unimportance of the analytical distinctions traditionally drawn between public and private organizations, stimulated the search for theories that encompass organizational life in general. The organizational theorists lent understanding to group behavior by demonstrating its *systemic* character—that is, by showing that it can be cast into grand theory.

From a different vantage point, social psychologists have contributed a vast amount by studying the behavior of small groups. "Small groups," according to three of the prime researchers in this area, "are groups that are small enough so that the individual partici-

pant can 'get all the way around' and fill out his relationship to each other person by some direct interaction with him."[3] This, then, means groups much smaller than most interest groups.

The point of these observations is not to initiate a commentary on the basic literature now in print concerning the behavior of large organizations or small groups. The point is to observe that each research field undoubtedly relates to political interest group behavior in certain ways and under certain circumstances. In the years to come, an important task for political researchers can be to bring the theory more closely to bear on the behavior of interest groups. However, it appears unlikely that much professional attention will be aimed in this direction; of the more than eight hundred political science dissertations under way or completed in 1965, for example, fewer than ten titles specifically related to political interest groups.

RESEARCH PROSPECTS: PARTIES

The outlook for study of political parties is equally modest. Using the same index of current interest, and omitting studies dealing with electorate party preference, only seven titles were listed treating parties as organizations. Dissertation topics, of course, reflect the main emphasis of graduate education, which in turn will affect the nature of professional research in coming years.

Political parties continue to be a slippery subject for research, in part because of the definition problem mentioned in Chapter Four. Since this volume concentrates on popular relationships to party organizations, the readings have not covered such matters as the significance of party identification and party leadership for the internal operations of legislative bodies and for the relationships between such bodies and executives. Yet this is an area of high interest to many contemporary political scientists, especially when the terms "legislative bodies" and "executives" are translated into "Congress" and "President." This particular substantive emphasis reflects the exceptionally powerful role the national government has played in American society in the 1960's.

By contrast, there is little evidence of new interest in political parties at the state level.

[3]Paul Hare, Edgar F. Borgatta, and Robert F. Bales, *Small Groups* (New York: Alfred A. Knopf, 1955), p. v.

The death of V. O. Key, Jr., in 1965, exposed the extent to which he dominated that field. State systems offer an unusual opportunity for the development of extensive studies in comparative government, thereby enabling a deeper understanding of the significance of variations in governmental forms and political cultures. This opportunity to date has been seized mainly by those who work with election data. It remains to be exploited adequately by those whose interest is in obtaining comparative data on the operations of parties as organizations. Current comparative research at the international level offers both a model and a standard of scientific procedure that needs translating into American inter-state research.

Because urbanization and its attendant problems continue to be a public concern in the United States, it is possible that research on the impact of parties on urban society will proceed with greater vitality than will research on parties at the state level. In one way or another, the massive research on urban politics that has dominated the 1950's and 1960's is likely to continue to yield more and more information about parties in local settings. But, as has been the case to date, this information is likely to be gathered rather haphazardly as a marginal by-product of investigation of such other phenomena as governmental form (e.g., the council-manager form), influence patterns ("power structures"), and local "political cultures." Few analysts have made local political parties central to their purpose in studying local politics.[4] It is possible, but not likely, that interest in local parties will move from marginality to centrality in coming years.

SUMMARY

What should be apparent from our brief attempt to project current research trends into the immediate future is that political science research is subject to motifs, or fads. (In this respect it differs not at all from intellectual inquiry in other disciplines). Which themes receive most emphasis depends on many considerations, two of the most powerful being a sense of public urgency and the availability of research money from governmental and private sources. These two considerations, of course, are related.

Another way of saying that "a sense of public urgency" lends direction to the profession would be to say that most political scientists do not feel comfortable operating as "pure scientists." Most are willing to concede the validity of arguments for paying some attention to the "pure science" side of political research and theory-building, but a healthy proportion find themselves unwilling, personally, to apply their own efforts in that direction. This is perhaps just as well, since society's problems are substantial and since social scientists are in scarce supply. The price paid is an unevenly developed comprehension of the totality of our political system. But, in the last analysis, if the more programmatic studies can effect concrete improvements in the condition of society, such imbalance of theoretical knowledge is a minor price to pay.

[4] One of the few is Phillips Cutright; see especially his "Measuring the Impact of Local Party Activity on the General Election Vote," *Public Opinion Quarterly*, XXVII (1963), 372-386.